A PRACTICAL PSYCHOANALYTIC GUIDE TO REFLEXIVE RESEARCH

A Practical Psychoanalytic Guide to Reflexive Research offers an accessible guide to enriched qualitative research. In this novel approach, the researcher's feelings and empathy in relation to participants take centre stage, leading to fresh, exciting and usable research findings. The psychoanalytic concept of reverie refers to those startling and unexpected images, feelings and daydreams which can come to mind as we interact with other people in the world. Qualitative research involves interacting with human subjects, and the book shows how uncanny or troubling reverie experiences can be turned to good use by being linked back to deeper research questions and hypotheses.

Joshua Holmes critically explores the role of self-reflection (reflexivity) in psychoanalysis and qualitative research. Practical guidance is offered while *planning* research; *conducting* research interviews; *analysing* interview data; *teaching* methods which foster the capacity for reverie; and in relation to *research groups*. Examples are given throughout, including the author's own missteps along the way, in which he shares the importance of learning from experience. The book breathes life into research processes, offering much-needed clinical relevance. The method moves away from one-size-fits-all, formulaic research procedures and brings tenor, colour and texture into the research process, to create vivid, real-life meaningful findings.

A Practical Psychoanalytic Guide to Reflexive Research is essential reading for undergraduate and postgraduate qualitative researchers wishing to enhance their reflexive practice, while psychotherapists and psychoanalysts will find a genuinely psychoanalytic research method, where their clinical skills become vital capacities rather than an awkward hindrance.

Joshua Holmes was awarded his PhD in Psychoanalytic Studies in 2015 and now works as a Child and Adolescent Psychotherapist in the NHS, while continuing to write and research. He has published papers in psychoanalytic, psychotherapy and qualitative research journals. He won the *Journal of the American Psychoanalytic Association* New Author Prize in 2015.

'Psychology has a long history of trying to be an objective science that mimics particle physics, DNA sequencing, or whatever. Here Josh Holmes says, Hey, wait a minute, what would happen if we dropped all that mimicry? This book takes us off the predicted track, immersing us in thinking through the use of the researcher himself as the subjective instrument. Thus, it plots the convergence of "being a person" with being a scientific probe. It takes us a step forward from the pseudo-solutions of behavioural and cognitive psychology, to keep us focused on that unsettled question of how we can know the human mind.'

– **Bob Hinshelwood**, *Professor Emeritus, University of Essex, UK*

'This is a very welcome addition to the growing literature on psychoanalytically informed qualitative research. This is a book packed full of useful concepts and techniques. The author writes with equal authority on research and psychoanalysis in an engaging, clear and accessible way. The use of Bion's and Ogden's work on reverie offers the researcher valuable new insights and approaches. It also challenges the naïve view that clinicians and qualitative researchers are different species rather than different animals within the same species of collaborative inquiry.'

– **Paul Hoggett**, *Emeritus Professor of Social Policy, University of the West of England, UK*

'In this thoughtful and absorbing work, the complex concept of reverie is examined and mined for its potential to inform psychoanalytically oriented qualitative research. The book is studded throughout with rich and illuminating examples of reverie at work and which bring the concept to life. The Reverie Research Method sits well with other contemporary multi-modal research approaches which seek ways to better capture experiential life through harnessing the imaginative, affective and meaning-making abilities of the researcher. A timely and relevant book.'

– **Dr Virginia Eatough**, *Birkbeck University of London*

'For any researcher interested to discover what psychoanalysis can offer their work, this book is an essential read. It sets out the theoretical basis for a "reverie-informed" approach to interviewing, which places subjectivity at the very heart of the research process. It is not only a practical guide to reverie-informed research, but raises fundamental questions about the role of subjective experience in our attempts to understand the human experience.'

– **Nick Midgley**, co-director of the Child Attachment and Psychological Therapies Research Unit, UCL/Anna Freud National Centre for Children and Families

"Based on a rigorous re-reading of Freud's text on fetishism, and on the fundamental psychic mechanism at its source, Verleugnung *(disavowal), which simultaneously links belief and non-belief in an undesirable perception and the maintenance of a counter-belief, Alan Bass achieves the great feat of showing how all thinking about fetishism (from de Brosses, through Comte, Heidegger, Merleau-Ponty and even Heisenberg's principle of uncertainty) remains haunted by this question. If fetishism in the strict sense takes the ersatz, the substitute, for the missing thing itself, every experience of substitution of one representation in the place of another—their distinction and their connection—clarifies the fundamental process of differentiation itself, of a thinking of difference (Derrida), and of the very process of symbolization. New consequences for the understanding and interpretation of any transference are given their full importance and are perfectly elucidated."*

—**Rene Major**, Director, Institute for Advanced Psychoanalytic Studies, Paris, France.

"With great skill, the author plots his course through a dazzling array of writers and texts, although the overall effect is not to register dispersion as much as to trace out complex and sometimes unexpected connections across a wide body of literary and philosophical work. In fact, the book is very well choreographed, bringing together those philosophical and literary voices with a great deal of elegance and poise. As much as it is an intellectually challenging book, it is also a highly readable one, and beautifully written."

—**Simon Morgan Wortham**, PVC Dean, Faculty of Arts and Social Sciences, Kingston University London, UK.

"Alan Bass's book provides an example of the finest comparatist work in the humanities and attests to the remarkable illumination that true interdisciplinary work can produce. I believe this unusual and provocative book will appeal to scholars of literature, philosophy, and psychoanalysis, as well as to historians and political theorists. The breadth of this book will make it a precious resource for students and teachers alike. It provides an invaluable rethinking of the extraordinary legacy to contemporary thinking that is the concept of fetishism."

—**Elizabeth Rottenberg**, DePaul University, USA.

FETISHISM, PSYCHOANALYSIS, AND PHILOSOPHY

Fetishism, Psychoanalysis, and Philosophy explores how and why Freud's late work on fetishism led to the beginnings of a re-formulation of the theory and practice of psychoanalysis. Freud himself, however, was unaware of the long history of the concept of fetishism, a history crucial to understanding it.

This book contains three main thrusts. One is historical, tracing the development of the concept of fetishism from the sixteenth century onwards. The focus here is on two important thinkers: Charles de Brosses from the eighteenth century and Auguste Comte from the nineteenth. The second thrust is philosophical. Fetishism is always about the relation between the mind and things. Martin Heidegger, Jacques Derrida, and Maurice Merleau-Ponty have made essential contributions in this area, contributions which have important scientific relevance. The third thrust integrates the historical, philosophical, and psychoanalytic investigations of fetishism. It also looks at Wallace Stevens' poetic meditation on mind and thing, which helps illuminate everything that precedes.

This comprehensive book features careful integration of the historical, philosophical, and psychoanalytic investigations of fetishism. It will contribute to opening new ways of thinking about the mind and how it is structured so that fetishism is possible. *Fetishism, Psychoanalysis, and Philosophy* will appeal to psychoanalysts and psychoanalytic psychotherapists as well as philosophy scholars.

Alan Bass, PhD is a psychoanalyst practicing in New York City. A training analyst and faculty member at the Institute for Psychoanalytic Training and Research and the Contemporary Freudian Society, he is also on the graduate philosophy faculty of the New School for Social Research. He is author of two previous books (*Difference and Disavowal: The Trauma of Eros* and *Interpretation and Difference: The Strangeness of Care*), translator of four books by Jacques Derrida, and editor of *The Undecidable Unconscious, A Journal of Deconstruction and Psychoanalysis.*

FETISHISM, PSYCHOANALYSIS, AND PHILOSOPHY

The Iridescent Thing

Alan Bass

Routledge
Taylor & Francis Group
LONDON AND NEW YORK

First published 2018
by Routledge
2 Park Square, Milton Park, Abingdon, Oxon OX14 4RN

and by Routledge
711 Third Avenue, New York, NY 10017

Routledge is an imprint of the Taylor & Francis Group, an informa business

British Library Cataloging-in-Publication Data
A catalogue record for this book is available from the British Library

Library of Congress Cataloging-in-Publication Data
Names: Bass, Alan, author.
Title: Fetishism, psychoanalysis, and philosophy: the iridescent thing / Alan Bass.
Description: Abingdon, Oxon; New York, NY: Routledge, 2018. | Includes bibliographical references and index.
Identifiers: LCCN 2017035536 (print) | LCCN 2017045375 (ebook) | ISBN 9781315150062 (Master) | ISBN 9781351368667 (Web PDF) | ISBN 9781351368650 (ePub) | ISBN 9781351368643 (Mobipocket/Kindle) | ISBN 9781138556409 (hardback : alk. paper) | ISBN 9781138556416 (pbk. : alk. paper)
Subjects: LCSH: Fetishism–History. | Fetishism–Philosophy. | Psychoanalysis.
Classification: LCC GN472 (ebook) | LCC GN472 .B27 2018 (print) | DDC 202/.109–dc23
LC record available at https://lccn.loc.gov/2017035536

ISBN: 978-1-138-55640-9 (hbk)
ISBN: 978-1-138-55641-6 (pbk)
ISBN: 978-1-315-15006-2 (ebk)

Typeset in Bembo
by Deanta Global Publishing Services, Chennai, India

CONTENTS

INTRODUCTION

This is my third foray into the inexhaustible topic of fetishism. My point of departure for this work is Freud's embryonic rethinking of his entire theory in relation to fetishism. In his very late work, Freud surprisingly came to see fetishism as the model of all psychic conflict. Because Freud had almost always taken neurosis as his model, the late shift to fetishism potentially dislodges all his basic ideas, starting with the nature of unconscious processes themselves. My two previous books, *Difference and Disavowal: The Trauma of Eros* and *Interpretation and Difference: The Strangeness of Care,* attempted to articulate and extend these shifts.

To recapitulate: Starting in 1924 (a, b), Freud was newly interested in the ego's capacity to act in self-contradictory ways, apparently knowing and not knowing the same thing. He described this phenomenon as simultaneous registration and repudiation of reality, such that the ego "splits itself." In the paper on fetishism (1927), Freud extended this idea, calling disavowal (*Verleugnung*) the defense mechanism responsible for ego splitting.

Difference and Disavowal dealt with this theory in relation to a difficult clinical problem. There are patients who seek out analysis, and who at first seem analyzable, but who demonstrate intense resistance to symbolization and interpretation once in analysis. Often called "concrete," these patients take the analytic process to its limit, because they specifically defend against the analyst's major therapeutic tool—interpretation itself. The analyst either has to decide that they really cannot be helped by an interpretive therapy or that interpretation itself has to be rethought.

Following Freud on the notion of disavowal, my contention was that such patients manifest a complex defensive structure of registration and repudiation of reality. However, departing from Freud, I contended that this defense is directed not against reality conventionally conceived, i.e., reality as objectivity. Rather, it is directed against the process that structures symbolization and interpretation. Symbolization and interpretation depend upon a process of connection and separation: a given phenomenon has a connection to, but is separate from, something else. For example, any interpretation of transference assumes that the patient experiences the analyst as connected to, but separate from, someone else. Simultaneous separation and connection is the fundamental sense of difference. Different things are separate from, but connected to, each other. "Concrete" patients substitute for the non-objectifiable reality of any form of difference an extreme objectivity—things are only what they are, there is no possible other meaning.

I was not the first to compare this defensive objectivity to fetishism. However, I did add to this comparison the idea of defense against differentiating process. I came to this conclusion through a close reading of Freud on fetishism (1927). He notoriously thought that the reality disavowed by the fetishist was the "reality of castration." Clearly, castration is a fantasy, however emotionally powerful. But, based on Freud's description of a particularly complex case, I came to see fetishism itself as a disavowal of sexual difference. There is a double form of splitting within fetishism: the registration and repudiation of (sexual) difference and the substitution for it of phallic monism, in which (*pace* Freud) there is a fantasy-based, concrete conviction of the objective reality of castration, which the fetishist then also registers and repudiates. I extended this revision to the problem of concreteness, understanding it as a defensive response to any possibility of differentiation. Like the fetishist, the "concrete" patient substitutes for differentiation a fantasy-based objectifying logic of relieving presence and threatening absence.

Such dynamics create a difficult task for the analyst. If he or she does not move beyond the assumption that reality equals objectivity, then the analyst is as "concrete" as the patient. The analyst then will not be able to understand the patient's extreme objectivity as a defense, and will not be able to interpret concreteness effectively. The usual result is that the analyst will be caught in a power struggle with the patient over whose version of objectivity is correct.

This clinical issue has implications for the entire theory of unconscious processes. Freud's is a theory of mind, psychopathology, and treatment founded on the idea of defense. Throughout his life, he maintained that the defense of repression is the "cornerstone" of psychoanalysis. The theory of repression unified the understanding of the unconscious and justified the use of interpretation as a therapeutic measure, because repression can produce symptoms that are symbols, and thus, interpretable. But Freud's surprising ultimate thought was that all defense has to be understood in terms of disavowal and splitting, which is why fetishism became the model for all psychopathology. This is why the specific use of a revised theory of fetishism to explain resistance to interpretation, and a newly generalized status of fetishism, lead to major revisions of the theory of unconscious processes. It becomes a question of rethinking the unconscious and interpretation in terms of registration and repudiation of difference. A major implication of this idea is that "the unconscious" simultaneously knows and does not know non-objective reality. This idea seems to contradict basic assumptions about "the unconscious" as a "buried" part of the mind, mostly out of touch with reality. It implies that there is unconscious registration of real, but non-objective differentiating processes.

In writing *Difference and Disavowal*, I knew that the clinical theory I was elaborating was an aspect of the idea that difference is the unthought of metaphysics, to use Heidegger's famous phrase. *Interpretation and Difference* was the integration of the clinical theory with the deconstructive thinking of difference. Nietzsche, Heidegger, and Derrida all read the history of philosophy "symptomatically," as a kind of registration of a logic of difference always at work in the most fundamental metaphysical concepts. This logic has always been repudiated because it disrupts the very concepts it structures. Thus, there is a bridge between the clinical problem of disavowal of difference and its very wide philosophical import. If the generalization of fetishism leads to the idea that disavowal of difference is the most general unconscious process, then all the thinking about difference as the unthought of metaphysics has to inform the (clinical) rethinking of interpretation. Nietzsche, Heidegger, and Derrida have made essential contributions to this question.

Nietzsche (1968) gives us a theory of active, differentiating interpretation. Active interpretation has to be freed from the presumptions about causality built into the metaphysical identifications of reality with objectivity and mind with consciousness. Active interpretation understands all phenomena in terms of unconscious interactions of force. It disrupts the reactive reduction of force that is the aim of metaphysical, identificatory equations. To return to the clinical point: resistance to interpretation can be understood as an attempt to defend against the differentiating force of interpretation. Insistence that x can only mean x, and never y, that x is either there or not there, is, in Nietzsche's sense, a reactive assertion of identity. Such identities eventually must be disrupted if there is to be analytic change. Importantly, following Nietzsche, the analyst's use of active interpretation also has to be freed of typical assumptions about causality, if it is not to perpetuate the patient's defensive objectivity. This is difficult for the analyst, given that so much psychoanalytic thinking, beginning with Freud, also presumes causality.

Heidegger, in *Being and Time* (1996), gives us a theory of descriptive, phenomenological interpretation, also freed from assumptions about causality. Descriptive interpretation serves an analytic function in the "destruction" of metaphysics, i.e., in retrieving the question of being from its millennial forgetting. This implies deconstruction of presumptions about time and space, opening up new ways of thinking the spatio-temporal aspects of interpretation itself. What is surprising for the analyst here is that descriptive interventions, which do not make statements about the causal influence of the past, do have an analytic effect when the issue is defense against the spatio-temporal aspects of interpretation.

For the later Heidegger, this thinking of space and time becomes a question of the "open," about which, he says, metaphysics knows nothing (1972). The way in which concreteness closes off the possibility of interpretation can be understood as another way to know nothing about the "open," which itself structures the time and space of analysis as an interpretive process. As the theory of disavowal implies unconscious registration of non-objective reality, my hypothesis is that the open is "known" unconsciously, but not in the way that consciousness "knows," i.e., representationally. Just as the analyst has to free him or herself of presumptions of causality, from Heidegger's point of view, the analyst would also have to free him or herself from presumptions about representation—another concept usually taken for granted in psychoanalytic theory.

Nietzsche and Heidegger both think about interpretation and difference in relation to pain, another pivot for the integration of the clinical and the deconstructive. Once Freud made anxiety the central problem of neurosis (1926), rethinking defense as motivated by the attempt to avoid anxiety, analytic therapy inevitably became a voyage through anxiety. And in scattered places, Freud understood the tension raising, i.e., painful, aspects of difference itself. Integrating these references with Nietzsche and Heidegger on difference and pain, it is possible to understand resistance to interpretation as a response to its inevitable pain, a pain experienced as uncontrollably disruptive. In *Difference and Disavowal* (2000), I gave multiple examples of patients' experiences of nearly traumatic, uncontrollably disruptive anxiety when their concrete defenses are modified.

To be in the "open" time and space of interpretation is then to be in a painful, uncontrollable place. Heidegger in particular is a thinker of anxiety. In *Being and Time* (1962), he offers a rich theory of *Dasein*'s inevitable flight from itself, i.e., splitting of itself, in the face of existential anxiety, an anxiety greater than the everyday experience of anxiety. Existential anxiety is linked to the theme of *Dasein*'s structural uncanniness. Although Heidegger came to criticize many aspects of *Being and Time*, uncanniness itself remained central to his work, including all his thinking about the "open" and difference as the unthought of metaphysics. Uncanniness is also a great Freudian theme (1919). If so, then uncanniness too, would have to be part of a revised theory of the unconscious based on disavowal of difference.

Fetishism, however, is not a guiding question for either Nietzsche or Heidegger. They both refer to it, but neither sees its connection to the thinking of difference. For Derrida, it is otherwise. Derrida finds the possibility of a general, non-metaphysical theory in the oscillating structures which characterize fetishism for the late Freud. (Derrida himself, however, seems unaware of Freud's own generalization of fetishism.) In *Glas* (1986), Derrida begins a rethinking of sexual difference itself in relation to such oscillating structures, and in *Specters of Marx* (1994), he speaks of fetishism and uncanniness in relation to spectrality—the intermediate reality of what is other than presence or absence, the reality of a time-space conceivable only as self-dislocating, differentiating process. Spectrality is an extension of Derrida's key "concept" of *différance*—difference as the "becoming time of space, and the becoming space of time," to use the early formulation (1982, p. 8). Hence, Derrida offers a conception of what he calls "spectral interpretation," interpretation rethought in terms of the space-time of *différance*. Spectral interpretation, he says, modifies what it interprets (1994, p. 52)—clearly the aim of psychoanalytic interpretation. Thus, a conception of spectrality and uncanniness would also have to inform the rethinking of interpretation in terms of disavowal of difference. Both are related to the theory of general fetishism Derrida elaborates in *Glas*.

Here, I want to situate all the preceding in a wider context: the ways in which the history of the concept of fetishism opens onto the very large question of the relations of what we call "mind" to what we call "thing." My aim is to expand both the psychoanalytic and deconstructive analyses of fetishism, of the relation of "mind" to "thing." The long, astonishing history of fetishism has always been fascinated and/or confounded by this question. From the coining of the word in the sixteenth century by the Portuguese explorers of West Africa, who used it to describe veneration of everyday things; to its role in controversies about the origins of religion; to its emergence as a general concept in the work of French ethnologist Charles de Brosses in 1760; its entrance into sociological theory in the work of Comte; its critical place in Marx's *Capital* (1977); its adoption by nineteenth-century sexologists; and in its psychoanalytic examination, analyses of fetishism almost always move from seeing it as an aberrant relation of mind to thing to seeing it as a reflection of the general relation of mind to thing.

Because this general question is embedded in any analysis of fetishism, some thinkers have elaborated generalizations of fetishism itself—Freud embryonically; Comte, Marx, and Derrida in grander fashion. These generalizations conform to a pattern already noted by some scholars. William Pietz begins his series of essays on the history of fetishism by noting that fetishism is "always threatening to slide… into an impossibly general theory. Yet it is precisely in the surprising history of this word as a comprehensive theoretical term indispensable to such crucial thinkers as Comte, Marx, and Freud that the real interdisciplinary interest of 'fetish' lies" (1985, p. 5).

Why "impossibly general"? One needs to consider both words. Pietz says "impossibly" because of the pattern of a frequently "indiscriminate" use of the word, its application—or misapplication—to too many phenomena. How can one concept describe so many things in so many fields (theology, anthropology, philosophy, sociology, economics, sexology, psychoanalysis)? But, why the pattern of generalization, such that the founders of positivism, communism, and psychoanalysis ultimately find in fetishism their broadest concepts—to say nothing of its role in Derrida's thought?

Paul-Laurent Assoun (1994), in his brief, indispensable history of the concept, noted a similar pattern, and provided an explanation. Summarizing his findings, Assoun says:

> The reconstitution of the concept of fetishism, grasped in its ultimate psychoanalytic configuration, attests to its strange and edifying "destiny": everything occurs as if, reinvented by each of the "tribes" of knowledge—ethnologists, sexologists, sociologists, "artists," then psychoanalysts—it served as a "password" for a specific "code," at once identical—the same word insists, from one moment and one usage to another—and distinct: everything depends upon… the "associations"… it crystallizes and organizes, as well as upon the effects it produces on the basis of the "presuppositions" of the "fields" or territories concerned… It is in a way the "virtue" of fetishism to confront each discourse with *its* "object," organizing a chain reflection on the functions of alterity and of the subject… Comte's position pushes this logic to its ultimate

> consequences in proposing a neofetishism for the future. A confirmation that the discourses on Fetishism are "*mises en abîme*" of their own object!
>
> *(pp. 121–123)*

Mise en abîme is originally the heraldic term for infinite regress: the shield in the shield in the shield...; the term was made popular by Derrida (although he had reservations about it), who I assume Assoun to be citing here. Assoun is saying that as a concept always concerned with *things*, a given discipline's discourse on fetishism brings it into a reflection on its "thing," opening up a self-reflective process whose effects tend to spread over every *thing*. In other words, there has always been a pattern of self-reflexivity in the examinations of fetishism. The discourse on fetishism turns into a reflection on the discourse itself—hence the *mise en abîme*. To put it another way, there has always between a "meta-theoretical" aspect to analyses of fetishism. They lead to a discipline's thinking about its own thinking. The clinical problem of resistance to interpretation, of concreteness, is itself often understood in terms of difficulties with self-reflection, with thinking about one's own thinking.

Is self-reflexivity actually an aspect of fetishism—the relation of mind and thing? Is this phenomenon always stumbled upon, without knowing what to do with it, in any consideration of fetishism? Does this have anything to do with the way in which philosophy itself has always been "haunted" by the logic of difference, according to deconstruction? More pointedly: is this self-reflexivity itself an aspect of the structure of difference, which then is inevitably disavowed? Assoun, having noted the self-reflexivity of the discourse on fetishism, also agrees with Freud that fetishism is the mark of inevitable splitting (1994, p. 124). But the splitting of what? Here Assoun follows Freud literally, seeing fetishism as the inevitable repudiation of the "reality of castration" in the widest sense, i.e., of everything that is "lacking in man," either as individual or as social being. For Assoun, the fetish functions as whatever is used to stop up the hole. As with Freud, seeing the fetish only in terms of "castration" disavows its relation to difference in the wider senses of Nietzsche, Heidegger, and Derrida. Assoun's statement then becomes another symptomatic statement in the history of what he accurately describes as a self-reflective, *en abîme* encounter with the functions of alterity and the subject. In *For a Critique of the Political Economy of the Sign*, Baudrillard noted that discourse on fetishism, "[i]nstead of functioning as a metalanguage for the magical thinking of others... turns against those who use it, and surreptitiously exposes their own magical thinking" (p. 90).

Pietz provides a great deal of historical material relevant to such questions. The word "fetish" comes from the Portuguese *feitico*, which originally referred to the popular tradition of magical practices, and itself derives from the Latin *factitious*, the adjectival form of *facere*, to manufacture. Even before its use by the explorers, the word already had the connotations of magic, manufacture, and facticity. Pietz specifies that the Portuguese in West Africa coined a pidgin word, *fetisso*, which carries particular connotations: the encounter with African religious practices in the context of colonialization, the slave trade, and new forms of commercial interaction (1985, p. 5). Many contemporary anthropologists dismiss the word and the concept as a corrupt, failed attempt to translate into European terms something the explorers could not understand. This critique began with Mauss in 1906. In reaction to what he saw as indiscriminate use of the word, based on the observer's prejudices, Mauss called fetishism an "immense misunderstanding" (1974, p. 244).

The early incomprehension of African religion became a convenient justification of colonial, exploitative aims. Pietz makes this point, but also advocates looking at the colonial texts themselves as novel productions resulting from the abrupt encounter of radically heterogeneous worlds; as descriptive records, they are often phantasmal (i.e., they expose the "magical thinking" of their authors, as per Baudrillard), but because of this, it is possible to view them as remnants of the creative enactment of new forms of social consciousness. Similarly, the pidgin word *Fetisso* as it developed in the cross-cultural spaces of the West African coast may be viewed either as the failed translation of various African terms or as something in itself, a novel word responsive to an unprecedented type of situation (1987, p. 6).

Looked at in this way, from the beginning, the word carried the sense of an inconceivable relation of mind and thing. How could ordinary, everyday things be venerated? This sense of the word led to its eventual usage, centuries later, to characterize the logical error of "misplaced concreteness," in Whitehead's phrase (ibid.). This apparent logical error, a major theme throughout the history of fetishism, again describes the clinical problem of resistance to interpretation, reinforcing the link between them.

Pietz makes another very important point: "the discourse on fetishism represents the emerging articulation of a theoretical materialism quite incompatible and in conflict with the philosophical tradition... The first characteristic to be identified as essential to the notion of the fetish is that of the fetish object's irreducible materiality" (1987, pp. 6–7). Pietz here refers to Deleuze's reference to fetishism in *Difference and Repetition* as an "affirmative term of fundamental theoretical significance congenial to that book's Nietzschean project of radically revaluing and 'reversing' the tradition of Western philosophical thought. This is not at all accidental, but is the result of the historical origin and development of the word" (p. 7, n.8). The irreducible materiality of the fetish was always going to divide it between primitive, illogical concreteness and a challenge to received notions of materiality.

This challenge resides in what Pietz calls the fetish's "untranscendent materiality." When Charles de Brosses coined the term "fetish*ism*" in the mid-eighteenth century, he used it to describe what he saw as the original form of worship, as opposed to those who thought that the first forms of religion were polytheistic. For de Brosses, fetishism was the primal religion, because it does not move beyond the terrestrial: the thing is the god. This first religion is unorganized and lacks reference to universality. The African worships the "first thing that comes along," arbitrarily projecting his own fancy into things, without reference to a truth beyond their materiality (1987, p. 8). This untranscendent materiality also makes the fetish irreducibly singular.

But even if untranscendent, the fetish certainly has a psychological component. Pietz:

> The fetish has an ordering power derived from its status as the fixation or inscription of a unique originating event that has brought together previously heterogeneous elements into a novel identity... But the heterogeneous components appropriated into an identity by a fetish are not only material elements; desires and belief and narrative structures establishing a practice are also fixed (or fixated) by the fetish, whose power is precisely the power to repeat its originating act of forging an identity of articulated relations between certain otherwise heterogeneous things.
>
> *(ibid.)*

Pietz here has outlined another central paradox. The untranscendent, irreducible materiality of the fetish is nonetheless also irreducibly "mental": it embodies desires, beliefs, narratives, and "fixates" them.

From a psychoanalytic point of view, it could not be otherwise. The privileged materiality of the fetish derives from its embodiment of the subject's fantasies; starting with Freud, fetishism demonstrates the material effects of unconscious processes. However, this psychoanalytic explanation glosses over exactly what Pietz describes: the very possibility of relatedness between what is "otherwise heterogeneous"—in the widest sense, the relatedness of "mind" and "thing." I am not a rock or a shoe. But it is always possible that I can worship a rock or be sexually aroused by a shoe. Typically, this is explained as projection. But if the rock or the shoe can embody my subjectivity, my projections, could there be common elements between myself and the rock or the shoe? Are they related in their heterogeneity?

Pietz makes a series of points about this question. He speaks of an "active relation" of the fetish object to the "living body" of the individual. But how can a "thing" be "active"? Pietz does not answer this question, but does say that the relatedness of object and living body "subverts the ideal of the autonomously determined self" (1987, p. 23). This is another aspect of the way in which the coinage of the word carries with it a confounded, dismissive response to the "alien":

> The alienness of African culture, in particular its resistance to "rational" trade relations, was explained in terms of the African's supposed irrational propensity to personify material (and especially European technological) objects, thereby revealing a false understanding of natural causality. A complementary principle said to characterize Africans was their supposed attribution of causal relation to random association.
>
> *(ibid.)*

Resistance to rational trade relations, i.e., commensurate forms of exchange, was understood by the colonialists, and then by philosophers, as resistance to rationality in general, particularly rational causality. When the trivial is idealized, causality apparently goes out the window. This is why early on, Kant reflected the general consensus about fetishism:

> The problem was especially expressed in the category of the trifling: European traders constantly remarked on the trinkets and trifles they traded for objects of real value (just as the socioreligious orders of African societies seemed to them founded on the valuing of "trifles" and "trash"). When he tried to formulate an aesthetic explanation for African fetish worship in 1764, Kant decided that such practices were founded on the principle of the "trifling" (*lappisch*), the ultimate degeneration of the principle of the beautiful because it lacked all sense of the sublime.
>
> *(1987, p. 9)*

Much later, in *Religion Within the Limits of Reason Alone* (1960, [1793]), Kant was to describe fetishism as the magical attempt by primitive man to obtain for himself divine satisfaction.[1] All these descriptions parallel the clinical descriptions of "concrete" and/or fetishistic patients: idealization of the trivial; skewed causality; resistance to rational forms of exchange (if patient says x, and the analyst says it means y, both have tacitly agreed that this is what the patient is paying for); immediate satisfaction; and blindness to the projection of one's own thoughts, wishes, and desires into an idealized object.

The point here is not to make the "African" or the concrete patient into a deconstructive hero, who challenges European—and hence, psychoanalytic—reason. This could all too easily "fetishize," i.e., idealize them. And it would do an injustice to what is accurate even in the most pejorative descriptions of fetishism. This accuracy however is itself grounded in presumptions about universal truth, an equally "fetishistic" operation. (Nietzsche, in fact, was to use the word "fetishism" in just this way; he spoke of belief in the reality of reason and the ego as metaphysical fetishism.) The point is subtler, to see whether there are indeed resources for another kind of thinking in the way in which the encounter of European rationality and what is called fetishism produces both incomprehension, impasse, *and* the pattern of generalization and self-reflection. Freud's generalization of fetishism points psychoanalysis in this direction.

Again, all of this concerns the relation of "mind" and "thing." Pietz describes how the functioning of fetish challenges the conventional view of materiality.

> Each fetish is a singular articulated identification (an "Appropriation," *Ereigenes* [sic], in Heidegger's language, unifying events, places, things, and people, and then returning them to their separate spheres)… Certain structured relationships—some conscious, others unconscious—are established, constituting the phenomenological fabric (the "flesh" in Merleau-Ponty's sense in *The Visible and the Invisible)* of immediate prereflective experience…

> the fetish is a special type of collective object... just as for Heidegger the work of art reveals, and hence is, the truth of "the thing."
>
> *(1987, pp. 13–14)*

The Heidegger references are to *Identity and Difference* and "The Origin of the Work of Art." While the use of *Ereignis* here might be technically incorrect—it contains no reference to being itself—the idea that fetishism might open itself to the kind of thinking represented by Heidegger and the late Merleau-Ponty is essential. Without "fetishizing the fetishist" does fetishism provide insight into "immediate prereflective experience"?

Difference and Disavowal (2000) and *Interpretation and Difference* (2006) both argued for something like this. The apparently irrational, because undifferentiated, nature of the fetish or of concreteness, was understood as the defensive response to a non-conscious, i.e., "prereflective," "immediate experience" of differentiating process. Because such "experience" is pre-reflective, it also has to be non-representational, as Heidegger said. This is an aspect of what I call "unconscious registration of non-objective reality." The impasse of the encounter of traditional rationality and fetishism can be understood in terms of reflective, representational thought having to open itself to "pre-reflective," non-representational thought.

The difficulty resides in understanding the interaction of the pre-reflective and non-representational with the reflective and representational. These are explicit questions for Heidegger's and Derrida's thinking of difference, questions which have an important practical import. The deconstructive point that there cannot be rationality without a logic of difference helps to explain why what is empirically different or "alien" is repudiated: it resonates with the disruptive effect of difference itself. (Freud did note a generally defensive response to difference, but said he had no explanation of it [1921, p. 102]). This is true across the board: European rationality must have seemed just as irrational to the "African" as the analyst's rationality seems to the concrete patient. The concrete patient usually—and justifiably—accuses the analyst of precisely what is ascribed to him: when you interpret, you are projecting your own fantasy for your own needs. What the explorers and the philosophers after them called irrational and non-causal, what the analyst may consider a failure to develop the capacity for abstract thought and self-reflection, is a refusal to consider another set of causal explanations.

In *Totem and Taboo*, Freud understood animism—the projection of the human spirit into objects of the natural world—as an attempt to project human causality into nature in order to control it via magic. Unfortunately, he did not link his thoughts about animism to his analysis of fetishism. Much of the history of fetishism is about this issue: spiritualization of material things as a form of control of the natural world. Heidegger, in his analysis of technology, sees all of metaphysics in relation to the mastery and control of nature. Whether from a psychoanalytic or deconstructive point of view, there is an emphasis on the inevitable attempts to control the uncontrollable. Without an understanding of this issue, discourse on fetishism tends to become fetishistic—an assertion of the superiority of "my" form of control, or in Freud's or Baudrillard's terms, "my" magical thinking. Inevitably, there is then accusation on both sides (explorer and African, philosopher and fetishist, analyst and patient), of failure to understand causes and reasons: you do not accept the obvious truth of my causality and hence my form of control. You are alien, anxiety provoking, uncanny. I must control you by relegating your difference to what de Brosses in 1760 called "the excess of superstitious stupidity" of fetishism—which he also saw as a "general religion, spread over the entire earth" (1988, pp. 12–13). De Brosses articulated precisely the confounding nature of fetishism for the European mind: "Fetishism belongs to the genre of those things which are so absurd that one can say that they leave no room for the reasoning that would contest them" (p. 95). If one understands that this accusation can always be reversed, one can take into account Pietz's point about the challenge of the fetish's irreducible materiality. If this materiality can indeed express a relatedness of mind and thing as a form of control, embedded within it is a "materialism of pre-reflective experience." What are mind and thing if they are also related in this way?

To sharpen this question let us take two of the many statements about the essence of fetishism, chosen because they recapitulate basic issues. On the question of self-referentiality, Laurent Fedi, in a book on fetishism, philosophy, and literature, says: "The primordial and immediate adhesion of the sign to what is shown, the fusion of the sign and the signified in the folding back upon itself of the auto-referential object, constitutes, in sum, the kernel of signification of fetishism" (2002, p. 314). On the question of the overall relation of mind and thing, Michael Taussig writes: "Fetishism elucidates a certain quality of ghostliness in objects in the modern world and an uncertain quality of fluctuation between thinghood and spirit" (1993, p. 217). These citations summarize the basic trends in the history of fetishism: the self-referentiality of the fetish is a fusion of sign and signified, indicative of the functioning of the primitive mind; the fetish is an equally primitive, "animistic" attribution of "spirit," of "mind," to things themselves, and not only in the modern world. But, can the apparently self-referential, "concrete," nature of the fetish elucidate the "uncertain fluctuation between thinghood and spirit," or even open onto an uncertain relation between "thinghood and spirit"? In other words, is there a shared, "ghostly" self-referentiality to the usually opposed categories of thing and mind? Would this transform the understanding of both? Is the potentially shared ghostly self-referentiality of mind and thing the source of the "meta-theoretical" aspect of discourse on fetishism? Is there an unthought relation between the self-referentiality of the fetish, immediate pre-reflective experience, and self-reflexive generalizations of fetishism?

These are my guiding questions here. In the introduction to *Interpretation and Difference* (2006), I said that it was not really a book separate from *Difference and Disavowal* (2000), because the necessary rethinking of interpretation demands integration with the deconstruction of metaphysics as the elaboration of a thinking of difference. And because all of this is related to the history of the concept of fetishism, the same holds for the relationship of this book to the preceding two.

Any reader familiar with the previous books will find repetition here: repetition of themes, and particularly repetition of certain passages in Freud, which continually open up for me.

Unless otherwise indicated, translations from French are my own.

Note

1 We will return to Kant on fetishism in Chapter 2 on Comte.

1

DE BROSSES

Universal fetishism[1]

Charles de Brosses coined the word "fetishism" in *Du culte des dieux fétiches* (1760, reprinted in 1988). His book was influential in a way not well appreciated today, except by scholars of fetishism. Who was he? A defender of the rights of the aristocracy against the crown, de Brosses was also a proto-anthropologist. He first presented work on fetishism to the Academy of Bordeaux in 1756. He sent the manuscript to Diderot, who esteemed it highly. Diderot in turn told de Brosses about Hume's *Natural History of Religion*. De Brosses contacted Hume, and there was then correspondence between all three, leading to de Brosses' decision to write his book (David, 1966). Given his political positions, the possibly controversial nature of the book, and the public burning of Helvetius' *De l'esprit* in 1758, de Brosses had *Du culte des dieux fétiches* published abroad, and introduced into France anonymously.

De Brosses' major thesis is that fetishism was the original, universal, but irrational form of religion. This posed an immediate problem for a Christian who conceived his religion as rational. If everything is created by God, one has to explain how the original, irrational form of worship could evolve into rational religion. Is the possibility of worship of an abstract, symbolic god somehow contained within worship of a concrete thing? If not, where does an abstract deity come from? De Brosses proposed to answer the question via scientific ethnology: "It is not in possibilities, but in man himself that one must study man; it is not a question of imagining what he could or should have done, but of what he does" (1988, p. 143).

De Brosses had predecessors in the study of fetishistic religions. By the time he wrote *Du culte*..., there had been more than two centuries worth of information about religious practices in Africa, the Americas, and Asia, much of it from the observations of explorers, traders, and priests. In 1704, Bosman had written about the relationship between "Guinean" (African) fetishes and prohibitions against eating certain meats, but found himself unable to explain it (Iacono, 1992, p. 12). (One already sees here the evidence for what Mauss in 1906 would call the "immense misunderstanding" embedded in discourse on fetishism.) Europeans apparently could not accommodate the relation between apparently non-symbolic worship of things and complex social practices. Iacono, like Pietz (see the Introduction), stresses that European incomprehension produced disapprobation and blindness:

> The Western observer's inability to understand and to explain… makes him present the behavior of the men he observes, the inhabitants of Guinea, as confused and arbitrary. The prohibition of which Bosman speaks supposes important symbolic codes and functions, but Western prejudices against the mentality of the "savages" hide from his perception and comprehension the relation between "fetishes" and prohibitions. The miscomprehension or negation of the symbolic value of "fetishes," and, in general, of the role of "fetishes" in African religious practices, corresponds to the picture of a "primitive" mentality having no faculty of symbolization or representation, or of having it at a very low level.
>
> *(1992, p. 12)*

This is the question that arises throughout the history of discourse on fetishism, including, eventually, the psychoanalytic. If one observes an apparently non-symbolic worship of things themselves, does this exemplify the mind of the primitive or the child, not yet capable of symbolism or abstraction? If so, one is obliged to account for the emergence of symbolism, or the possibility of rational, abstract religion—precisely de Brosses' problem.

There had been strong hints in this direction in the work of another important predecessor, Pére Lafitau (1724). His title, *Moeurs des sauvages américains comparées aux moeurs des premiers temps* (*Customs of the American Savages Compared to the Customs of the Earliest Times*), makes the point that there is a basis for comparison of contemporary primitives to early man. The primitive mind is constant, the same both then and now. Lafitau called the fetish a "talisman," whose function was akin to the manitous of the American Indians and to the practices of the barbaric peoples of the East Indies and of the island of Formosa (Iacono, 1992, p. 14). The fetish itself, however, was still specifically African.

As a Christian, Lafitau confronted the problem which was to preoccupy de Brosses. Given the conviction of one true God who created everything, Lafitau posited a unique origin of humanity with knowledge of divinity. His aim was to demonstrate the correspondence between the American Indians and Biblical texts, via common descent from the "Pelagians." The "Pelagians" were hypothetically descended from the Biblical Peleg, himself a descendant of Shem, one of the three sons of Noah. This is important for Lafitau's argument, as it will be for de Brosses. Of Noah's three sons who repopulated the earth after the flood, only Shem's descendants carried the memory of belief in the one, true God, the God who saved Noah and his family from the otherwise complete destruction of humanity. Shem's descendants, like his brothers', branched out in many directions, eventually producing the Semites, and hence Abraham, the patriarch of Judaic monotheism. But if the "Pelagians" were also descended from Shem, one can allege a link, however distant, between them and those who founded, or returned to, the religion of the one, true, *abstract* God. Primitive religions, then, were degenerations of the first, pure religion. Belief in the fetish or the manitou was belief in minor gods (Iacono, 1992, pp. 22–25), but contained within it the possibility of belief in the one, true God. As far-fetched as this might sound, it is an answer to the basic question: via common descent there is a distant memory of an abstract creator even in some forms of worship of things. Hence, the correspondence between "Pelagic" American Indians and the Bible.

In the four years between de Brosses' initial presentation on fetishism (1756) and the clandestine publication of his book (1760), he absorbed Hume on the origins of religion. Some of Hume's points re-appear in de Brosses. "[T]here is no tenet in all paganism, which would give so fair a scope to ridicule as this of the *real presence*: For it is so absurd, that it eludes the force of all argument" (Hume, 2007, p. 67). Given his rationalism and religious beliefs, Hume was quite willing to mock the absurdity of "real presence" wherever he saw it. He enjoys the anecdote of the Catholic priest who mistakenly gives a counter instead of a wafer for communion. The communicant says, "I wish you have not given me God the Father: He is so hard and tough there is no swallowing him" (p. 68). But Hume is also aware that those who see the irrationality of "true presence" will also practice some version of it. "[I]n a future age, it will probably become difficult to persuade some nations, that any human, two-legged creature could ever embrace such principles. And it is a thousand to one, but these nations themselves shall have something full as absurd in their own creed, to which they will give a most implicit and most religious assent" (ibid.). Hume intuits that there is something about the mind that makes what de Brosses will call fetishism inevitable.

Hume made the important point that religion is the result of the fear of primitive men confronted with unpredictable nature; hence, both the diabolization and divinization of natural phenomena.

> The primary religion of mankind arises chiefly from an anxious fear of future events; and what ideas will naturally be entertained of invisible, unknown powers, while men lie under dismal apprehensions of any kind, may easily be conceived... Every virtue, every excellence, must be ascribed to the divinity, and no exaggeration will be deemed sufficient to reach those perfections, with which he is endowed... Here therefore is a kind of contradiction between the different principles of human nature, which enter into religion. Our natural terrors present the notion of a devilish and malicious deity: Our propensity to adulation leads us to acknowledge an excellent and divine. And the influence of these opposite principles is various, according to the different situation of the human understanding.
>
> *(2007, p. 77)*

Hume here sounds a note that will echo in psychoanalysis. One can hear Freud on animism: the attribution of "spirit" to uncontrollable, terrifying nature in the attempt to control it (1913). And one can hear Klein on the good and bad breast, the idealized source of everything good and the evil source of all deprivation (1932), derived from the "contradiction between the different principles of human nature," i.e., the propensity toward adulation and terror. Hume makes another point that will dominate psychoanalytic thought: the mind develops from the inferior to the superior (Iacono, 1992, pp. 32–37). Hence, a position such as Lafitau's—the distant memory of abstract religion in the descendants of Noah—does not make sense, nor does the Biblical literalism it requires. For Hume, original religion had to be polytheistic nature worship, *without* a possibility of abstract monotheism, which could only develop with the slow progress toward reason. This position seems quite sensible: like the development of the child into the adult, mankind develops from the concrete to the abstract. There is no need to posit the possibility of the abstract at the origin. But then what about cumulative ethnological evidence of universal worship of things? How would one even get from fetishism to polytheism? (One eighteenth-century answer was that once man began to worship the stars ["Sabism"], belief in powers that reside in a realm beyond man became possible.)

De Brosses will agree with Hume on the progression from the lower to the higher, from irrationality to rationality, but will disagree on the polytheistic origin of religion. This will place him between Lafitau and Hume, creating an even more extreme version of Lafitau's problem: the abstract form of worship has to be contained within the concrete. "Fetishism" is named for the first time as a universalization of its African exemplar:

> [T]he cult… of certain terrestrial and material objects called *Fetishes* among the Black Africans, among whom this cult subsists, and that for this reason I will call *Fetishism*… [A]lthough in its proper meaning [the Fetish] is related in particular to the belief of the Black Africans, I signal in advance that I count on making use of it in speaking of any other nation in which cult objects are animals or inanimate beings which are made into divinities… all these ways of thinking have at bottom the same source, and this latter is only the accessory of a general Religion extended at great distances over the entire earth.
>
> *(1988, p. 11)*

Why is fetishism the universal, primal form of religion, found in all places at all times? Because, like Hume, de Brosses thinks that the constancy of the primitive mind is an index of the universal childhood and irrationality of humanity:

> [T]here is no superstition so absurd or so ridiculous engendered by ignorance joined to fear… Nations of the Orient in their first centuries were no more exempt from this puerile cult, that we will find generally spread over the entire earth, and maintained especially in Africa. It owes its birth to the time when peoples were pure savages ensconced in ignorance and barbarism. With the exception of the chosen people, there is no Nation which has not

> been in this state… [Fetishism] is practiced by peoples who spend their lives in perpetual childhood.
>
> *(p. 13)*

While the chosen people may be the exception to the general rule of fetishism, de Brosses concedes that individual examples of fetishism can even be found in the Old Testament. How could this not be, if fetishism reflects childhood itself? De Brosses here uses the argument that will be echoed across centuries: the child initially lacks capacity for abstraction, symbolization, and representation.

Like Hume's idealized and terrifying gods, the fetish can act for good or evil and can protect or harm. In a passage that was to influence Marx, de Brosses recounts:

> No other Divinity of this type was so baleful to the Savages than gold, which they believed certainly to be the Fetish of the Spanish, judging of that species' belief by their own, and by the profound veneration that they saw in them for this metal. The Barbarians of Cuba, knowing that a flotilla from Castille was going to descend on their island, judged that it was first necessary to conciliate the God of the Spanish, and then to distance it from them. They assembled all their gold in a basket. Here, they said, is the God of these strangers; let us celebrate a festival in its honor to obtain its protection; after which we will make it leave our island. They danced and sang in their religious fashion around the basket, and then threw it in the sea.
>
> *(1988, pp. 30–31)*

There is no irony in de Brosses' account here, as there eventually would be for Marx. Or even as there already was for Hume, when he said that those nations that denounce the error of "real presence" "shall have something full as absurd in their own creed, to which they will give a most implicit and most religious assent." For de Brosses, the Spanish, having advanced beyond universal childhood, and bringing the true religion to the savages, could not be fetishists; they have a rational belief in the value of gold. But belief in the evil of the gold-fetish is superstition, as absurd as the belief that it could be propitiated.

Much of *Du culte…* is concerned with demonstrating the fetishistic nature of Egyptian religion. Many of de Brosses' contemporaries thought that the Egyptians had been a superior, intellectual people, along the lines of the argument that the possibility of abstraction had to be part of God given endowment. De Brosses' position is complex. He will agree that the possibility of abstraction has to be inherent in man, but he finds it absurd to think that Egyptian animal worship is itself an abstract religion. Looking at the conflicts among Egyptians who worshiped different animals, de Brosses wrote:

> Among the Egyptians there was no way for the worshipers of the rat to live on good terms with the worshipers of the cat. But these wars give new proof that it was a question of the animal taken in itself; and not considered

> as an arbitrarily chosen emblem of the real Divinity: for then there would have been no reason for discord; all these types relating to the same object, like different words of several languages when they signify the same thing... Egyptian zoolatry is very ancient. The Bible portrays it not as an emblem or an allegory, but as a pure, direct Zoolatry... Mosaic law prohibits nothing with more threats than fornication with this Fetishistic cult.
>
> *(1988, pp. 52–53)*

The childish mind cannot encompass that "*chat*" and "cat" can mean the same thing. The word is the thing; the animal or the thing is the god. This is the core of concreteness as a logical error. As Mosaic law is founded on iconoclasm, the religion of the chosen people is the only one before Christianity exempt from this error. This does not mean that individual Jews were free from fetishistic beliefs. The stories of Jacob and Rachel attest to such lapses: Jacob believed in the power of a greased stone, Rachel stole her father's household idols on leaving his house (p. 73). One has to distinguish between the sacred and the profane even in the Old Testament: "For example the bronze serpent erected on the orders of [Moses] (de Brosses gives: Jaoh) himself, the sight of which was a protection against the bites of desert serpents, certainly had nothing in common with Fetishism; while the two calves of the ten tribes, one placed in Dan, the other in Bethel, were marks of fetishism, as scandalous as they are certain" (p. 75). The distinction seems meaningless: why wouldn't belief that sight of a bronze serpent protects against snake bites be as a fetishistic as the two golden calves of the ten tribes? De Brosses here relies on the presumption that Moses, inspired by the one, true God, cannot practice the renegade fetishism of the ten tribes.

However, taking de Brosses at his word, the co-existence of fetishistic and non-fetishistic beliefs, particularly among the "chosen people," is not a casual question. Rather, it indicates the central bind of his argument. How to reconcile a position such as Lafitau's (original knowledge of the one true God who created man) with Hume's (progression of humanity from the inferior to the superior, from the concrete to the abstract)? Observation and logic support Hume:

> When one sees men, in such distant centuries and climates, who have nothing in common between them except their ignorance and barbarism, with such similar practices, it is much more natural to conclude that thus is man made, that left in his natural brutish and savage state, not yet informed by any reflected idea or by any imitation, he is the same in his primitive customs and ways of doing things in Egypt as in the Antilles... [The explanation of this is] the constant uniformity of savage man with himself, his heart perpetually open to fear, his soul ceaselessly avid with hopes, which give free rein to the disorder of his ideas, pushing him into a thousand actions without sense; his mind without culture and without reason is incapable of perceiving how little link there is between certain causes and the effects he expects from them. Since one is not astonished to see children not raise their minds any higher

> than their dolls, believing them animate, and acting with them in consequence, why would one be astonished to see peoples, who constantly spend their lives in a perpetual childhood and who are never more than four years old, reason without any accuracy, and act as they reason?
>
> *(1988, p. 96)*

However much the contemporary reader may agree with Iacono (see above) and Pietz (see Introduction) that de Brosses here provides a rationalization for colonialism and the slave trade, any developmentally informed reader would also be struck by the accuracy of this description—as it applies to children (see Piaget's developmental stages)[2] and to adults who have problems with symbolization (see most of the psychoanalytic literature on concreteness). Children do treat their dolls as animate and act accordingly; children do have difficulty with rational relations of cause and effect; are prone to terrible fears; and do invent strange explanations (fantasies in psychoanalytic language) to explain the world. Concrete adults do treat words as things and often have difficulties with conventional cause and effect. The Indians of Cuba may have accurately observed Spanish fetishization of gold, but they were certainly wrong if they thought they could protect themselves by throwing that gold into the sea.

But, does this mean that God created man as a naturally fetishistic child? This is de Brosses' bind. He cannot agree with his contemporaries who thought that Egyptian religion was "pure and intellectual," so that even if their religion degenerated into worship of material objects, a small number of wise people would have maintained the original knowledge of a supreme being (1988, p. 98). From a historical, developmental point of view, this reasoning is the inverse of the natural order of progression from the concrete to the abstract (p. 99). But de Brosses knows that he has to account for the reverse possibility, that man was created so that he could rise above infantile fetishism. That possibility too must have been part of his nature.

Like Lafitau, de Brosses resolves the dilemma via the flood:

> The error in this respect, it seems to me, comes from considering man as he initially emerged from the hands of his creator, in a state of reason and well informed by divine providence; instead, one must consider the human genus only posterior to the almost total destruction, and deserved punishment, which, overcoming the surface of the earth, and abolishing everywhere, except at one single point, the acquired knowledge, produced a new state of things. Of the three Chiefs of generations who repopulated an earth newly emerged from beneath the waters, only the family of one conserved the knowledge of the primordial cult and healthy ideas of Divinity. The posterity of the two others, more numerous and more spread out than that of the first, lost what little remained of knowledge… All was forgotten, all became unknown. This new state of such a large part of the human genus, *which has its forced cause in a unique event* [my emphasis], is a state of childhood, a savage

> state out of which some nations raised themselves only little by little, and from which others have still emerged only quite imperfectly.
>
> *(1988, pp. 99–100)*

If Christianity is the *telos* of humanity, God had to have created man with the capacity to evolve toward it. Man had to have a "healthy" knowledge of an abstract divinity, "in a state of reason and well informed by divine providence." Thus, man had to be endowed with the capacity for symbolization, the differentiation of thing and word, object and god; God's chosen people were iconoclasts. But God also created man with the possibility of a fall, which did not lose knowledge of him, but did transgress his law. Once the extent of the transgressions became unendurable for him, he chose to destroy humanity, excepting the one man who remained righteous—Noah—and his family. But as only one of Noah's sons, Shem, maintained the true belief—why?—the rest of humanity was repopulated by those who lost it. So, the "forced cause" of a "unique event" created the co-existence of a small monotheistic minority "in a state of reason" *and* the universally observable, unreasonable, childish worship of things. Only some nations might progress back to the original "state of reason," acquiring the intellectual maturity necessary for true religion: "the more a people is deprived of common sense, the less it knows Divinity" (p. 104). If the Egyptians were polytheistic animal worshipers, their religion could not be rational.

What if one were to reject de Brosses' concrete Biblical literalism (or, one might say with Baudrillard, his magical thinking), and were to read his account symbolically? In that case, one would have a more complicated picture: the end of development—abstract reason, common sense, divinity independent of man—would have to be contemporary with its beginning. Catastrophe, the "forced cause" of a "unique event," divides the originary possibility of symbolization from fetishism. Certainly, this makes fetishism a kind of avatar of the fall, but it also addresses a question that Hume's logic glosses over: one has to account for the possibility of the *co-existence* of the concrete and the abstract. This co-existence is divinely mediated, an attribute of man independent of man.

If one translates this problem into the question of the difference between a thing and the god it embodies, then de Brosses is placing difference—the possibility of symbolization—at the origin, literally, the creation. Difference, then, is a "transcendental" possibility, which can only be eliminated by a transcendental catastrophe—the "forced cause" of a "unique event." Those who remain in the post-catastrophe state of irrational fetishism can only emerge toward reason and abstraction via the counter-force of conversion (colonialism, slavery). But the co-existence of non-symbolic and symbolic forms of worship is structurally necessary if fetishism is universal and monotheism exceptional.

De Brosses is blind to the implication of his argument: he needs *catastrophe* to account for the universality of fetishism as the fall away from original monotheism. This is not far from my argument in *Difference and Disavowal* that concrete or fetishistic patients, who do seem to conflate word and thing, and who do have difficulties with symbolization, are defending against any form of differentiation that is experienced as catastrophic. Hence, the clinical paradox: such patients are never consistently concrete. Just as the hysteric, for Freud, is only apparently asexual, because hysterical symptoms express repressed sexuality, so the concrete patient is only apparently non-symbolizing, because concrete symptoms express disavowed difference. This is why the description of fetishism in de Brosses is in many ways accurate, and corresponds to the description of concrete patients. But such descriptions themselves become fetishistic, concrete, or literalizing when they cannot encompass difference itself as the non-transcendental possibility of symbolization.

Hence, de Brosses is more right than he can possibly know when he separates symbolization from fetishism by catastrophe. Once he assumes both original difference (abstract divinity) and universal non-difference (fetishism), he has placed difference at the origin.[3] If original difference is not God given, then de Brosses would have a conception that contradicts reason: difference itself cannot be original. It has to be secondary to original unity. Post-catastrophe, difference *is* secondary, and there is a Humean progression from the error of "real presence" to symbolic reason. This is why de Brosses is incoherently forced to consider an original differentiation that is then described fetishistically—an imaginary flood, a catastrophe, taken as literal fact to explain the co-existence of apparently original, universal fetishism with "truly" original worship of an abstract god.

But this complexity does allow de Brosses to accommodate the ethnological evidence with Humean common sense, and scientific reason:

> [the idea that] all peoples [i.e., including the Egyptians] began with correct notions of an intellectual Religion that they then corrupted with the most stupid idolatries... has nothing in conformity with the natural progress of human ideas, which is to proceed from sensory objects to abstract knowledge, to go from the near to the far, to mount from the creature to the Creator, not to descend from a Creator which they do not see to the nature which is before their eyes. A profound Philosopher, who having said, *I think, therefore I am*, elevates himself in one step by this single idea to the knowledge of spirituality and to the conviction of the existence of a single immaterial God who is first cause, had behind him thousands of ideas that helped him to step across this enormous interval. But those who would ascribe to Savages the minds of Plato or Descartes—would they be judicious critics?
>
> *(1988, p. 101)*

How seriously should one read this passage? On one hand, de Brosses is stating the obvious. It is absurd to attribute the kind of capacity for abstract thought one finds in Plato or Descartes to a child or a "savage." (In clinical practice, this seems to be the problem of the concrete patient.) But in contrasting the universally fetishistic mind to Plato as the predecessor of Cartesian rationality, one would have to suppose that Plato maintained the knowledge of antediluvian humanity, kept alive by the descendants of *one* of the sons of Noah. The progression from Platonic abstraction to Cartesian self-reflection as the epitome of rational, abstract religion is inevitable. But so is irrational, concrete, non-self-reflective, childish, and primitive fetishism. Hence, de Brosses has to exclude Plato, Descartes, and himself from the possibility of fetishism.

One hears all the racial, colonial implications of the encounter of European and non-European peoples in this exclusion. De Brosses cannot see that gold is indeed the fetish of the Spanish, just as he cannot see that nothing prevents the fetishization of apparently abstract thought. (Could Hume have applied his own observation of the "fetishistic" practices of those who denounce fetishism to himself?) The equation of the transcendental with the reality of ideal forms can be called the fetish of Plato; the equation of self-reflection with the reality of one true God as first cause can be called the fetish of Descartes; and the amalgamation of Plato and Descartes with Biblical literalism can be called the fetish of de Brosses.

This reasoning was first Nietzsche's. As already noted, he called metaphysical belief in the reality of reason and the ego—the linchpins of Cartesianism—a form of fetishism. Nietzsche's remark is as ironic as Marx was to be in retelling the story about gold as the Spanish fetish. But does Nietzsche understand what de Brosses, however incoherently, understood—that fetishism itself is irreducible? That to call certain metaphysical beliefs fetishes might function as a traditional denunciation of fetishism, without understanding the conundrum built into it, that it embodies both the concrete and the abstract?

In the Introduction, discussing Assoun and Pietz, we came upon some of the effects of this conundrum. Assoun spoke of the *mise en abîme* effect of discourses on fetishism. While Assoun meant the way in which discourses on fetishism tend to become examinations of their own objects, de Brosses also shows the reverse: discourses that analyze fetishism tend to repeat it when they cannot examine some of their own presuppositions. (This is conspicuously true of Freud on fetishism as disavowal of "the reality of castration.") Pietz spoke of the materiality of the fetish in relation to immediate pre-reflective experience, and, like Assoun, of discourse on fetishism tending to become an "impossibly general" theory.

Reconsidering these points, there is another conundrum. *Mise en abîme* implies reflection, even if uncontrolled, infinitely regressive reflection. Immediate pre-reflective experience seems to close off the space of reflection. The fetish object itself, in its conflation of thing and referent, has been described as self-referential. Again: "The primordial and immediate adhesion of the sign to what is shown, the fusion of the sign and of the signified in the folding back upon itself of the self-referential object—this is what, in sum, constitutes the kernel of meaning of fetishism" (Fedi, 2002, p. 314). Iacono (see above) said that this "miscomprehension… of the symbolic value of 'fetishes'… corresponds to the picture of a 'primitive' mentality having no faculty of symbolization or representation, or of having it at a very low level," and served to justify colonialism. Such justifications had to assume that reason itself excludes fetishism.

Once this assumption is made, discourse on fetishism inevitably repeats fetishism. When de Brosses said that "Fetishism belongs to the genre of those things which are so absurd that one can say that they leave no room for the reasoning that would contest them" (1988, p. 95), he could not see why he is right. How could one reason with the Indians of Cuba to show them that throwing gold into the sea will not protect them from the Spanish? How could one reason with de Brosses to show him that his Biblical literalism is a concrete response to the possibility of original difference? In psychoanalysis, this becomes the problem of how to interpret when the patient resists interpretation.

In each instance, the difficulty is the apparent exclusion of self-observation. Iacono addresses this issue in writing about the relation between de Brosses and Marx on fetishism:

> In an article in the *Rhenish Gazette* (November 3, 1842) Marx refers to the story of the savages of Cuba, which he found in de Brosses… The fact that Marx attributes the reference to an image [i.e., gold as fetish] to an active process indicates that the modification of the image [i.e., its literalization] hides or makes one forget an essential moment of reflection, that of self-observation, by means of which subjects not only produce an activity of symbolization, but also have the faculty of seeing this very activity of symbolization as an object… the fetish character of merchandise [in *Capital*] expresses the absence of this moment of self-observation on the part of those subject to the phenomenon. From this point of view Marx literally repeats de Brosses' definition… Inanimate things or animals are considered directly as gods and not as representations or symbolizations of abstract and invisible gods [i.e., capitalist forms of exchange are just as concrete as the beliefs of "primitives"]… the link that would make self-observation possible is broken… the analogical function of the concept of fetishism… serves to make observable a phenomenon which occurs unconsciously and equally affects the observer.
>
> *(1992, pp. 86–87; p. 99)*

This is a good description, but perhaps does not delve sufficiently into the "phenomenon which occurs unconsciously" and "affects the observer." One can reconfigure the conundrum in relation to self-reference and self-observation. The former seems to be non-reflective and the latter reflective. De Brosses, without knowing it, gives an allegorical account of this issue when he makes both fetishism (universal childhood concreteness) and the possibility of symbolic abstraction (Cartesian self-observation as the epitome of original knowledge of divinity) irreducible aspects of mind. The difficulty is that one cannot so easily separate non-reflection and reflection, i.e., fetishism and abstract reason, even if one cannot attribute Cartesian rationality to the child.

This problem haunts psychoanalysis. The analyst treating the concrete patient often feels that the patient is being unreasonable in the extreme, or is even attacking the analyst's sense of reason. ("Fetishism belongs to the genre of those things which are so absurd that one can say that they leave no room for the reasoning that would contest them.") From one point of view this is true: the patient's refusal to consider the possibility of alternate meaning, particularly in an interpretive therapy, seems senseless. But, from the point of view that fetishism itself is a complicated structure of differentiation and concreteness, the analyst who thinks that reason excludes fetishism is as wrong as de Brosses when he assumes that his own thinking excludes fetishism—or as wrong as Freud on "the reality of castration." It is this assumption that almost inevitably produces the fetishistic elements of the discourse that critiques fetishism. The analyst's difficult task is to question why reason itself leads to a logical and/or clinical impasse. To undertake this task is to question the fetishistic sense of control and security derived from applying unquestioned assumptions to a paradoxical phenomenon. To return to Iacono's formulation: the analyst must sustain the space of self-observation in which the patient's apparent self-reference unconsciously affects the analyst. This means that the analyst must observe within him- or herself the movement away from self-observation to defensive self-referentiality about the superiority of abstract reason. The analyst's own sense of reality and reason must change to include the inextricable relatedness of self-reference and self-observation.

This also means changing the analyst's conception of phenomena that occur unconsciously. The critical change is the conception that there is an unconscious process of "registration of difference," even where it appears to be absent. Such a conception is actually built into Freud's theory. Once the unconscious is linked to memory, it is precisely, as Freud says early on, that part of the mind which is materially differentiable, and is capable of forming *Bahnungen*, differentiated pathways. Schmidt-Hellerau, in her rigorous analysis of Freudian metapsychology, calls the unconscious "phenomenologically differentiable." Derrida says that the Freudian unconscious is always "open to the effraction of the trace" (1978, p. 201). This way of thinking is counter-intuitive, as it implies an unconscious process of registration of those aspects of reality which themselves are not present or objectifiable (time, space, separation, connection, difference). In a non-theological (non-"de Brossian") way, this is a form of thinking difference at the origin, the fundamental "axiom" of deconstructive thought. It is an important corrective to some aspects of psychoanalytic theory. While it may be the case that from the point of view of direct observation of consciousness the human child develops from the concrete to the abstract, from the irrational to the rational, this does not mean that there are not unconscious processes of registration of difference. If the analyst does not understand such a process, then, as in the entire tradition of discourse on fetishism, the analyst will see the concrete patient as simply primitive and childish. Once this is so, the analyst, unconsciously, will use reason the same way the patient uses concreteness: to control a potentially painful, even catastrophic, paradoxical, and uncontrollable process.

Or the same way that much of the European discourse on fetishism protected itself from forms of thought it could not encompass. De Brosses, like Hume, thought that fetishism was a response to the fear generated by uncontrollable nature. What he could not imagine was that the Cartesian reason prepared by Plato might be similarly motivated. When Nietzsche called belief in the subject and reason a fetish, he was extending his idea that Christianity is "Platonism for the people." In his account, the devaluation of unconscious, instinctual, differentiating, and uncontrollable forces in favor of a non-bodily, abstract realm of truth did eventually lead to the Cartesian self-certainty of the subject, which produces scientific reason as proof of the existence of an abstract God. For Nietzsche, this was why a certain science and certain theology were united in their "no" to difference. All of Heidegger's thinking is based on the idea that metaphysics is an inevitable forgetting of the question of being, which is symptomatically expressed in the privileging of presence. This gives added weight to Hume on the error of "real presence" in relation to the fear of uncontrollable nature. When Heidegger, in his late work, sees technology as the end of metaphysics, he too addresses the inevitable attempt to dominate and control nature. Heidegger is explicit that technology was prepared in Platonism, which reaches one of its pinnacles in Descartes' explicit attempt to make men the "masters and proprietors of nature" (cited, Heidegger, 1987, p. 135). Metaphysics would be no less fetishistic than any other attempt to control the uncontrollable via belief in "real presence." The psychoanalyst can act in ways that Nietzsche could characterize as theologically scientific, or that Heidegger could characterize as technological, if he or she does not understand the possible use of interpretation to control a threateningly uncontrollable patient, who him- or herself is in conflict with precisely the same issue.

De Brosses understood that the uncontrollable and the unpredictable were built into the fetish's presence, and its capacity to act for good or for evil. He explains this theoretically:

> We know of man's natural penchant to conceive beings similar to himself, and to suppose in external things the qualities that he feels in himself. He willingly and unreflectingly ascribes goodness and evil even to the inanimate causes that please him or harm him… impelled by fear to suppose invisible powers, and led by the senses to fix his attention on visible objects, he reunites two opposite and simultaneous operations, attaching the invisible power to the visible object, without distinguishing in the crude context of his reasoning the material object from the intelligent power he supposes in it… Once admitted for certain objects, this way of thinking generalizes itself without effort and extends to many others, especially in circumstances in which chance, that is, unforeseen accidents, have a great deal of influence.
>
> *(1988, pp. 110–111)*

This passage anticipates major psychoanalytic ideas. The tendency to see external things as versions of oneself is what Freud called narcissism. In *Totem and Taboo*, Freud understood animism as a narcissistic projection of man's own wishes onto unpredictable nature—chance, unforeseeable events—in an attempt to control it. Generalizing this conception, Freud called animism the first *Weltanschauung*, and saw in it the origin of science, particularly of scientific determinism (1913, pp. 64–65). (This is not so far from Heidegger on technology as the mastery and control of nature.) Although Freud does not speak of narcissism and animism in his analyses of fetishism, like de Brosses he thinks that the fetish contains opposite ideas. It is both the antidote to castration fears and an expression of them. Analogously, Klein (1932) theorizes an infant whose feelings of satisfaction and frustration are projected onto a good and a bad breast, which are the sources of all good and all evil, intentionally feeding or depriving. Like de Brosses, subsequent psychoanalysts and developmental theorists understood these operations as the result of the infantile mind's exclusive attention to the immediate and the sensory. And all this thinking assumes that the reality of "chance," of "unforeseen accidents," provokes anxiety, which then produces fantastically incoherent attempts to master it: the reuniting of "two opposite and simultaneous operations" in the visible object.

An important investigator of the origin of religion after de Brosses, J.A. Dulaure (1825) had similar ideas about fetishism:

> In the infancy of societies, everything that operated a strong impression on the senses; everything that to a high degree produced pleasure or pain, admiration, astonishment, fear; everything that was capable of procuring good, of distancing evil: elements, natural phenomena, animals, vegetables, inanimate substances, became at first so many cherished, feared, and revered objects; and then, through long habituation, were considered as filled with an occult force, a supernatural power, and became the objects of a cult.
>
> *(p. 32)*

> Mountains, objects of acknowledgment and of terror, of fear and hope, alternately harmful and beneficial... how could crude and savage men not see in them a supernatural power, a divinity?... Was it possible that mountains, the dwellings of the gods, furnished symbols of divinity, as Maxime de Tyr thinks? He attributes to the first mortals the opinions of his own century. Symbols result from a combination of ideas, from knowledge of the object symbolized; and the first mortals were incapable of combinations, without such knowledge.
>
> *(pp. 44–45)*

Symbols *combine*. The worshiped animate or inanimate object of immediate sensory impression does not; it *alternates* between contradictory assumptions. In different ways, Freud and Klein were to characterize this operation as splitting derived from the projection of internal states onto external objects that do not function as symbols. From within the assumptions of reason such descriptions are correct. But they can prevent reason from observing its own limitations, another of which is implied in the alternation of opposites consistently observed in fetishism. Reason says that good and evil, help and harm, hope and fear, castration and non-castration cannot be embodied in the same thing. This is the principle of identity.

Freud makes the case that the unconscious ignores the principle of identity, that unconscious fantasy allows a thing and its opposite to be the same. This is why he says that the way in which the fetish embodies opposite ideas—the woman is castrated; the woman is phallic—is made possible by the unconscious laws of thought. But Freud never challenges the principle of identity in relation to external reality; a thing can be itself and its opposite only in fantasy. De Brosses or Dulaure might say that the fetish's capacity to combine opposites is simply knowledge of the immediate experience of nature: it can always help or harm. For them, the logical error of fetishism is to generalize this possibility onto all things. But, what if the alternating opposites of the fetish (divine/demonic; phallic/castrated; idealized/persecutory) and self-referentiality (non-symbolic structure) were themselves structured by a registration of real, but non-objectifiable difference? Difference that is paradoxically the "opposite" of itself, simultaneously separation and connection, relation and otherness? And if this were why, beyond conventional reason, the fetish combines differentiation and non-differentiation, as an instance of mind itself combining self-observation and self-reference? And if this were why the unconscious relation to things necessarily opens the question of a process both abstract (self-observation) and sensory (self-reference)? And related to the uncontrollable or the catastrophic?

Throughout *Difference and Disavowal*, I emphasized the nearly traumatic, "catastrophic" anxiety related to disavowal of difference. Clinically, one sees evidence of this in the fear of uncontrollable chaos related to modification of defenses against difference, i.e., of the analyst's interpretive function—"trees flying through the air," the "world falling apart," to cite several patients. In *Interpretation and Difference*, I attempted to understand such anxieties in relation to Heidegger on *Dasein*'s flight from itself, its "self splitting," in reaction to *Angst* and uncanniness: the generalized dread and strangeness of being-in-the-world as "being outside" oneself, eventually the "outsidedness," or even "outsidingness," *ek-stasis*, of primordial time. Critically, such dread and strangeness concern what *Dasein* is—care, being-in-the-world. But as being-in-the-world, *Dasein* is neither an internal subjectivity nor an external objectivity, and finally not even specifically human (time itself as the structure of care). But this relatedness to something other is not about a relation to a transcendental god, a god seen as the creator of the possibility of such a relation ("abstraction"), nor is it immediate, sensory experience of the objectively present.

Heidegger (1969) called metaphysics onto-theology—i.e., the system of thought dominated by conceptions of universal substance and highest principles. This was a way of describing metaphysics as the forgetting of the difference between being (time not conflated with the present) and beings (the objectively present). Again, metaphysics is a larger version of what Hume called the error of "real presence," but of presence itself as a symptomatic expression of a difference that is other than presence. Heidegger, one can say, avoids the trap of Humean common sense, which posits that the abstract develops slowly out of a concrete beginning, and the de Brossian trap of explaining that the concrete and the abstract can co-exist only as a theological, Biblically literal idea.

Derrida, extending Heidegger on difference as the unthought of metaphysics via the problematic of the trace, took Rousseau's *Essay on the Origin of Language* as one of his great "symptomatic" readings of this issue (in *Of Grammatology* [1974]). The question of difference is always the question of "the unity of opposites," perhaps in a way not appreciated by Heidegger, even in his own deconstruction of the principle of identity. Derrida's early work famously emphasizes that the trace, "writing" in an extended sense, as the differential, non-meaningful play that makes it possible for language to have meaning, is consistently found to be both necessary *and* threatening in metaphysics. The great example in *Of Grammatology* is Rousseau's characterization of writing as a dangerous supplement—"supplement" in French combining the contrary senses of that which necessarily makes up for a lack and of that which is extra, not necessary, and even dangerous. For Derrida, a thinking of difference as "original," as that which structures apparent oppositions, such that aspects of reality are "themselves and their opposite," means encompassing what is a "catastrophe" for reason itself: not only is presence an effect of difference, but all phenomena are constituted by internal division. Whatever the differences between de Brosses and Rousseau, both their arguments require a *divine* catastrophe when they encounter the question of "original difference," and both have to disqualify the belief that a thing can embody opposite characteristics, even as they observe this phenomenon.

This is why Noah's sons are as important to Rousseau as they are to de Brosses. In accounting for the possibility of different languages, Rousseau, like de Brosses, speaks of what Derrida calls "a catastrophic event annulling progress and compelling repetition, [so that the] structural analysis can recommence from zero" (1974, p. 254). As Rousseau puts it: "Adam spoke, Noah spoke, so be it. Adam had been instructed by God himself. In going their separate ways, Noah's children abandoned agriculture, and the common language perished along with the first society. This would have happened even if there had never been a tower of Babel" (p. 254; trans. mod.).

But there is an even greater divinely created catastrophe that accounts for the origin of different languages. For Rousseau, there is nothing within archaic barbarism that would impel it toward the development of society. Something from the outside had to push it in that direction. God is central to Rousseau's genealogy of society out of the state of nature: "He who willed man to be social, by the touch of a finger shifted the globe's axis into line with the axis of the universe. With this slight movement I see the face of the earth change, deciding the vocation of the human race" (1974, p. 256, trans. mod.). Why? Because there were now different seasons, as opposed to an original eternal springtime. Now man is compelled to cultivate the land, so there will be enough to eat when cultivation is not possible. All society emerged from this terrestrial revolution. But this differentiation depended upon "the finger of God." As Derrida puts it: "As the catastrophe... of seasonal differentiation could not be logically produced from within an inert system, one must imagine the unimaginable: a flick of the finger perfectly exterior to nature... The negative, the origin of evil, society, articulation come from the outside" (p. 256, trans. mod.). But this theological outside also permits the realization of faculties dormant in man (p. 256). Which leads to Derrida's question: "Who will ever say if the lack in nature is *within* nature, if the catastrophe by means of which nature *separates itself from itself* is still natural? A natural catastrophe conforms to the law to overturn the law" (p. 258). In other words, the play of difference that accounts for society and different languages is an internal possibility made actual via catastrophe that has to come from the outside, if reason says that difference itself cannot be original. But to speak of "original difference" is already to contradict the principle of identity: the "origin" is its "opposite," that which comes after the origin.

If this catastrophe for reason is contained within reason, if, as Derrida says via Rousseau, "supplementarity [in its contradictory senses] is irreducible to logic, and first of all because it includes logic as one of its cases" (1974, p. 259, trans. mod.), one then either has to place this possibility in the transcendental beyond of man, which has always defined theological investigation, or one has radically to revise what both man, and what is other than man, might be. This implies something like a transcendental approach, even if it deconstructs the transcendental. On some occasions, Derrida has called this approach "quasi-transcendental," notably when analyzing another famous instance of the blind conceptualization of writing, trace, difference, as intrinsically containing opposite properties: Plato's *pharmakon*, simultaneously remedy and poison. (Writing simultaneously "cures" an essential deficiency of spoken language and balefully infects it. [Derrida, 1981a, *passim*.])

Note the similarity to the long history of observing that worship of things, animate or inanimate, was linked to both hope and fear, influence for good or evil; and note too the similarity to the psychoanalytic ideas that the fetish is both phallic and castrated, or the breast both idealized and persecutory. The long history of observation of fetishism is dominated by the same idea, seen as universal evidence of childish irrationality. If adult rationality has to emerge from this state, the two have to be connected, either by divine catastrophe (e.g., de Brosses) or the overcoming of primal anxieties (Freud, Klein). But psychoanalysis generally attributes this overcoming to a kind of Humean natural progression toward reason, which can always misfire, producing the unreason of something like fetishism. The problem is that the necessary co-existence of the abstract and the concrete, the differentiated and the non-differentiated, is not accounted for—despite all the (clinical) evidence for it.

Psychoanalysis potentially could think about this issue, without positing divine intervention, via Freud's original conception of the unconscious not only as the realm of irrational fantasy, but as the possibility of differentiation itself. This implies theorizing unconscious processes beyond, or prior to, the principle of identity: unconscious processes are "larger" than reason not only because they are primordially irrational, as are "children and savages," but also because they include reason as "one of their cases." To wit: they register the reality that exceeds the opposition rational/irrational, the reality of differentiating processes that contravene the principle of identity. But such registration must be thought in relation to catastrophe: the catastrophe of registration of an uncontrollable otherness, the catastrophe of inevitable pain. It is not difficult to understand why such realities would be attributed either to a transcendental beyond *or* to a present thing that acts for good and evil. Both possibilities place the catastrophe *outside*.

Does one then place the catastrophe inside? From within the conventional use of such terms, yes. But the conventional sense will not do here, because it risks making this process the property of an internal subject. Here, one must return to something like Heidegger's being-in-the-world, a structure of "outsidedness" that one nevertheless *is*. Psychoanalytically, I have tried to link being-in-the-world to primary narcissism, conceived not in the usual sense of a self-enclosed monad, but in the sense of an organization in which inside and outside, subject and object are not relevant terms. *And* in a sense that has to include the differentiable unconscious, the unconscious which primordially registers the trace of the breast in Freud's theory. The breast, in this conception, is then not only the first source of self-preservation (food) and pleasure, as in Freud's conception, but is also the *differentiating thing that one is.* (In Freud's posthumous formulation: "'The breast is a part of me, I am the breast.' Only later: 'I have it'—that is, 'I am not it'" 1941, p. 299.) This differentiating thing is no more an external object than the baby is an internal subject—the "being-in-the-world" of primary narcissism. It inhabits fantasy as its condition of possibility—as in Freud's conception that the proto-dream is the hallucinatory revival of the memory trace of the breast. But it is a memory that cannot know itself as memory: as in any hallucination, the thing is there now. It is an object perceived, even if fantasmatically. Structurally, then, the "differentiating thing that one is," a kind of "abstraction," co-exists with the concrete perception of an object. The capacity for hallucination, for dreaming, is what makes the "error of real presence" inevitable. As the differentiating thing "becomes" more and more a fantasy object, it can act for good or evil, can be idealized and persecutory as for Klein, or phallic and castrated as for Freud. It can become a theological object. It will be worshiped and feared, the apparent source of salvation and catastrophe. And it will be the apparent source of both unreason and reason—whether in the accounts of a god who created man with the co-existent possibilities of concreteness and abstraction or in the developmental progression from "fantasy" to "reality."

When Freud described animism in terms so similar to those found in all the discourses on fetishism—the projection of human spirit onto uncontrollable nature in the attempt to control it magically—he could not see what was "true" in animism. The original relation to a thing—the differentiating breast of primary narcissism—is an unconscious relation to a living, erotic *thing*, which is not an external object, and which "traces itself," opening a pathway of memory. In other words, the irrational, magical belief in the power of things, or even the erotic arousal by things, is also the memory of the original, different thing, a memory "overlaid" with theological fantasies of good and evil, of external difference. This is another "secret of fetishism." The fantasy driven idealization of things, analyzed in various ways in the discourse on fetishism, carries the memory of a real, *living thing.*

The "living thing" is a prime example of the uncanny for Freud, the uncanny which brings us back to the unity of opposites, to the familiar as the unfamiliar, the fictive as the real, the thing as alive. It is not usually noted that Freud derived uncanniness from primary narcissism. Discussing the uncanny in terms of doubling, identification with another to the extent that one is in doubt as to which one's self is, so that one might "substitute" oneself for the other, Freud derives it from "the primary narcissism that dominates the mind of the child and primitive man" (1919, pp. 246–247). He does not integrate this derivation with the theoretically necessary differentiating memory trace of the breast, the living thing that one is ("I am the breast"). If the uncanny is the unfamiliar at the heart of the familiar, then one has here a prime example of it: the uncanniness of the universally ordinary experience of the baby and the breast. Remarkably, Freud proceeds to derive the possibility of self-observation from uncanny doubling. He speaks of the "fact that... man is capable of self observation," as making it "possible to invest the old idea of a 'double' with a new meaning" (1919, p. 247). I am interpreting this "new meaning" of doubling as the oscillation within it of self-reference and self-observation, the structural co-existence of the abstract and the concrete. This would have to be linked to Freud's generalization of fetishism at the end of his life. If the worshiped thing or the sexualized thing—the fetish in the usual sense—is the model for all symptom formation, and if such a relation to a thing carries the memory of the "different thing that one is," then all symptoms—conventionally symbolic or concrete—also carry within them the possibility of self-observation and self-reference. Certainly, to different degrees. But there will be alternation between these apparently opposite possibilities in every analysis. Analytic "reason" cannot exclude this possibility.

De Brosses, in making universal fetishism co-exist with abstract reason via catastrophe, unwittingly gives an account of the quasi-transcendental or uncanny nature of what we call mind. Mind is originally capable of both self-reference and self-observation. For a certain reading of Freud, identity is quasi-transcendental or uncanny: it is originally a relation to a differentiating thing that one is. Mind and identity, then, are made possible by the structure of fetishism—hence its inevitable generalization.

Notes

1 Chapters 1 and 2 of this book are both based upon "On the History of Fetishism" by Alan Bass and are reproduced from *The Undecidable Unconscious: A Journal of Deconstruction and Psychoanalysis*, vol. 2, 2014, with permission from the University of Nebraska Press. © 2016.

2 In Chapter 6, we will see Merleau-Ponty elaborate an important challenge to this position.

3 Difference as original is, of course, the idea that guides Derrida's work, which will be discussed further.

2

COMTE

Neo-fetishism[1]

Comte's "neo-fetishism" is in part a reaction against what he calls "superb Germanic doctors." So we will begin, briefly, with Kant and Hegel. Pietz (see Introduction) had cited Kant on fetishism as worship of the trifling. This is from his early *Observations on the Feeling of the Beautiful and the Sublime* (1960a [1763]). Kant supported the slave trade, so his initial formulations about fetishism are consistent with the colonial and racist thinking that dominates the encounter of Europe and Africa. Here is the entire passage:

> The Negroes of Africa have by nature no feeling that rises above the trifling. Mr. Hume challenges anyone to cite a single example in which a Negro has shown talents, and asserts that among the hundreds of thousands of blacks who are transported elsewhere from their countries, although many of them have even been set free, still not a single one was ever found who presented anything great in art or science or any other praiseworthy quality, even though among the whites some continually rise aloft from the lowest rabble, and through superior gifts earn respect in the world. So fundamental is the difference between these two races of man, and it appears to be as great in regard to mental capacities as in color. The religion of fetishes so widespread among them is perhaps a sort of idolatry that sinks as deeply into the trifling as appears to be possible to human nature. A bird feather, a cow's horn, a conch shell, or any other common object, as soon as it becomes consecrated by a few words, is an object of veneration and of invocation in swearing oaths. The blacks are very vain but in the Negro's way, and so talkative that they must be driven apart from each other with thrashings.
>
> *(pp. 110–111)*

Note the inconsistency: even though some freed Negroes "among the whites" have "superior gifts," difference of color equals an essential difference of mental capacity. That is, Kant cannot see the possibility that the equation of visible, present color with inferior mental capacity is as "trifling" as what he ascribes to Negroes. And that this equation is a form of "fetishism," in which the ascription of one's own ideas onto the object gives one an unquestioned right to abuse it. (As in de Brosses, the fetish can be beaten or destroyed.) Negroes' trifling talk, their insistent chattering to each other, demands the whip.

Many years later, in *Religion Within the Limits of Reason Alone* (1960b [1793]), Kant returns to fetishism in a broader context. He defines fetishism as the attainment of divine approval by oneself, the fulfillment of one's desires. (A psychoanalyst hears the narcissism of immediate wish fulfillment.) Kant characterizes this kind of gratification as irrational and immoral: "between solely physical means and a morally efficacious cause there is no connection whatsoever according to any law of which reason can conceive" (p. 166). This is the "service of God" as "mere *fetishism*" (p. 167). But now this understanding of fetishism extends to any organization of religion in which obedience to a clergy predominates: "*Clericalism*, therefore, is the constitution of a church to the extent to which a *fetish-worship* dominates it... Now there are, indeed, various types of church in which the fetishism is so manifold and so mechanical that it appears to crowd out nearly all of morality, and therefore religion as well, and to seek to occupy their places; such fetishism borders very closely on paganism" (pp. 167–168). Similarly, compulsory service to precepts judged unconditionally necessary is a "fetish faith through which the masses are ruled and robbed of their moral freedom by subservience to a church (not to religion). The structure of this hierarchy can be monarchical or aristocratic or democratic... its constitution is and ever remains despotic" (p. 168). Typically for Kant, a moral religion must conform to natural law:

> Every initiatory step in the realm of religion, which we do not take in a purely moral manner but rather have recourse to an *in itself* as a means of making us well-pleasing to God and thus through Him, of satisfying all our wishes, is a *fetish-faith*. This is the persuasion that what can produce no effect at all according to either natural laws or to moral laws of reason, will yet, of itself, bring about what is wished for, if only we firmly believe that it will do so, and if we accompany this belief with certain formalities.
>
> *(p. 181)*

While Kant does not use overtly racial categories in this passage, how can one not hear them in the use of words like "paganism" and "fetishism"? One might say that there is a kind of "African" propensity to mankind, i.e., an irrational desire to equate ritual, "certain formalities," and belief in magic, with the fulfillment of wishes, prescribed by an equally "African" clergy. As always, one hears the permanence of the mind of the savage, even in forms of contemporary religion. Which is not to say that Kant's comparison of fetishism to ritualistic clericalism is unjustified. But how can one not also hear a rationalist justification for religious prejudice, analogous to Kant's linkage of fetishism to justification of the slave trade? As always in analyses of fetishism, a compelling logic (fetishism, magic, wish fulfillment), co-exists with a blind incapacity to grasp the illogic at the heart of the argument.

Hegel will repeat some of these themes, which were commonplace in European discourse, due to what he calls the "copious and circumstantial accounts of Missionaries" (1956, p. 93). How could one doubt the uniform, voluminous reports of the Christian observers "in the field"?

> The peculiarly African character is difficult to comprehend, for the very reason that in reference to it, we must quite give up the principle that naturally accompanies all *our* ideas—the category of Universality. In Negro life the characteristic point is the fact that consciousness has not yet attained to the realization of any substantial objective existence—as for example, God, or Law—in which the interest of man's volition is involved and in which he realizes his own being... We must lay aside all thought of reverence and morality—all that we call feeling—if we would rightly comprehend him; there is nothing harmonious with humanity to be found in this type of character.
>
> *(p. 93)*

Without European universality, there is no true religion and no morality, nothing truly human. If there is some form of religion, lacking the idea of the universal, it "exhibits man as the highest power, regarding him as alone occupying a position of command over the power of Nature" (ibid.). This is what will be called animism, as in Freud, and Hegel's understanding of it is identical: "Although they are necessarily conscious of dependence upon nature... yet this does not conduct them to the consciousness of a Higher Power: it is they who command the elements, and this they call 'magic.'" (p. 94). The inevitable result of this non-abstract form of worship is fetishism:

> The second element in their religion, consists in their giving an outward form to this supernatural power—projecting their hidden might into the world of phenomena by means of images. What they conceive of as the power in question, is therefore nothing really objective, having a substantial being and different from themselves, but the first thing that comes in their way. This, taken quite indiscriminately, they exalt to the dignity of a "Genius"; it may be an animal, a tree, a stone, or a wooden figure. This is their *Fetich*—a word to which the Portugese first gave currency, and which is derived from *feitizo*, magic. Here, in the Fetich, a kind of objective independence as contrasted with the arbitrary fancy of the individual seems to manifest itself; but as the objectivity is nothing other than the fancy of the individual projecting itself into space, the human individuality remains master of the image it has adopted. If any mischance occurs which the Fetich has not averted, if rain

> is suspended, if there is a failure in the crops, they bind and beat or destroy the Fetich and so get rid of it, making another immediately, and thus holding it in their own power. Such a Fetich has no independence as an object of religious worship; still less has it aesthetic independence as a work of art; it is merely a creation that expresses the arbitrary choice of its maker, and which always remains in his hands. In short there is no relation of dependence in this religion.
>
> *(ibid.)*

As in de Brosses, and implicitly in Kant, projection of "the fancy of the individual" makes the individual "master of the image it has adopted," which can be beaten or destroyed should the individual's wishes fail to be realized. The fetish is not really *different* from its creator and it has no real objective existence. Two points must be noted. First, the problem of difference arises, as in any discussion of the relation to a thing which seems to be other, but which embodies one's own mentality. Difference itself is equated with objectivity. Second, Hegel, like Kant, does not take up de Brosses' conundrum: the universality of this non-universalizing form of worship. What would either do with this question? Would either arrive at de Brosses' position that abstraction, difference, and fetishistic concreteness necessarily co-exist?

Inevitably in this context, there is the question of slavery. Hegel: "Negroes are enslaved by Europeans and sold to America. Bad as this may be, their lot in their own land is even worse, since there a slavery quite as absolute exists; for it is the essential principle of slavery, that man has not yet attained a consciousness of his freedom, and consequently sinks down to a mere Thing—an object of no value" (1956, p. 96). How does Hegel know that the African slave is worse off in his own land than in America? Even assuming that the Negro has no consciousness of his freedom, would the African slave, given the choice, prefer to stay where he is or to be transported to America? For Hegel, it would seem that the slave is better off in America, just as for Kant Africans only show their "superior gifts" among the "whites":

> [S]lavery is itself a phase of advance from the merely isolated sensual existence—a phase of education—a mode of becoming participant in a higher morality and the culture connected with it. Slavery is in and for itself *injustice*, for the essence of humanity is *Freedom*; but for this man must be matured. The gradual abolition of slavery is therefore wiser and more equitable than its sudden removal.
>
> *(p. 99)*

In other words, the slave in America should remain a slave until such time as absorption of the necessarily and uniquely European idea of freedom occurs.

Comte will stand all this on its head.

The usual account of Comtean positivism divides it into two phases. According to Comte's most enthusiastic supporters, such as Littré and Mill, only the early part was to count as true positivism. The second part, in which fetishism plays a dominant role, was an aberration. Comte himself thought the opposite. Never abandoning his famous conception of the three phases of human development—the theological or fictive; the metaphysical or abstract; the scientific or positive—Comte understood his late project for a "positivist religion" as the culmination of his entire effort to regenerate humanity. To combine positivism and religion was to give new weight to the earliest theological or fictive stage—fetishism. "The better one compares fetishism and positivism," he wrote in the *System of Positivist Politics* (*Système de politique positiviste*, 1853), "the more one recognizes their fundamental affinity" (p. 119).

The source of this affinity is the subjectivistic nature of fetishism. This might surprise those who think of positivism as the most anti-subjectivistic conception of science. Comte did not doubt that early man had an inevitable tendency to attribute his own sense of himself to what he found in his world. But he disagreed with all the previous thinkers who saw this as irrational. Comte saw it as the possibility of a reason superior to the reason of the metaphysical or abstract age of humanity: "the definitive reconciliation of feeling and reason [the goal of the positivist religion free of metaphysical abstraction] was even announced in the fetishistic synthesis, in which the preponderance of the first [feeling], and the impotence of the second [reason] were equally spontaneous, without inciting any mutual oppression" (ibid.). How and why this is so, culminating in Comte's neo-fetishism, requires explanation.

The ironically titled *Positivist Catechism* (*Catéchisme positiviste*) of 1852 offers this integration of positivism and fetishism:

> All healthy logic is reducible to a single rule: always formulate the simplest hypothesis compatible with acquired information. Now, theological thinkers, and even fetishists, applied this rule better than most of our modern doctors. Proposing to penetrate causes, they limited themselves to explaining the world by man, the only possible source of all theoretical unity, attributing to all phenomena superhuman will. Such a problem, by its nature comports no other solution... primitive theology opened the human mind to the only exit from our initial situation. Even though it could never lead us to the determination of causes, the provisional links established between facts led us spontaneously to the discovery of laws.
>
> *(pp. 47–48)*

This will be Comte's theme: before theology became metaphysics, the conviction that things in the world were animated by the same forces that primitive man felt in himself led to intense involvement with these things, involvement that produced practical, not abstract, knowledge. This is the knowledge Comte calls "lawful," i.e., understanding of how things work, without knowledge of their true "causes." Metaphysical abstraction, placing causality in the gods, i.e., in a realm beyond man and things, loses practical, lawful knowledge, and can never arrive at true causes.

Hence, the positivist religion will find its most potential adepts among the Africans who have not yet passed through a polytheistic or monotheistic phase of belief in gods beyond man:

> Fetishists occupy a vast region in the middle of Africa completely inaccessible to our civilization. Positivist missionaries will find there the situation most likely to stimulate theoretical efforts and practical zeal, proposing to extend the universal religion directly among these naive populations, without imposing upon them any monotheistic, or even polytheistic, transition. The possibility for this kind of success results from the profound affinity of positivism with fetishism, which differ… only in the adoration of materials instead of in products. In all spontaneous or directed human formation fetishism constitutes the mode of the fictive regime which is truly inevitable, because it emerges at a time when the species or the individual is incapable of any reflection.
>
> *(1852, p. 322)*

Incapacity for reflection, and "adoration of materials" are historically the traits used to disqualify fetishism. Reflection for Comte, however, is consubstantial with metaphysical abstraction. This is why immediate, pre-reflective experience contains the germ of the "true logic" of the future:

> The mental efficacy of fetishism consists in spontaneously founding the subjective method, which, initially absolute, will increasingly preside over our normal state. True logic, in which feelings dominate images and signs, therefore has a fetishistic origin. When any given passion impels us to seek the causes of phenomena whose laws we do not know, in order to anticipate and modify them… we directly attribute to these beings human affects, instead of subjecting them to external forces. Fetishism is therefore more natural than polytheism.
>
> *(1852, p. 333)*

The impetus to causal knowledge is "passion." We are compelled, moved, to understand why things happen if we are to "anticipate and modify them." We then attribute a similar passion, affect, to these things; hence, we engage with their internal operations in a more direct way than if we suppose them to be acted upon by non-human, external forces. This is why there was initially no "mutual oppression" of feeling and thought: the "affects" attributed to the internal working of things produced intimate knowledge of them. When fetishism became belief in gods who determine what things are, and how they work, attention was diverted away from subjectively understood things themselves, and instead to "images and signs." The polytheist had to understand the influence of the gods on himself and his environment. This influence is external; one becomes preoccupied with the gods rather than with the internal "passions" of things. Feeling and thought then have to be segregated.

Both Kant and Hegel had reflected the consensus that the fetishistic equation of things and oneself meant that there was no universal abstraction in fetishism; each man could worship the first thing that caught his fancy. If immediate feeling is all there is, then there is nothing between man and the object of worship. Kant, we have seen, saw fetishism even in extreme clericalism. Comte's view of clericalism is in some ways similar. Once there is polytheism, and eventually monotheism, a priesthood mediates between man and god via reflection on universal principles. The transition to polytheism, and to a religion that required a priesthood, came with the veneration of the stars ("Sabism"). As the stars are beyond our reach, residing in a realm above us, we cannot understand them the way we understand the things around us. A special class is needed to interpret their will, and how they determine things and events. While this development certainly fostered observation of the heavens, it alienated man from the world around him. Stars became gods; religion became polytheistic. Eventually, this polytheism became monotheism, which culminated in the metaphysical age, the ultimate divorce of thought and feeling; as Comte sees it, the clergy became doctors of philosophy. Reflection is then speculation, losing the immediate engagement with things of subjective experience. (This is where Comte departs from Kant.) Positivism will overcome this divide, integrating irreducible subjectivity with causal science.

The positivist surmounting of the divide between feeling and intellect has a large result for the study of man. Comte is generally credited as the founder of sociology. Man, he thought, must be studied collectively, because the notion of an individual divorced from humanity at large was the result of metaphysics. Fetishism gave the impetus to this eventual sociology, having initiated the passage from pastoral to agricultural life, from nomadism to a sedentary state of families and collectivities. "This great transformation, whose difficulty is no less misconstrued than is its importance, certainly belongs to fetishism, according to the profound attachment it inspires in us for our native soil" (1852, p. 334). What fetishism could not encompass was the actual state of our minds: "Fetishism, essentially relative to the material world, could not directly embrace our intellectual and moral existence" (p. 336). But the positivist religion will rectify this failure, while promoting sociological study and the glorification of Humanity.

Sociological study will include mental illness. Given his own experience of breakdown in 1826, and his convictions about the primacy of emotion, Comte thought that "mental alienation" was an innate human possibility. Sounding very much like Freud, he thought that the nature of dreams could illuminate the nature of "alienation." He understood dreams as transitory states of madness, in which subjective impulses dominate involuntarily (1852, p. 152). Because the "heart directs the mind during the waking state, despite external impressions, it must dominate the mind even more when these impressions are suspended" (p. 153). Freud: because the perceptual apparatus is not preoccupied with external stimuli during sleep, it is more receptive to internal, instinctual, affective stimuli. Sounding even more like Freud, Comte thought that to see dreams as brain functions would make them interpretable: "One can hope that cerebral theory will finally lead to real interpretation of dreams," although he then hoped for something Freud thought was impossible: "and even to modification of them, according to the premature wish of all antiquity" (ibid.). (None of this contradicted Comte's passionate belief in phrenology.) What distinguishes Comte and Freud (on fetishism, dreams, and madness) from de Brosses (who formulated the idea shared by all that fetishism reveals the universal childhood of man) is that Comte and Freud are open to a scientific, "positivistic" analysis of fetishism. Such analysis reveals the universal functioning of the mind—and even of the brain. The question was always whether the universal structures of the infantile mind/brain could be surpassed or whether they were always active, providing essential resources for mature, collective functioning. Comte did not hesitate to say that man is fetishistic during childhood, metaphysical during adolescence, and positivist in maturity, but this maturity has to understand its roots in childhood, in order to overcome adolescence—and potential metaphysical madness.

The *System of Positive Politics* (1853) extends this analysis. Fetishism becomes the interface of instinct, emotion, materiality, and action in the world. The fetishistic age, says Comte, is characterized by the spontaneity of the "fictive synthesis" (p. 78), and by a principle of "harmony." The essence of this harmony is to act through feeling and to think in order to act: "When instinct impels us to modify the external world, activity dominates, and intelligence is limited to counseling it. This being the most essential and frequent case, I have had to formulate human harmony on this basis" (ibid.). The next most general case of intelligence in the service of feeling is the communication of emotion. There, "the mind is elevated to the dignity of principal minister of the heart, and activity is limited to furnishing the means necessary for material expression, which only intelligence can employ" (p. 80). These inverse functions—action and communication—always co-exist. The first belongs to "fetishistic spontaneity" and the second to "theological systematization" (p. 81). But the latter is less harmonious than the former. It inhibits spontaneous action, because it understands the relation to materiality as passive submission to supernatural powers—again the result of the transition to polytheism (pp. 81–82).

In all these ways, Comte's views of affect and intellect seem to be the opposite of Kant's. For Comte, affect is active; as sensory reception, for Kant, it is passively received. For Comte, to make "intelligence" the "principal minister of the heart" produces theological passivity; for Kant, concept formation, the intellect, is spontaneous, producing the possibility of "religion within the limits of reason alone." Hence, from Comte's anti-metaphysical point of view, Kant inevitably and conventionally dismissed fetishism: the fetish as a trifling object with no relation to the sublime; the fetish as a magical attempt by primitive man to obtain divine satisfaction. Comte is proud that his view of fetishism flaunts philosophical convention: "I must especially compare these two general states of primitive philosophy to demonstrate, contrary to the dominant prejudice, that the first [fetishism] surpasses the second [theological systematization] as much in rectitude as in spontaneity" (1853, p. 82).

His insistence on the "fictive" for the development of reason is equally contrarian. The superiority of fetishism to systematic theology is due to:

> spontaneity, which constitutes the principal property of the fictive synthesis as the primitive guide of human reason... In taking complete positivity as the normal type of mental maturity, the fetishist is located at much less distance from it than any theologist. His general approximation of reality is more exact in that it is more natural: we surpass it only in the scientific state. This is why fetishism would still prevail everywhere, if social necessities had not forced our ancestors to take the route of theologism in their necessary preparation of positivism. This conception is directly contrary to all current opinion.
>
> *(1853, p. 85)*

Fetishism, then, is the relation to things most natural to man, and closest to "reality." But it is not yet science, which is reached via the alienating detour of the "theologism" imposed by social necessity. Why is this conception "directly contrary to all current opinion"? For the evident reason that it sees in a non-reflective, putatively irrational practice something more "realistic" than the putatively rational, reflective thought in which abstract reason integrates science and theology. Compare Kant and Hegel.

But even though Comte's views necessarily seem to be the inverse of theirs, all are preoccupied with the same question: how is mind constituted such that it can gain knowledge of things. I am emphasizing Kant here, because it seems to me that Comtean positivism is more of a response to him than to Hegel, and because we will have more to say about Kant in subsequent chapters. In the *Critique of Pure Reason*, Kant's question is: how does a finite being, man, come to have knowledge of things he did not create, things that have their origin in an infinite being, God. As is well known, this led Kant to his conception of the *a priori* synthesis. Comte's fetishistic "fictive synthesis" plays a similar role: it is the original possibility of scientific knowledge, because of its freedom from (theological) abstraction. "Fictive" in Comte means subjective, but subjective in the strong sense of direct engagement with oneself and things as the source of true objectivity. "Thus, the fetishistic method opens the normal progression to true logic, from which the theological method diverges radically. The one spontaneously limits itself to the degree of subjectivity which is indispensable to us; instead, the other becomes much more subjective than its theoretical destination requires" (1853, p. 86). The hyper-subjectivity of the theological method derives from making man and things *subject* to abstractions that are outside them, the metaphysical abstractions mediated by clerical doctors of philosophy. Their "hyper-subjectivity" makes them more concerned with the abstractions developed in their own minds than with things themselves.

For Comte, that way lies madness. He thinks that "mental alienation, especially of the chronic kind, is much more frequent and stubborn in theologists than among fetishists" (1853, p. 87). Thus, he thought that his own experience of breakdown was a kind of theological regression, which then had to lead back to healthy positivism.

Kofman cites his account of the "sad experience" of madness in 1826. He claimed to have descended "from positivism to fetishism, stopping first at monotheism and then even more at polytheism... I slowly rose from fetishism to polytheism, and from the latter to monotheism, from whence I promptly returned to my previous positivity" (cited, p. 183).

The metaphysical abstractions derived from theology are not only potentially mad in their abstraction, they are intellectually inadequate: "the humble thinkers of central Africa are more estimable, even in rationality, than the pompous verbiage of superb Germanic doctors. For it is the result of a real feeling, however confused, of the precocity of such theories for whoever remains without a scientific basis, from which our metaphysicians are more shamefully estranged than the slightest blacks" (1853, p. 99). In other words, Kant's and Hegel's pejorative dismissals of African mentality are a kind of metaphysical madness.

No accident, then, that Comte's appreciation of fetishism is linked to denunciation of the slave trade: "Fetishism, even in our day, has everywhere inspired a stubborn attachment... among the deplorable victims of an infamous traffic" (1853, p. 113). Comte did believe in the superiority of European reason—provided it was positivist. His missionaries too, were to convert Africans to the true faith. Again, this is why fetishism as the original form of worship is so important. As Comte so consistently says, positivism is more akin to the "African" mind than to the metaphysical, "European" mind. In terms of his epigenetic theory, this means that the childish African is closer to nature than the adolescent metaphysician and his potentially mad abstractions; true adulthood belongs to the positivist who returns to nature more scientifically, drawing upon the resources of the original "subjective synthesis."

The sanity of the fetishistic synthesis makes it the true possibility of integrating synthesis and system, perhaps another aspect of Comte's apparent anti-Kantianism.

> Lacking the systematic relativity that only positivism emphasizes, fetishism is still reproached for a tendency for which true philosophers should be profoundly grateful, when it is accused of granting feeling too much ascendency over intelligence... In this way one forgets that the initial synthesis, necessarily deprived of an objective basis, found itself forced to borrow from the heart its theoretical principle. According to the fundamental doctrine established in this treatise on the true nature of unity, the final coordination of human speculations also rests upon affect. For such is the unique source of universal systematization, without which the theoretical synthesis would remain impossible.
>
> *(1853, p. 93)*

To put it axiomatically: Kant's *a priori* synthesis could not be the kind of fictive synthesis Comte envisages. Kant as logical epistemologist is *too* systematic: he creates an architectonic and an *a priori* synthesis deprived of an authentic affective foundation. Even if the Kantian system is a justification for Newtonian science, it would lack the necessary relativism (i.e., constant adjustment according to the actual nature of things) of true science, possible only for positivism.

> Thus, synthesis is more important than system. The fetishistic regime, although more spontaneous than the following regimes, was really more synthetic, without for that being systematic... If we always regard the qualities of synthetic and systematic as connected, this is due to a confused perception of the normal state, forgetting the preparatory regime, in which these two attributes had to be profoundly contrasted. The definitive reconciliation of feeling and reason was even announced in the fetishistic synthesis, in which the preponderance of the first, and the impotence of the second were equally spontaneous, without inciting any mutual oppression. The better one compares fetishism and positivism, the more one recognizes their fundamental affinity. Even though these two extreme syntheses are the one spontaneous and the other systematic, they offer an equivalent subjectivity, the necessary condition for any universal connections. Their essential opposition can be reduced to the general contrast between the absolute character of the first and the relative spirit of the second, in conformity with their respective tendencies toward causes or laws, as with their proper use of the human type, individual or social... Under all essential headings, the philosophical influence of fetishism finds itself admirably in conformity with the best precepts of positivism... The fundamental preponderance of the heart over the mind, which the final systematization established laboriously in a milieu vitiated by theology and metaphysics, emanated without effort from primitive spontaneity.
>
> *(1853, p. 119)*

Positivism, like metaphysics, is systematic, but in a superior way: it draws upon the fetishistic synthesis of feeling and reason. The disadvantage of fetishism is its absoluteness and its view of man as an isolated individual. Only positivism achieves true scientific relativism and a view of man as social. This is the only possible access to true knowledge of "causes and laws."

Another resource of the "fictive synthesis" is its understanding of matter itself. The fetishist was guilty of the "very excusable" error of seeing man as too similar to animals, and even vegetables; the theologist is guilty of the not so excusable error of exaggerating their differences. True understanding of living beings and matter is not possible in abstract metaphysics:

> In representing living beings as essentially passive, in order to explain all real activity by supernatural influences, the second [metaphysical] regime of causes distances us directly from the true scientific state, toward which the first [fetishistic] one impels us. Human existence finds itself irrationally separated from the ensemble of beings into which fetishism had assimilated us too much... The theological doctrine is therefore more distant from the truth

> than the fetishistic doctrine in relation to the living world. As concerns "inert nature," fetishism is less satisfying, although again excusable. From the point of view of science, its error consists in... not distinguishing life properly called from spontaneous activity... This confusion distances us less from the true than does, in the opposite sense, the cosmological hypothesis introduced by theologism, in which matter is always supposed to be passive.
>
> *(1853, pp. 87–88)*

Comte then denounces the "murky hypothesis" (*hypothèse ténébreuse*) of "inert matter" (1853, p. 87).

The hypothesis of "inert matter" is "murky" because it understands matter only as acted upon by external, divine forces; the truly objective laws of matter's own functioning are not in question. Positivist logic will subjugate the subjective to the objective correctly by reviving the spirit of fetishism, which "impels man even to the adoration of matter" (1853, p. 91). The adoration of supernatural beings, on the other hand, "transposes onto imaginary motors the wills that fetishism supposed to be in real bodies" (ibid.) Hence, theologism tends to dispense with "all true submission to the natural order" (ibid.).

True submission to the natural order, whether fetishistic or positivistic, demands recognition of the immutability of all species and substances:

> One must... equally grant to fetishistic philosophy the capital notion of the fixity of all natural species, which, too altered under theologism, and poorly respected by scientific empiricism, furnishes the last necessary preamble to positivism. In directly attributing to real bodies all directing wills, fetishism consecrates the independence and perpetuity of each of them. This immense service, without which we would tend toward unlimited divagations, was radically compromised when theologism transported superhuman influences onto purely imaginary beings, capricious masters of a matter become entirely passive... There is danger to human reason in the esthetic seductions of metamorphoses... any notion of a real order would necessarily dissolve if species, that is substances, could change arbitrarily.
>
> *(1853, p. 125)*

It is not difficult to grasp Comte's reasoning. Species and substances passively subject to the whims of the gods can be changed arbitrarily—metamorphosis. Their specific, lawful, internally governing principles remain unknown, even inconceivable, as they typically are for the doctors of philosophy. "Everyone today should easily be able to conceive this tendency, on the example of the difficulty experienced by so many doctors to feel the invariability of the laws relative to the most modifiable phenomena. Since the real order seems incompatible with modifiability, fetishists had to consolidate its initial conception by means of a total fatalism" (1853, p. 122).

Reality would dissolve into chaos, science would be impossible, if *theological* mutability were the law. Fetishistic "fatalism" before the immutable nature of things is more realistic than the inability to see permanent lawfulness even in "modifiable phenomena." Kofman summarizes Comte's position: he believed in the fixity of species composed of clearly distinct terms, separated by unbridgeable intervals (1978, p. 270).

Here, one knows that Comte is wrong. Science was to move progressively in the direction of the mutability and connections of "species and substances." Comte was writing only a few years before *The Origin of Species*; pre-Darwinian conceptions of evolution were already "in the air." After Comte, and with the progressive understanding of the atomic structure of matter, the mutability of elements (half-life, particle emission) became the nature of physical reality. Immutably fixed species and substances imply timeless governing principles. Here, Comte is perhaps more Kantian than he might wish. The function of the *a priori* synthesis is to justify the existence of a timeless cogito, which produces Newton's immutable, universal scientific laws. Positivism too, asserts that the "real order" is fixed.

One cannot reproach Comte for being unaware of scientific ideas unavailable to him (evolution, atomic structure). But one can ask a question: if species and substances were mutable, what would happen to his understanding of fetishism? For de Brosses, reason demanded that the fetish had to exclude difference; for Comte, positivism demands that it has to exclude time, change, and connection. And just as there is a certain correctness to de Brosses on the undifferentiated aspect of the fetish, so too there is a certain correctness to Comte's timeless fetish: what Comte calls the "total fatalism" of fetishism shows up clinically in the apparent indifference to time of the conspicuously concrete patient. The clinical literature on concreteness almost always notes the strange willingness of such patients to stay in analysis interminably with no change, no concern for the passage of time. And we have seen the fear of uncontrollable chaos that emerges when fetishistic certainty is modified. Could the Comtean praise of fetishism's affinity to positivism also be an expression of the fear of uncontrollable chaos linked to time itself as connecting synthesis? This will be a major topic of the next chapter.

This question is "deconstructive." It puts synthesis, time, and difference as connection within phenomena, within both mind and matter. Nietzsche's conception of "metaphysical fetishism," of fixed, immutable reason and subjectivity, led him to reject all timelessness; he is a thinker of becoming. He thought that the concept of timeless substance was a projection of metaphysical subjectivity, and dismissed Comte (1968, p. 432) as a proponent of a new version of Christian morality. Heidegger was to put time as the possibility of synthesis at the heart of the allegedly timeless Kantian *cogito* in *Kant and the Problem of Metaphysics*. All of this to say that the places where discourse on fetishism repeats the defensively controlling aspects of fetishism (de Brosses, Freud) are places where even a general theory of fetishism encounters its "unthought." For Comte, this is the question of fixity, of whether there is a temporality of the thing.

For Comte, fetishistic fixity renders a crucial service. It counters innate human destructiveness:

> The destructive instinct is more energetic in us than the constructive instinct, by virtue of our cerebral constitution, and of our carnivorous habits... The

immense benefit of fetishism is to preserve many animal and vegetable species, in contrast to the destructive ardor which civilized men brutally develop, when exceptional circumstances sufficiently suspend the continuous repression of this powerful instinct… primitive alliance was always principally due to the fraternal customs that fetishism made predominant toward animals… No other absolute doctrine could be as favorable as fetishism to the direct and continuous rising up of our sympathetic instincts. Emanating from internal inspiration, its principle was necessarily personal, like that of any fictive synthesis, always incapable of consecrating social existence, which only positivism was to systematize.

(1853, pp. 103–108, passim*)*

In other words, individualistic, destructive, carnivorous man needs repression in order to prevent the "war of all against all" (see Freud in *Civilization and its Discontents* [1930]), which is inevitable if carnivorousness remains unchecked. Fetishistic veneration of animals prohibits killing them. The "primitive alliance" derived from "fraternal customs toward animals" is not yet truly "social"; its inspiration is "necessarily personal." Unlike de Brosses, who emphasized the "wars" between the worshippers of the rat and the cat, Comte says that "the mutual hostility of fetishists cannot in any way modify their respective faiths" (1853, p. 113). That is, as fetishism is individual, but does provide the first check on unfettered aggression, the "worshippers of the rat and the cat" will live on uneasy, peaceful terms with each other. This is certainly preferable to the "destructive ardor which civilized men brutally develop, when exceptional circumstances sufficiently suspend the continuous repression of this powerful instinct." Only positivism, with its sociological understanding of collective man, can make harmony between men systematic. But, as always for Comte, fetishism is the original possibility of this harmony because it *fixes* relations to animals, families, and communities. Fetishistic "fatalism," its belief in the atemporal immutability of species and substances, makes the fetishist less potentially barbaric than metaphysical man, who uses the questions of abstraction and universality to justify slavery (Kant, Hegel).

Fetishism is not only the first barrier against unfettered aggression; it is also responsible for linguistic fixity. Speech, the "phonic art," says Comte, was naturally incapable of perpetuating its "impressions." Thus, it had to make the transition to writing, and did so via painting and sculpture, which already fixed images. For Comte, then, as for so many others, writing was originally hieroglyphic.

[W]riting… remained for a long time in the hieroglyphic state, in which visual language, although subordinate to oral language, remained fully distinct from it, constituting a system of directly appreciable signs. The more complete subordination [of writing to oral language], by means of which forms are limited to translating sounds in order to fix them, in alphabetic or syllabic language, was established much later, and determines the entire systematization of human language. Except for this final institution, which only

> belongs to polytheism, fetishism certainly presides over all these successive transformations, from which results the decisive foundation of the language proper to humanity... Even taking one's point of departure from our current languages, one can recognize that their common basis necessarily goes back to the first fetishistic age.
>
> *(1853, p. 134)*

This analysis of the relation of writing to speech contains some de Brossian conceptions. Hieroglyphic, "fetishistic" writing is "directly appreciable." That is, it lacks the analytic abstraction necessary for the systematic fixing of spoken language. This analytic abstraction is as necessary and inevitable as positivism. But, precisely because it is a question of making the sensory abstract, the initial impetus toward phonetic writing comes only with the abstractions of polytheism, just as theology and metaphysics prepare positivism. In one sense, Comte here repeats the entire metaphysical tradition of seeing alphabetic writing as the best relation of writing to speech, linked to the possibility of reason. (All of Derrida's early work on centered on the questions of metaphysics as phonologism.) In another sense, Comte is saying something else: even abstract, "alphabetic or syllabic," languages have their "common basis" in fetishism.

This is where, like de Brosses, Comte has to account for the co-existence of concreteness and abstraction. Fetishistic, hieroglyphic writing has to contain within it the possibility of polytheistic abstraction, otherwise there would be no phonetic writing. As "directly appreciable," hieroglyphics are close to the self-referential. They are a "fictive synthesis" of subject and object, representative and represented. Phonetic, non-pictorial language is (apparently) not self-referential. But as the theological abstraction derives from fetishistic concreteness, fetishism has to inhere in all language.

This inherence of fetishism in phonetic language allows Comte to spell out why universal phonetic language is the possibility of a universal positivist religion:

> The two principle elements of human discourse are already abundant in all fetishistic languages, generally rich in nouns and even in verbs, in conformity with the dominant tendency possessed at that time by concrete appreciation... [Fetishistic languages] everywhere present the common attributes which bear witness to the domination of feeling over intelligence and of private life over public life. Despite their natural diversity, which superficial observers have greatly exaggerated, their fundamental affinity already intimates the final liaison between the universality of religion and the universality of language, simultaneously sketched out in fetishistic spontaneity.
>
> *(1853, p. 135)*

The "concrete appreciation" of the world evident in all fetishistic languages is more important than the diversity of languages. In a sense, Comte wants to overcome the "Babelian" problem. Less important than linguistic diversity is the universal fetishistic principle of fixing language—writing, in its original, hieroglyphic sense. This universal attribute is what will make individualistic fetishism, the first, universal form of worship, the foundation of universal, social religion, i.e., of positivism itself: the synthesis of feeling and thought.

Thus, Comte's ultimate neo-fetishism will apply what is best about the fictive synthesis—its appeal to sensory experience—with instruction in all forms of knowledge. Mathematics will be taught poetically. Neo-fetishism will overcome the limitations of original fetishism:

> Whatever the great intellectual and moral properties of fetishism, and despite its grand theoretical or practical results, its profound political insufficiency represents it as a purely provisional state, admirably suited to our childhood, but then tending to perpetuate it… [B]y consecrating an exclusively synthetic observation, fetishism only instituted a pure empiricism, as sterile in practice as it is incompatible with theory… [F]etishism could not subsequently direct the elaboration of natural harmony, consisting of the relation of succession or similarity between diverse phenomena… the immutability of the arrangement of phenomena in the midst of their changes of degree necessarily escapes the concrete [note the word] contemplation exclusively consecrated by fetishism… [fetishism] always leaves us floating between complete immobility and unlimited disorder.
>
> *(1853, pp. 148, 150)*

The "complete immobility" of fetishism refers to its "total fatalism" (mentioned previously); its "unlimited disorder" refers to its inability to explain causes, "the relation of succession or similarity between diverse phenomena." Taking these limitations into account, neo-fetishism will draw on all the esthetic possibilities of fetishism to develop "a fictive anchoring in a re-enchanted reality" (1853, p. 265). But to apprehend this "re-enchanted reality" is to escape the twin traps of sterile empiricism and unlimited disorder. Immutable, fixed laws can also be "fictive" in their potential esthetic delight.

Hence, neo-fetishism is a new alliance of poetry and philosophy (Fedi, 2002, p. 177). There will be an integration of religious, cultural, and pedagogic practice. Instead of the "puerile speculations" of (adolescent) metaphysics, there will be an awakening of the moral and esthetic—subjective—interest of practical studies, without which abstract science is "dry." Positivist pedagogue-priests will judiciously use these fictions to stimulate the emotions that will enliven study, while guarding against their wandering off into pure imagination. In this way, the "complementarity" between knowledge and love, allegedly unknown to philosophers (a dubious claim), will regenerate human knowledge.

This is where Comte's own, phonetic, writing becomes self-referential. The "final liaison between the universality of religion and the universality of language, simultaneously sketched out in fetishistic spontaneity," is embodied in Comte's writing itself. Fedi describes:

> For Comte, language being simultaneously a link between the inside and the outside (logic as a means of access to the real) and a mode of communication (language as a collective, transmissible capital), the articulation thereby revealed and systematized is to guide our practice of the sciences as much as our amorous conversations. Through the play of this articulation, the new logic becomes a social logic, with which one not only "reveals truths," but also "inspires conceptions," that is, reacts on thought by activating it from the inside, from a moral point of view... Comte illustrates this by presenting the new logic as the definitive systematization of the algebraic geometry invented by Descartes... the poetico-algebraic composition of the *Subjective Synthesis* [is] a complicated illustration of this new logic, in which writing plays by attaching "representative signs" onto the "corresponding emotions." This strange text in effect obeys an inapparent principle of writing as follows: each chapter is constructed as an assemblage of sections beginning respectively with A, B, C, D, E, F, G, H; the first letters of the new paragraphs of each section, placed end to end, form a key word belonging to French or to a European language, for example "Clartés" [clarities], in the hypothesis of a third section; if one then casts one's glance within a paragraph, one will discover that the first letters of the sentences give a new word, and since "Clartés" covers seven paragraphs, there will be a total of seven words; in the chosen example "*Certo*," "*Louis*," "*ardue*," "*relatio*," "*trova*," "*émois*," "*sacré*." Out of this emerges an arborescent structure offered to the reader like a rebus... [W]as it not a question too, of in a way fetishizing the hidden interior of writings as if to confect a sophisticated neo-fetishistic Bible?... To comment upon Comte in terms which are foreign to him, but which reflect the climate of his last writings, let us say that his intuitionism is not an anti-rationalism, as the return to fetishism might lead one to understand, but rather a form of hyper-rationalism whose consequences are difficult to measure.
>
> *(Fedi, 2002, p. 187)*

This perceptive analysis requires commentary. When Fedi speaks of the "hidden interior of writings" one can refer to the necessary relation of phonetic to hieroglyphic writing—as always in Comte, the fetishistic, "directly appreciable" origin of true abstraction. As Fedi says, this "intuitionism," this pre-reflective, fetishistic aspect of language, would not contradict rationality, but would make it more rational, overcoming both the "dryness" and limitation of thought divorced from feeling. This kind of writing then does not lose what is essential to Cartesian mathematics, but expands it. In de Brosses, of course, it was the opposite: fetishistic concreteness is to be divorced from Cartesian abstraction. ("Those who would ascribe to Savages the minds of Plato or Descartes—would they be judicious critics?") If Cartesianism is the foundation of the modern subject reflecting on itself, then Comte inevitably has to find a way to integrate self-reflection with self-reference. His does this through his writing itself. Here, self-reference (call it "poetry") and self-reflection (call it "mathematical logic") are integrated.

This integration is itself an "arborescent structure," a kind of rebus. The psychoanalytic reader might be struck by a resemblance to Freud's idea that the manifest content of the dream is like a hieroglyph or a rebus constructed by an endlessly intersecting—arborescent—chain of associations. Should one pause before a comparison between forms of writing and a natural object? Recall Comte's and Freud's thoughts about "cerebral science" providing a method of dream interpretation. For both Comte, in his final work, and Freud, from the beginning, there had to be a physiological link between the supposed origin of writing in sensory images and non-linear, endlessly entwined thoughts. A generalized fetishism is the potential explanation of this link for Comte. A generalized fetishism in which the apparent limitation of self-referential writing becomes an opening to scientific reason.

Kofman cites Comte's thought that the writing of the *Synthèse subjective* was to erase all structural differences between "poetical volumes and philosophical tomes" (1978, p. 242). Mill called this a "fantastical and tyrannical" regimentation; it was rejected by most of Comte's disciples (p. 243). Can this fetishistic writing still include the timelessness and fixity that Comte attributes to the natural order? It was Comte's intent to give back to reflective certainty its esthetic underpinning. But is this intent undermined by the necessary synthesis of poetry and philosophy, with the inevitable thought that the truth of philosophy is as much in its poetic writing as in its reflective certainties? Does Comte perform, without knowing it, the deconstructive/scientific gesture of finding in self-referential writing another kind of truth? Is this one of the consequences that is "difficult to measure"? Comte may have wished to impose a "fantastical and tyrannical" regimentation on his writing, but does not this very gesture produce a writing that creates an undecidability between what it purports to describe and what it is? Eventually, Godël would demonstrate undecidability via a system of self-referential notation and would put a certain kind of intuitionism at the heart of mathematics itself (Goldstein, 2005).

Like evolution and physics, contemporary brain science has made mutability—"plasticity"—an essential part of its conceptual foundation. Doubtless, Comte would be alarmed by such a conception. But he might also be gratified that the segregation of feeling and thought (*Descartes' Error* to use the title of Damasio's book) has been shown to be neuro-physiologically unfounded. The mutable, feeling-thinking, bilateral brain has been shown to be more than anything else a self-referential organism. As neuro-physiologist, Gerald Edelman puts it: the brain is "in touch more with itself than with anything else" (1992, p. 19). It is primarily auto-affective, "a self-organizing system" (p. 25). The "matter of the mind interacts with itself at all times" (p. 29). The strange possibility opens up that Comte was more right than he could have known when he sees self-referential fetishism as a better apprehension of reality than metaphysical abstraction that separates feeling and thought. Comtean fetishism, and neo-fetishistic writing, might be an unwitting intuition of the functioning of the brain itself. But, then, as opposed to everything Comte believed, this is a mutable, plastic brain, a temporal brain, which like evolution itself, according to Edelman, "has a generator of diversity" (p. 78). As in evolution, then, there can be no unbridgeable intervals in this brain. Thus, the paradox within Comtean neo-fetishism: he cannot see that the bridgeable interval between feeling and thought, poetry and philosophy, would have to make positivism a theory of mutability, time, and connecting intervals.

Freud purposely abandoned speculation about the brain after the 1895 *Project*. What would happen if one returned to such speculation on the basis of his own theory of generalized fetishism? My own contention has been that to understand fetishism itself as the disavowal of (sexual) difference, and then to apply this understanding to apparently self-referential concreteness, calls for a modification of the theory of mind. It implies an unconscious that registers the reality of non-present difference. I have argued that this modification can be integrated with Freud's early understanding of *Bahnung*, the process of forming differentiated memory traces in a "phenomenologically differentiable" unconscious (2006, pp. 13–14)[2]. A differentiable unconscious that starts from an organization of "integration with environment," being-in-the-world, primary narcissism. This unconscious, perhaps this brain, writes itself "neo-fetishistically" in a *revised* Comtean sense. Its affective-cognitive self-referential structure is temporal.

Here, perhaps, Comte escapes Nietzsche's criticism of him. Nietzsche understood fetishism in the usual way, applying the concept to metaphysical abstractions themselves as something to be denounced. He did not see within fetishism what Comte saw. There is a reversal here: Nietzsche, the trenchant critic of positivism, in the name of becoming and unconscious differentiating processes, did not see a possibility of generalized fetishism; Comte, the positivist, does, even if in the name of (metaphysical) fixity. But once fetishism is generalized, unpredictable effects are released; there are consequences difficult to measure. This was as much the case for Comte as it was for Freud.

Notes

1 Chapters 1 and 2 of this book are both based upon "On the History of Fetishism" by Alan Bass and are reproduced from *The Undecidable Unconscious: A Journal of Deconstruction and Psychoanalysis*, vol. 2, 2014, with permission from the University of Nebraska Press. © 2016.

2 Canguilhem noted that Comte's theory of fetishism captured the obligatory alignment of milieu and organism (cited, Kofman, 1978, p. 127, n.77). Analogously, Macherey sees Comte as "the hero of a veritable revolution in thought, which, no less than the one operated by Kant, which moreover it joins on certain points, deserves the name of Copernican revolution. His attempt to present science, in the absence of a rational foundation or absolute real, as a progressive formation of the exchanges between man and the world—one might almost say between a living being and its milieu—culminating in a complete social integration of knowledge, rises to the level of one of the great historical forms of culture: it is the one which, in the nineteenthth century, takes the place in France of the one occupied two centuries earlier, with different aims, by Cartesian rationalism" (1989, p. 6).

3

THE HEIDEGGERIAN THING

The handkerchief and the fetish

Comte's understanding of fetishism situated man in direct relation to his environment. In *Being and Time* Heidegger elaborates a conception of *Dasein*, the human mode of existence, as being-in-the-world not mediated by traditional philosophical abstractions. In that context he briefly considers fetishism, but as a temptation to be avoided. How? Why?

We are in Division One. The aim is to prepare the analysis of *Dasein* and temporality. To restate the well-known themes: *Dasein* is always already *in* a world, a world which is not objectively present for a subject. Rather the "worldliness" of world—what the "in" of being-in-the world means—is itself constitutive of the existential structure of *Dasein*. Introducing the analysis of worldliness, Heidegger asks the question of where to take his point of departure: "Which beings are to be our preliminary theme and established as a pre-phenomenal basis? / We answer: things" (1996, p. 63). While it would be a mistake to equate *Dasein* with "mind," Heidegger's point of departure is nevertheless related to my fundamental theme: the relation to things.

The fetish as thing will be discussed as a possible example of this point of departure, a possibility to be dismissed. The reasons for this dismissal will also concern another fundamental theme: the history of the European encounter with fetishism, which is always a conception of the "primitive." Heidegger is no exception, so one must attend to his remarks about the role of ethnological data in the existential analytic. The context is his justification for the analysis of everyday *Dasein*, which will eventually yield the structure of care, *Dasein*'s being. He asks whether everydayness is a "primitive stage of *Dasein*, that we become acquainted with empirically through anthropology" (1996, p. 47). The answer is no, because everydayness is "a kind of being of Dasein" even in "a highly developed culture" (ibid.). Nonetheless, "primitive Dasein" has its own forms of "noneveryday being… and its own specific everydayness" (ibid.). There might be an advantage to orienting the analysis of *Dasein* toward "the life of primitive peoples":

> "primitive phenomena" are often less hidden and complicated by extensive self-interpretation on the part of the *Dasein* in question. Primitive *Dasein* often speaks out of a more primordial absorption in 'phenomena' (in the pre-phenomenological sense)
>
> *(ibid.)*

In other words, primitive absorption in phenomena is free of the objectifying, theoretical relation to phenomena, the kind of relation that obscures the existential analytic. This is not so far from Comte on fetishism as non-metaphysical, direct engagement with things.

But our knowledge of "primitive peoples" is compromised by its source, ethnology itself:

> [E]thnology already moves in certain preliminary concepts and interpretations of human being in general... We do not know whether commonplace psychology or even scientific psychology and sociology, which the ethnologist brings with him, offer any scientific guarantee for an adequate possibility of access, interpretation, and mediation of the phenomena to be investigated... Ethnology itself already presupposes an adequate analytic of Dasein as its guideline. But since the positivistic sciences neither "can" nor should wait for the ontological work of philosophy, the continuation of research will not be accomplished as "progress"; but, rather, as the *repetition* and the ontologically more transparent purification of what has been ontically discovered.
>
> *(ibid.)*

From within the entire project of the "destruction" of metaphysics, this is a clear point. If the history of metaphysics is the history of the forgetting of being, then any empirical discipline which does not engage its metaphysical presuppositions inevitably repeats that forgetting. All anthropologies, including the great ones of Kant and Hegel, participate in this structure. They "presuppose an adequate analytic of Dasein," which they do not possess. Thus, they will have to misconstrue "primitive Dasein," because they do not understand *Dasein* itself. The ethnological data requires ontological "purification." This "purification" is not the acquisition of more data, but rather the rehearsing, the repetition, of that data from the ontological point of view. Hence, it is an "illusion" to think that knowledge of the "most exotic and manifold forms of existence" (p. 48) will itself be of any use in elaborating the conception of the world necessary for the analytic of *Dasein*. Here, the "primitive" is not excluded from the existential analytic; excluded, rather, is the compromised knowledge we have of it.

The brief discussion of fetishism itself will be a complement to the discussion of primitive *Dasein*. It will be introduced by a knot in a handkerchief. The knot will be an example of everyday *Dasein*'s relation to things, Heidegger's point of departure.

Things are in the world. The worldliness of the world is revealed through the analysis of things as tools or equipment. Everyday *Dasein* always already *is* in the mode of using things—I use the doorknob to open the door. Phenomenological access to beings encountered this way must reject the "interpretational tendencies" that cover over "'taking care' of things in general, and thus even more of beings *as* they are encountered of their own accord *in* taking care" (1996, p. 63). Calling the things we encounter in taking care "useful," Heidegger says that there is "no such thing as *a* useful thing" (p. 64). Rather, there is a totality of useful things, of things used "in order to" do something. "In order to" always contains a "*reference* of something to something" (ibid.). In other words, because reference itself is not a specific being, yet belongs to the totality of useful things (the world), the structure of reference is ontological; it reveals the worldliness of world.

To sharpen this point, Heidegger uses the example of a broken tool, an unusable thing. A broken hammer is just there, in its "unyielding objective presence" (1996, p. 69). Apparently, the referential structure of the "in order to" is disturbed:

> But in a *disturbance of reference*—in being unusable for...—the reference becomes explicit... circumspect noticing of the reference to the particular [i.e., ontic] what-for makes the what-for visible and with it the context of the work, the whole "workshop" as that in which taking care of things has always already been dwelling. The context of useful things appears not as a totality never seen before, but as a totality that has continually been seen beforehand in our circumspection. But with this totality world makes itself known.
>
> *(p. 70)*

Heidegger consistently uses this kind of argument: a global disturbance of what something is reveals what it is. The apparently "unyielding objective presence" of the broken hammer does not demonstrate that usefulness and reference are attributes added to objective presence. Rather, it demonstrates that world as reference is "always already disclosed for circumspection" (p. 70). "Disclosure" itself means "'to unlock'—'to be open'" (ibid.). Anyone familiar with *Being and Time* will grasp the portent of this remark. Heidegger is preparing the analysis of truth as disclosure, which always means the understanding of "opening" as the existential space for the possible encounter with the thing.

Heidegger now defines being-in-the-world as "circumspect absorption in the references constitutive for the handiness of the totality of useful things" (1996, p. 71). Because "reference" is the pivotal concept, and reference points to something beyond specific use, i.e., to usefulness in general, Heidegger looks at the "sign structure" of reference. Signs themselves are "useful things with manifold references ...the sign structure itself yields an ontological guideline for 'characterizing' any being whatsoever" (p. 72). By "signs" as useful things, Heidegger means *things* that *indicate*, such as signposts, flags, or the directional signal of a car. Indication is the "ontic concretion" of the ontological determination "of the useful thing *as* a useful thing" (p. 73). Signs, then, are "*useful things which explicitly bring a totality of useful things to circumspection so that the worldly character of what is at hand makes itself known at the same time"* (p. 74). Because reference and signs reveal the "worldly character of what is at hand," and because the structure of worldliness is constitutive of *Dasein* as being-*in*-the-world, they intimate the structure of existential space, the "in" of being-in-the-world. "Signs address themselves to a specifically 'spatial' being-in-the-world" (ibid.).

Heidegger then envisages an inevitable objection. What is taken as a sign (e.g., the south wind as a sign of rain), must have become accessible first before the sign is established (there has to have been a south wind). Yes, he says, what is taken as a sign does indeed have to "be there in some way or another" (1996, p. 75). But what is essential is not to assume that something present at hand which is *not yet* a sign is something "merely objectively present" (ibid.).

As an example, Heidegger takes making a knot in a handkerchief as a reminder of something to do. (Stambaugh renders Heidegger's "Knopf in Taschentuch" as a "string on one's finger" [1996, p. 76], which is more familiar to the English reader, but loses the feel of the example.) One might, however, forget what one is supposed to remember. The "knot" then does not entirely lose its "sign character, but rather acquires the disturbing obtrusiveness of something near at hand" (1996, p. 76). The broken tool was also a disturbance of the structure of reference, a disturbance that could mislead one into assuming the priority of objective presence. Instead, this very disturbance illuminates the ontological status of reference.

The disturbing knot is the hinge to fetishism. Let us consider it. Heidegger wants to show that something unusable that is apparently "just there" cannot be divorced from the sign structure of useful things. Even if I have forgotten why I put the knot in the handkerchief, I know that I wanted to *use* it as a reminder, just as I know that the broken hammer was a useful thing. But Heidegger seems to gloss over a difference between the broken hammer and the perplexing knot. If I forget what I have put the knot in the handkerchief for, but of course I know that I wanted to use it as a reminder, I am reminded of why I put a knot in the handkerchief in the first place: I might forget something. I know that memory is fallible. I might be able to compensate for this fallibility with a thing. This could certainly reinforce Heidegger's point about the sign structure of useful things. But it also raises the question of the relation to the memory aid.

The psychoanalyst will always wonder whether forgetting what one wanted to remember is a slip. If so, then the perplexing knot is another kind of sign—a sign that for reasons I am not aware of, I might not want to remember what I intend to remember. (Heidegger would reject this point, as he makes clear in his refutation of the Freudian theory of slips in the much later *Zollikon Seminars*.) The knot in the handkerchief is then a symptom in the fabric of the mind. Whether for psychoanalytic or putatively non-psychoanalytic reasons, the knot then refers to mind referring to itself. I know that my mind is not consistently reliable. In fact, it is so unreliable that I might even forget how I have tried to compensate for that unreliability. I cannot remember why I put the knot in the handkerchief. There is nothing like this in the example of the broken hammer.

After the knot, new paragraph, first sentence: "One could be tempted to illustrate the distinctive role of signs in everyday heedfulness for the understanding of the world itself by citing the extensive use of 'signs,' such as fetishism and magic, in primitive Dasein" (1996, p. 76). "Primitive" immediately alerts one to the earlier discussion of ethnological data. Heidegger at first seems to follow his previous line of reasoning, stating that "the establishment of signs that underlies such use of signs does not come about with theoretical intent and by way of theoretical speculation" (ibid.). He is typically describing a relation to things not obscured by the theoretical distancing that assumes that things are objectively present. The use of signs in fetishism and magic "remains completely within an 'immediate' being-in-the-world" (ibid.). But the temptation to use fetishism and magic as an illustration of the sign structure is to be avoided: "when one looks more closely, it becomes clear that the interpretation of fetishism and magic under the guideline of the idea of signs is not sufficient at all to comprehend the kind of 'handiness' of beings encountered in the world of primitives" (ibid.).

If reference and sign disclose the worldliness of world, and if the handiness of fetishism and magic cannot be a sign, then there is no possible ontological status of fetishism and magic. This is what Heidegger goes on to explain, using a variant of the argument of the broken tool:

> With regard to the phenomenon of signs, we might give the following interpretation, that for primitive people the sign coincides with what it indicates. The sign itself can represent what it indicates not only in the sense of replacing it, but in such a way that the sign itself always *is* what is indicated. This remarkable coincidence of the sign with what is indicated does not, however, mean that the sign-thing has already undergone a certain "objectification," has been experienced as a pure thing and been transposed together with what is signified to some region of being of objective presence. The "coincidence" is not an identification of hitherto isolated things, but rather the sign has not yet become free from that for which it is a sign. This kind of use of signs is still completely absorbed in the being of what is indicated so that a sign as such cannot be detached at all. The coincidence is not based on a first objectification, but rather upon the complete lack of such an objectification. But this means that signs are not at all discovered as useful things, that ultimately what is "at hand" in the world does not have the kind of being of useful things at all. Perhaps this ontological guideline (handiness and useful things), too, can provide nothing for an interpretation of the primitive world, and certainly for an ontology of thingliness. [Macquarrie and Robinson render this sentence: "Perhaps even readiness-to-hand and equipment have nothing to contribute as ontological clues in Interpreting the primitive world; and certainly the ontology of Thinghood even less" (p. 113)] But if an understanding of being is constitutive for primitive Dasein and the primitive world in general, it is all the more urgent to develop the "formal" idea of worldliness; namely of a phenomenon which can be modified in such a way that all ontological

> statements which assert that in a given phenomenal context something is *not yet* or *no longer* such and such may acquire a *positive* phenomenal meaning in terms of what it is *not*.
>
> *(1996, pp. 76–77)*

Heidegger here repeats the major aspect of the European encounter with fetishism: the fetish is what it indicates. The rock *is* the god. As in the entire tradition, Heidegger understands the fetish as not detached from, not free from, what it seems to signify. This is very close to Hegel on fetishism: the fetish "is therefore nothing really objective," is not really different, "detached from," the "fancy" of its creator. Heidegger's version is that the fetish does not have the sign structure of replacement. Whether from a philosophical or a psychoanalytic point of view, the consistency of this description cannot be avoided. The point is always to see what happens when it enters thought. We have seen the contrasting views of de Brosses and Comte. For de Brosses, it is a question of both an "excess of stupidity" that precludes reason, and of the aporias of accounting for the relation of the concrete and the abstract. For Comte, it is a question of a non-metaphysical absorption in things that could yield a scientific "subjective synthesis." For psychoanalysis, it is the analogous question of "concreteness."

For Heidegger, the primitive cannot even have metaphysics of objective presence. The fetish that it indicates is not a transposition of something objectively present to something else objectively present: there is no objectification at all. One might think that this would be all to the good for Heidegger; he has already accredited the non-theoretical, immediate "being-in-the-world" of primitive fetishism and magic. However, the lack of objectification means that signs themselves are not discovered as useful things. In other words, a sign that indicates only itself—the constant theme in the history of fetishism—lacks the referential structure that is essential to understanding the worldliness of the world. This is why Heidegger says "Perhaps this ontological guideline (handiness and useful things), too, can provide nothing for an interpretation of the primitive world, and certainly for an ontology of thingliness." But, extending the earlier remarks about the *Dasein* of primitive peoples, there has to be some way of conceptualizing their being-in-the-world. There has to be a "formal" idea of worldliness. Such a formal idea could yield positive ontological knowledge in terms of what it is not—as for the broken tool, or even the perplexing knot.

I will outline two readings of this passage.

The first might see Heidegger blindly repeating the entire history of the ethnology he rejects. In this history of fetishism, the self-referential, concrete nature of the fetish precludes the abstraction of symbolization. This is what Mauss called the "immense misunderstanding." In this view, the fetish cannot co-exist with symbolic structures. There is no possibility of symbolization, of the sign as replacement, in the primitive world. The ethnologist then overlooks the complex symbolic structures that co-exist with apparently non-symbolic fetishism. Analogously, Heidegger says that there is not even objectification in the primitive world, so that signs cannot be discovered as useful things. The self-reference of the fetish precludes reference. This is why Mauss protested: "The object which serves as a fetish is never, no matter what has been said about it, just any given object, chosen arbitrarily; rather it is always defined by the code of magic and religion" (1974, p. 216). In other words, the fetish is never exclusively self-referential.

And how could it be the case that "primitive Dasein" completely lacks the sense of the handiness of things as tools "for something"? Would "primitive Dasein" be unable to understand the south wind as a sign of rain, without confusing it with rain, even if wind or rain themselves might be worshipped? Or, inversely, would Heidegger say that even in an "advanced state of culture" there are no self-referential structures? The psychoanalyst encounters patients who simultaneously do not conflate signs with what they indicate, and yet who do resist symbolic interpretation, forming a fetishistic transference to the analytic process. And where does Heidegger get the idea that there simply is no "objectification" for "primitive Dasein"? He could be making the historical point that for "primitive Dasein," the "object" in the modern sense, which emerges out of the work of Descartes, does not yet exist. But he seems to be saying something broader: the conflation of indication and indicated precludes any possible objectification in the sense of *ob-ject* or *Gegen-stand*: that which stands against one, and hence, is separate from one—"free," in Heidegger's sense.

From a Nietzschean point of view, one could say the opposite. When Nietzsche says that "metaphysics begins in dreams," he means that the dream experience, the feeling of being visited by apparently real "spirits," initiates belief in a second, transcendent world (1995, p. 18). Historically, the argument about fetishism has always been that it has no possible relation to transcendence. However, it was precisely the persistence of fetishistic formations in modern religions, even with their belief in an abstract god, that led Hume to his statement about the universal error of objective presence. In other words, wherever there is belief in either real "spirits" or transcendence, there is conviction of a "world" apart from oneself, and hence some form of objectification. This is why Nietzsche ironically spoke of belief in the primacy of consciousness and in the reality of a second world as metaphysical fetishes.

One can extend Nietzsche's thought about dreams and transcendence to Freud's conception of the dream experience. To explain the "reality effect" of the dream, Freud emphasizes its hallucinatory nature. To experience a hallucination is to have the feeling of experiencing something objectively real. Hallucinatory reality is a product of what Freud calls perceptual identity and temporal immediacy (1900, pp. 542–544). If I see something now that is identical to something I have seen before, it is objectively real for me—even if it is a hallucination. The primal example is the hungry baby who hallucinates the image of the breast that previously fed it, an image stored in unconscious memory. Freud's conception of hallucination provokes the vexing problem of reality testing: to see something now cannot be the ultimate criterion of reality, because this is also true for hallucinations. But it also says that once there are dreams, there is always a version of objective presence—which would also have to hold for "primitive Dasein." Integrating Mauss, Nietzsche, and

Freud, to construe the fetish *only* in terms of lack of reference, transcendence, and objectification would be evidence of blindness to anything other than immediate self-reference, a blindness based on both prejudice and failure to consider how the fetish is constructed. Particularly from Freud's point of view, any symptom—whether in neurosis, in the slips of the psychopathology of everyday life, or in the construction of a fetish—is a compromise between knowing and not knowing. This is why at the end of his life he extends the construction of the fetish backward to account for the action of mind on itself that produces symptoms or slips.

But, one could object, if Heidegger says that the fetish is *not yet* a sign, just as the broken tool or the perplexing knot are *no longer* signs, then there would have to be a link between the self-reference of the fetish and the reference of the unusable thing. The fetish that is not yet a sign has to be capable of becoming one. This too, is a question examined throughout the history of fetishism. De Brosses' universalization of fetishism put him in the awkward position of having to account for the possibility of abstract monotheism across an apparently unbridgeable divide; recall his argument about the sons of Noah. Derrida commented on this issue in *Glas*, via Kant and Hegel. For Kant, the "teleological horizon of 'true and unique religion' is the disappearance of the fetish" (1960, p. 207). For Hegel, the fetish as African is foreign to historical consciousness. It belongs "to an unconscious that does not let itself be dialectized as such, that has no history... But this nondialecticalness, this ahistoricity can always be interpreted as negativity, as resistance proper to the dialectic economy, and consequently interned in the speculative process" (ibid.). Although Heidegger is making an argument about worldliness, not religion, like Kant and Hegel he sees the fetish as both foreign to reference, and as destined to reference, in its not-yetness. This is why there has to be a "formal" structure of worldliness that could account for "primitive Dasein," which does not yet encounter things as referential. If the fetish is poised between not being a sign and potentially becoming a sign, then the sign structure cannot be completely foreign to it. But does Heidegger explain how this is so? Or is he unable to do so, and hence the dismissal of fetishism? Is the fetish a perplexing knot for Heidegger?

If one grants this argument, there is a second way to read the passage. Heidegger does say that the fetish's lack of referentiality, even more than the broken tool or the perplexing knot, contains the possibility of an ontology of things that is wider than the one elaborated on the basis of handiness. Is Heidegger momentarily considering the universality of fetishism? "One could be *tempted* to illustrate the distinctive role of signs in everyday heedfulness for the understanding of the world itself by citing the extensive use of 'signs,' such as fetishism and magic, in primitive Dasein" (1996, p. 76 [my emphasis]). He imagines the possibility of an ontological status of the fetish, but resists it for the traditional reason of its self-referentiality, while knowing that there has to be a "formal structure" of being-in-the-world that would have to include the primitive. What if his resistance was misguided? Whether ethnologically or clinically, apparently non-abstract and closed self-referential structures always co-exist with apparently abstract and open symbolic structures. One cannot simply say that the fetish is foreign to symbolism.

This is the problem of self-reference: is it ever simply closed in on itself, ever simply concrete?

This is the central question: can the self-reference of the fetish open onto other ways of thinking what we usually call "mind" and what we usually call "thing"? Recall the perplexing knot, the thing that is both no longer a sign of what one was supposed to remember, and that is a sign of mind's fallibility, its action upon itself—which Heidegger does not consider. Heidegger would justifiably suspect the traditional concept of mind, but his point of departure from things to elucidate *Dasein*'s being rethinks "mind" and "thing" in terms of their relatedness. And this relatedness is always a question of finitude, a question itself always related to how "mind" acts on itself (This will become clearer via *Kant and the Problem of Metaphysics*.) As finite being-in-the-world, as always already related to things, the existential structure of world and things *are Dasein*.

And vice versa, when being-in-the-world as care becomes the structure of time. Care is temporality because both care and time are simultaneously being ahead (the existential future), being already (the existential past), and being together with (the existential present)—but not as a future present, a past present, and a present present or now. If that were the case, time would occur and elapse in an objective present, making time itself something objectively present—which it cannot be. Hence, Heidegger writes: "Temporality 'is' not a *being* [i.e., something objectively present] at all. It is not, but rather *temporalizes* itself... temporality [is] the *ekstatikon* par excellence. Temporality is the primordial 'outside' of itself... [I]ts essence is temporalizing in the unity of the *ecstasies*" (1996, p. 302). To paraphrase: the way in which *Dasein* exists only as outside itself, as being-in-the-world (existential space), as *ek-static*, as always already outside itself, *is* the structure of time as the reaching out toward each other, the *ek-stasis*, of past, present, and future. As none of this is objectively present, is not a being, is neither a subject acting on an object nor vice versa, time is this "outsiding." But although time is not an objectively present being, nonetheless, it is a kind of thing—*the ekstatikon* par excellence. This non-present thing is an auto-affective process—temporaliz*ing* itself.

Two critical strands come together here. The first is the understanding of the *being* of being-in-the-world. As being-in-the-world is always a relation to things, but things not objectively present, worldliness or thingliness must be integrated with the structure of time. Hence the paradoxical noun form of time temporalizing itself: *the ekstatikon* par excellence. The second is the understanding of time. If existential space *is* existential time, if being-in is being-outside, and if time itself is this "outsiding," then time has to have a non-objectively present spatial aspect. As spatial it is thingly, is a kind of *thing*—again, *the ekstatikon* par excellence. This kind of thing is auto-affective. Is the auto-affective thing completely foreign to the self-referential thing? Could being as time, as auto-affective thing, as care, as being-in-the-world, simply exclude fetishism?

From a psychoanalytic point of view, everyday universal phenomena, such as dreams and slips, reveal the basic structure of mind. Eventually, and unwittingly, Freud joins a long tradition of universalizing fetishism in order to say more about the basic structure of mind. Heidegger is tempted by fetishism, but then rejects it, based on the false premises that have characterized the metaphysics he wants to "destroy." Does the temptation speak to an intuition that fetishism does open onto the crucial ontological questions of the thing and time? What if Heidegger had known of the anthropological finding of the universality of fetishism? And had also known of Mauss' critique of traditional analyses of fetishism and that the apparently exclusive self-reference of the fetish always exists in the context of a symbolic code? And had been able to question the usual conceptions of the "primitive"? Could he have yielded to his temptation and used fetishism to expand his ontology of thingliness? And could this have been a place where Freud's universalization of fetishism would have had to encounter Heidegger on the thing?

The transcendental imagination: The iridescent thing

The questions of the relationship to things and the auto-affective structure of time are sharpened in Heidegger's reading of the *Critique of Pure Reason* (henceforth *CPR*) in *Kant and the Problem of Metaphysics* (henceforth *KPM*). To understand how, and to begin to examine the consequences, requires a detailed examination of that work.

Heidegger gives a clear indication of his "method" in general when he writes in *KPM*: "with any philosophical knowledge in general, what is said in uttered propositions must not be decisive. Instead, what must be decisive is what it sets before our eyes as still unsaid, in and through what has been said" (1953, p. 140). One can restate this in terms of Kant's guiding question in *CPR*: how does man, a finite creature, have knowledge of things he has not created, as creation of things belongs to the infinite reason of God? By ferreting out the unsaid in Kant's answer to this question, a question about the relatedness of mind and thing, Heidegger will make Kant's conception of mind and thing ontological, i.e., temporal. My contention will be that Heidegger's controversial reading of Kant has crucial resources for the psychoanalytic conception of "mind"; I began to lay this out in *Interpretation and Difference* (2006, pp. 77–83), and will have to return to that here. And because my major point is that Freud's late generalization of fetishism would have to affect his entire conception of unconscious processes, I am attempting to demonstrate that Heidegger's analysis of the unsaid in Kant is essential to the unsaid in the theory of fetishism, and even to the dismissal of fetishism in *Being and Time*.

Heidegger has to begin by contesting the traditional understanding of the *CPR* as an epistemological work. That understanding derives from Kant's well-known idea that the metaphysical foundations of natural science provide the means to understand the possibility of man's knowledge of things he has not created. However, when Kant says that the purpose of the *CPR* is to lay "the ground for metaphysics as a whole" (1953, p. 8), Heidegger takes him at his word. To lay the ground for metaphysics as a whole means "unveiling in the inner possibility of ontology" (ibid.). Specifically, it means that Kant's most general question about the possibility of knowledge—how are *a priori* synthetic judgments possible?—is itself the question of "the inner possibility of ontology."

This is why Heidegger consistently inflects Kant ontologically. For Kant, pure reason, reason which does not depend upon experience, is a faculty of knowing according to *a priori* principles. The issue is to determine how *a priori* synthetic judgments—i.e., judgments which add to knowledge—are possible. Heidegger says that this means that Kant is concerned with the "quiddity"—the whatness—of the thing, an ontological question. Quiddity, then, is itself a question of experience free synthesis. "… bringing forth of the determination of the Being of the being is a preliminary self relating to the being. This pure 'relation-to…' (synthesis) forms first and foremost the that-upon-which and the horizon within which the being in itself becomes experiencable" (1953, p. 10). Why "self relating"? Because every judgment, according to Kant, is an "I connect" (ibid.). Heidegger here is looking at Kant in terms of process. Whatever the content of the "I connect," it is a process of "mind" *relating to itself.* Heidegger's entire argument seeks to demonstrate that self-relating is actually the possibility of the *a priori* synthesis, "access" to the being, the thing. The demonstration itself will be guided by the auto-affective nature of time. To follow the complex structure of Heidegger's argument it is useful to know this in advance.

Continuing. Because human reason is finite, Heidegger zeroes in on Kant's initial statement about finite knowledge: "In whatever manner and by whatever means a knowing may relate to objects, *intuition* is that through which it relates itself immediately to them and upon which all thought as a means is directed" (cited, 1990, p. 15). Heidegger comments: "In order to understand the *Critique of Pure Reason* this point must be hammered in, so to speak: knowing is primarily intuiting. From this it at once becomes clear that the new interpretation of knowledge as judging (thinking) violates the decisive sense of the Kantian problem. All thinking is merely in the service of intuition" (ibid.).

If we know in advance that Heidegger will be concerned with auto-affection, we can see why he starts with Kant on intuition as a "knowing" that is an *immediate relating of itself to objects.*[1] But, to return to the order of Heidegger's argument, he is "hammering" in the point about intuition to justify the weight he will give to the very short transcendental aesthetic that begins the *CPR*. Intuition is sensory in the Greek sense, *aisthesis*. Kant, of course, is not concerned with empirical intuition, but with experience free, *a priori* intuition: hence, the *transcendental* aesthetic. Heidegger makes a crucial point about the necessity of a transcendental aesthetic:

> The essence of sensibility exists in the finitude of intuition… With this, Kant for the first time attains a concept of sensibility which is ontological rather than sensualistic. Accordingly, if empirically affective intuition of beings does not need to coincide with "sensibility," then the possibility of a non-empirical sensibility remains essentially open… if finite intuition is now to be knowledge, then it must be able to make the being itself as revealed accessible with respect to both what and how it is for everyone at all times.
>
> *(1990, p. 19)*

There is an enormous amount embedded in this comment. By taking Kant at his word, Heidegger approaches the "unsaid" in his thought: the paradoxical concept of "non-empirical sensibility" is the key to a new understanding of intuition as the primal relation to the thing. In combined Kantian and Heideggerean language: "the synthesis of thinking and intuiting accomplishes the making evident of the encountered being as object" (p. 20). Heidegger always questions the encounter of the "being as object." But by analyzing this encounter in terms of the "synthesis of thinking and intuiting," Heidegger will go beyond the being as object—and man as subject.

This takes us to the next crucial step of the argument. Kant famously characterizes thinking and intuiting, concept formation and sensory reception, as the "two basic sources of the mind," other than which there are "no others" (cited, 1990, p. 25). How can they be synthesized? Heidegger cites Kant from the beginning of the *Critique*: "... there are two stems of human knowledge, *sensibility* and *understanding,* which perhaps spring forth from a common, but to us unknown, root" (ibid.). He juxtaposes this statement with one from the conclusion of the *CPR*, in which Kant says that he has begun where "the common root of our power of knowledge divides and throws out two stems, one of which is reason" (cited, p. 26). Kant explicitly says that the purpose of the *CPR* is to "outline the *architectonic* of all knowledge arising from *pure reason*" (ibid.). This is why the *CPR* is usually read as an epistemological work. Heidegger, however, hears in these statements an opening to the unsaid:

> [T]he "sources" are understood as "stems" which spring forth from a common root. But whereas in the first passage the "common root" was qualified with a "perhaps," in the second the "common root" is reputed to exist. Nonetheless, in both passages this root is only alluded to. Kant not only fails to pursue it further, but even declares that it is "unknown to us." From this, something essential arises for the general character of the Kantian laying of the ground for metaphysics: it leads not to the crystal clear, absolute evidence of a first maxim and principle, but rather goes into and points consciously toward the unknown.
>
> *(ibid.)*

The rest of *KPM* will be a demonstration that the "common root" indeed exists, that Kant himself has embedded an explanation of it in the *CPR*, but that this explanation undermines his entire architectonic. It will be something from which Kant has to "recoil." My aim will be to show the importance of Heidegger's delineation of the common root for the psychoanalytic conception of mind in relation to fetishism.

If there could be a common root, it would have to explain the synthesis of the elements of pure knowledge—pure intuition and pure thinking (1990, p. 27). This would have to be a demonstration of the possibility of a pure, experience free, transcendental synthesis that requires "clarification of the original ground for the inner possibility of this synthesis" (ibid.). This original ground is what Heidegger means by "ontological." One knows that if it is ontological, it will depend upon the forgotten question of being (time) itself. This is why Heidegger says that the demonstration of a transcendental synthesis is a "projecting freeing of the whole, which an ontology essentially makes possible." It thus "brings metaphysics to the ground and soil in which it is rooted as a 'haunting' of human nature" (p. 29).

"Haunting" is a citation; Kant's word is *Heimsuchung.* Richard Taft adds an important translator's note about it:

> The German *Heimsuchung* is translated by Kemp Smith [the translator of the *CPR*] as 'visitation,' but the term also connotes a haunting or an obsession. I render it 'haunting' to show the sense in which the questions Kant asks are an inescapable and lingering part of human nature. We should at the same time be attuned to the literal sense of the word, which suggests the seeking of a home.
>
> *(1990, p. 29, n. 57)*

Whether as visitation, haunting, obsession, or the search for a home, Heidegger is emphasizing Kant's word to show that the question of being, the forgotten or unsaid of metaphysics, cannot not be at work in a critique of pure reason. It cannot not visit a laying of the ground for metaphysics, but this visit can be a visitation, comparable with the way a spirit or ghost insinuates itself. It cannot not haunt, or obsess, any attempt to find the home of metaphysics—a home that is foreign to it. A foreign home: the *unheimlich*, the uncanny, which is such an important theme throughout Heidegger's work. The *Unheimlichkeit* of this *heim,* the "unknown common root," will be the reason for what Heidegger will call Kant's "recoil."

Let us return to the stages of the argument. From within Kant's framework, the possible common root of pure intuition and pure knowledge must be a transcendental synthesis. And if all thought is in service to intuition, the "transcendental synthesis must be an intuition, and as *a priori* knowing, it must be a pure intuition" (1998, p. 30). Space and time are the pure intuitions of the transcendental aesthetic. Kant defines space as the pure external sense and time as the pure internal sense. Because Kant says that time "is the formal *a priori* condition of all appearances whatsoever." Heidegger says that time "has pre-eminence over space" (1990, p. 34). Hence, he is going to show how "time shifts more and more to the forefront in the course of the individual stages of the laying of the ground for metaphysics, and hereby first reveals its own particular essence in a more original way than the provisional characterization in the Transcendental Aesthetic permits" (ibid.). Heidegger justifies his approach:

> If in general the grounding of the universality of time as pure intuition is to be possible, this can only happen if it can be shown that although space and time as pure intuitions both belong "to the subject," time dwells in the subject in a more original way than space. Time immediately reduced to the

> givens of inner sense, however, is at the same time only ontologically more universal if the subjectivity of the subject exists in the openness for the being. The more subjective time is, the more original and extensive is the expansiveness of the subject.
>
> *(1990, p. 35)*

One hears the echo of *Being and Time.* Existential space, being-in-the-world as the relation to things, yielded existential time, ecstatic time temporalizing itself. Heidegger cannot literally accept Kant's characterization of time as subjective. Rather, he is pushing Kantian subjectivity to its limits, wanting to show how the temporality of the subject expands—or even explodes—it. (Again: this is the importance of the preliminary point about knowing as a *self relating* to the being.) The overall aim is the integration of expansive time, which opens the "subject" to the thing, with the delineation of the common root. Let us already envisage the integration of the common root with expansive time, the very relatedness of mind and thing, as the possibility of fetishism.

Proceeding carefully, Heidegger says that intuition and thinking as the elements of finite knowledge demonstrate a "pull of the elements toward one another" such that "their unity cannot be 'later' than they are themselves, but rather that it must have applied to them 'earlier' and must have laid the ground for them. This unity unites the elements as original in such a way that even at first in the uniting, the elements as such spring forth" (1990, p. 41). In other words, there has to be a "prior" synthesis of intuition and thinking that at the same time permits their distinction. The unity of intuition and thinking "may be sketched out initially in such a way that it shows how each of these elements structurally supports the other. They indicate seams [*Fugen*] which point in advance to a having-been-joined-together" (p. 43).

A seam joins and articulates. The seam of intuition and thinking indicates ahead of them that they can be separate. The seam, then, precedes what it joins. The seam is the "unknown common root." It is a synthesis that is "neither a matter of intuition nor of thinking" (1990, p. 44). Heidegger cites Kant on synthesis itself: "Synthesis in general, as we shall hereafter see, is the mere result of the *power of imagination*, a blind but indispensable function of the soul without which we would have no knowledge whatever, but of which we are seldom conscious even once" (ibid.).

"Seldom conscious even once." The psychoanalyst can wonder: unconscious? In the usual sense, no. Kant is not talking about anything like a dynamic unconscious in the Freudian sense, an unconscious that is the source of drives and wishes that inevitably place the mind in conflict. Rather, he is talking about a possibility of conscious knowledge, a possibility which itself does not operate consciously. In another sense, however, there is a link to Freudian thought. In an unusual passage of the paper on "The Two Principles of Mental Functioning," a passage that I have referred to in both *Difference and Disavowal* and *Interpretation and Difference,* Freud speaks of "originally unconscious thought." The passage is unusual in that Freud speaks of an unconscious source of the possibility of conscious knowledge.

This is the source of secondary process, which itself is the inhibition, the binding, of the tendency toward the immediate discharge of the primary process. In other words, it is the possibility of delayed gratification. Delay itself implies increase of the tension that discharge would release. "Originally unconscious thought" is not thought in the usual sense, involving connection to words. Rather it *is* the unconscious tendency toward binding of tension. And this unconscious tendency toward binding is synthetic. Freud specifies that as tension raising delay, originally unconscious thought also binds the *relations* of unconscious memory traces of "objects" (*Objekteindrucke*) (1911, p. 221). This is a unique moment in Freud's thought, whose many possible implications he does not pursue. Is originally unconscious thought a "blind but indispensable function of the soul"—*Seele*, psyche—of which we are never conscious? Has it any possible connection to a rethinking of time? For the moment, these are only questions.

To return to Heidegger on Kantian imagination and synthesis, he predictably speaks of them temporally. Time as the pure internal sense for Kant is synoptic, the *a priori* unification of time as succession. If pure knowledge itself is synthetic, and pure time synoptic, a "pure synthesis of the power of imagination" would not simply join intuition and thought. As per his conception of the "seam," Heidegger sees pure, i.e., transcendental, imagination as the structural center in which "the pure synopsis and the pure, reflecting synthesis meet and join together… [which is] the original, rich wholeness of one which is composed of many members" (1990, p. 45). One "composed of many members" recalls the structure of care as time—an articulated whole of *ek-static* future, past, and present that is itself *the ekstatikon*. This temporal "thing," we saw, is a process. The transcendental imagination as the possible unknown common root that is a temporal, articulated whole would also have to conceived in processive terms.

> The essential unity of ontological knowledge cannot be the conclusion, but must instead be the correct *beginning* of the laying of the ground for ontological knowledge. This ground-laying has been transformed into the task of bringing to light pure synthesis as such. But because it is an action, its essence can only become apparent to the extent that it is itself traced out in its springing-forth.
>
> *(p. 46)*

This process or action is the possibility of the relation to the thing for finite knowledge. "Finite creatures need this basic faculty of a turning-toward… In this original turning-toward, the finite creature first allows a space for play [*Spielraum*] within which something can 'correspond' to it. To hold oneself in advance in such a play-space, to form it originally, is none other than the transcendence which marks all finite comportment to beings" (p. 50). This is a complex point. Heidegger is saying that if we follow Kant on the finitude of human reason, then the "finite creature" structurally, transcendentally, *needs* something that makes possible any relation to a thing. This transcendental need is "fulfilled" by a process, the action of pure synthesis, itself a function of the transcendental imagination. This process itself, like the spatiality of being-in-the-world, is the opening to the thing, a play-space.

Heidegger does not immediately justify calling this opening a "play-space." If one is familiar with the rest of his work, one knows how important a notion play is, especially in the commentary on Heraclitus on time as play (cited Schurmann, 1990, p. 42). In the immediate context of *KPM*, one can at least be struck by the oddness of putting play at the center of the Kantian architectonic, whose aim is to lay the metaphysical grounds for deterministic science. But we already know that Heidegger's wants to show how the Kantian architectonic has to undermine itself. Once the self-undermining is demonstrated, Heidegger will say more about the *Spielraum*.

Proceeding step by step toward this undermining, Heidegger asks whether the pure synthesis of intuition and thought, a necessary Kantian question, has a place within the Kantian system:

> [P]ure synthesis falls neither to pure intuition nor to pure thought. For this reason, the elucidation of the origin of pure synthesis which is about to begin can be neither a transcendental-aesthetic nor a transcendental-logical one... But to which transcendental discipline, then, does the central problem of the possibility of ontology fall? This question remains foreign to Kant.
>
> *(1990, pp. 46–47)*

The foreignness of the question is precisely why Kant can envisage a common root, but say both that it is unknown and that it is "a blind but indispensable faculty" of "which we are seldom conscious, even once." Heidegger insists that if one reads the *CPR* without considering these issues, then it will always be understood as an epistemological work. "But precisely for this reason, the interpretation must free itself from the Kantian architectonic, and it must make the idea of transcendental logic problematic" (p. 47). The implications of this statement are large. If the transcendental logic is the metaphysical ground of Newtonian science, then Heidegger is saying that the transcendental logic cannot really account for its own ground. The possibility of the relation to the thing would be foreign to the conceptual framework of Newtonian science. Psychoanalytically, one can extend this statement: the possibility of something such as fetishism, a relation of mind and thing, cannot be conceived in terms of the logic of "classical" science. Is there any possibility that this could have to do with Freud's "originally unconscious thought"? Or with time?

Proceeding further toward the integration of time with the transcendental imagination, Heidegger undertakes an analysis of the transcendental deduction, one of the most difficult sections of the *CPR*. His daring move is to show that the transcendental deduction itself can be clarified via the relation of imagination to time, even if this "appears to contradict Kant's own explicit explanation of what deduction means" (1990, p. 53). The issue, as always, is the pure synthesis of pure intuition and pure thought, but from the point of view of the formation of the "play-space," which a finite creature *needs* in order to encounter any being at all. Here we come to the question of the transcendental apperception, the Kantian *cogito*, the "I think," (described previously as an "I connect"), which Kant calls "pure, original, unchangeable consciousness" (cited, 1990, p. 55). Kant also says that the transcendental apperception "presupposes a synthesis, however, or includes one" (cited, p. 56). Recall that Kant has already established that synthesis itself is a function of imagination—the non-conscious, blind, but indispensable faculty. The pure synthesis of pure intuition and pure thought cannot represent anything empirical. Rather, it is "formative *a priori*, i.e. purely productive" (ibid.). Again, this pure synthesis is an action, a process. Crucially for Heidegger, Kant says: "Thus the principle of the necessary unity of the pure (productive) synthesis of the power of imagination, prior to apperception, is the ground for the possibility of all knowledge, especially of experience" (ibid.). Heidegger can then remind us that if pure synthesis unifies *a priori*, *a priori* unification itself is a question of the pure intuition of time as synopsis. The elements fall into place: "the intuition which in advance is pure, given, and universal, and which takes things in stride is time. Hence the pure power of imagination must be related to it essentially. Only in this way is the pure power of imagination unveiled as the mediator between Transcendental Apperception and time" (p. 57). As Kant also says that "all modifications of the mind... are subject to time... as that in which they must all be brought... into relation with another" (cited, ibid.), Heidegger can now say that it is "striking" that Kant does not explicitly pursue "the *a priori* essential relationship of the pure power of imagination to time" (ibid.). He is implying that Kant could not pursue the relation of imagination to time because it is the "foreign home" of his entire system.

Kant himself registers discomfort: "That the affinity of appearances... only becomes possible by means of this transcendental function of the power of imagination is indeed strange" (cited, 1990, p. 58). Heidegger intensifies the strangeness via time as the "pure universal intuition... wherein things can be joined in general and [as] that wherein it is possible to form connections" (ibid.). Following the implications: if the "I think" is allegedly unchangeable, not subject to modification in time, but if it requires, as Kant says, "a pure power of imagination... which serves as basis for all knowledge *a priori*," and if the transcendental imagination as synthetic has to be relative to time—can the *cogito* really be unchangeable, timeless?

Heidegger moves more directly toward a temporal *cogito* when he looks at Kant's highest synthetic principle: "the conditions for the *possibility of experience* in general are at the same time conditions for the *possibility of objects of experience*" (cited, 1990, p. 84). Heidegger says that "at the same time" is more important than the italicized words. "At the same time" expresses "the full structure of transcendence," as the "horizon of objectivity in general," i.e., the relatedness to the being, the thing.

> This relatedness is a going-out-to..., which was previously and at all times necessary in finite knowing, and thus is a constant standing-out-from... (*Ecstasis*)... In itself, transcendence is ecstatic-horizonal. The highest principle gives expression to this articulation of transcendence unified in itself... The grounding principle... is the expression of the most

> original phenomenological knowledge of the innermost, unified structure of transcendence.
>
> *(p. 84)*

Heidegger is here integrating his reading of Kant's conception of time as the possibility of the relation to things with the analysis of time itself as *ekstasis*, i.e., the "outsiding," which accounts for *Dasein* as being-in-the-world (*Being and Time*). And we can ask again: would this not also be the possibility of fetishism, of the relatedness of mind and thing?

Heidegger then takes up the faculty of imagination itself. Kant says that the laying of the ground of metaphysics belongs to the human soul, so Heidegger looks at the discussion of imagination in the *Anthropology*. This recourse to the *Anthropology* will provide an essential insight into imagination, which Heidegger will then seem to disqualify, and then again to revalidate. The structure of this twisting argument is itself essential to understanding the relation of the transcendental imagination and time.

In the *Anthropology*, Kant defines imagination as "a faculty of intuition even without the presence of the object" (cited, 1990, p. 90). Heidegger reframes this definition: "imagination 'can' intuit, 'can' take the look of something in stride, without showing the intuited which is referred to" (p. 91). "Can" is in scare quotes to emphasize that the Kantian faculty is always a capacity, a power, an ability to do something. Here, it is the ability to "see," to take in a "look," without actually seeing anything. Heidegger: "we find in the power of imagination… a peculiar non-connectedness to the being" (ibid.). This leads him to a critical point about imagination, a point whose methodological status he will have to question:

> The power of imagination can hence be called a faculty of forming [*Vermogen des Bildens*] in a peculiar double sense. As a faculty of intuiting, it is formative [*bildend*] in the sense of providing the image [*Bild*] (or look). As a faculty which is not dependent upon the presence of the intuitable, it fulfills itself, i.e. it creates and forms the image. This "formative power" is simultaneously a "forming" which takes things in stride (is receptive) and one which creates (is spontaneous). In this "simultaneously" lies the proper essence of its structure. But if receptivity means the same as sensibility and if spontaneity means the same as understanding, then in a peculiar way the power of imagination falls between both. [Heidegger's footnote: Already in Aristotle's *De Anima*, book G3, *phantasma* stands "between" *aisthesis* and *noeisis*.] This gives it a remarkably iridescent [*schillernd, Kant und das Problem…*, p. 119] character.
>
> *(ibid.)*

If, following Kant, intuition is receptive–passive, and thought, concept formation, spontaneous–active, then imagination, in its power to "see," to form an image without actual presence, is receptive–spontaneous, active–passive. Iridescent. Shifting its color in and of itself.

But the *Anthropology,* unlike the *CPR,* is an empirical, not a transcendental investigation. "The way of Kant's Anthropology, which at first appears to be self-evident... has revealed itself to be the wrong way" (1990, p. 94). Nonetheless, "reference to transcendental structures always already lies in the empirical interpretation of the faculties of the soul, which properly speaking, can never simply be purely empirical themselves" (ibid.). If the iridescent imagination of the *Anthropology* is to have any relation to time, the "reference to transcendental structures" will have to be demonstrated.

Returning to the *CPR*, Heidegger isolates an important contradiction. As transcendental, imagination is the pure synthesis of intuition and thought. There are three basic transcendental faculties—sensibility, imagination, and thought. But we know that Kant also says that there are "two basic sources of the mind, sensibility and understanding," and that "aside from these two sources of knowledge, we have no others" (1990, p. 95). Using a significant word, Heidegger says that the "transcendental power of imagination is *homeless.* It is not even treated in the Transcendental Aesthetic where, as a faculty of intuition, it properly belongs. On the other hand, it is a theme of the Transcendental Logic where, strictly speaking, it may not be as long as logic remains confined to thought as such" (p. 95; my emphasis). Heidegger then cites other passages in which Kant speaks of three original faculties.

Two or three? Is Kant inconsistent? Relying on the previous analysis of the transcendental imagination as the original unification, the seam, of intuition and thought, which also allows their separation, Heidegger makes the essential point: "What if this original, formative center was that 'unknown common root' of both stems? Is it an accident that with the first introduction of the power of imagination Kant says that 'we ourselves, however, are seldom conscious [of it] even once'?" (ibid.). In other words, the "homelessness" of the transcendental imagination makes it the necessarily "unknown," foreign, home that "haunts" the *CPR* [*Heimsuchung*].

Is it iridescent? To answer, Heidegger returns to the transcendental aesthetic, where the transcendental imagination, as intuition, "properly belongs." Space and time are pure intuitions in that they do not allow any beings to "spring forth" (1990, p. 99). Rather, they "pro-pose [*Vor-stellen*] the look of time and space in advance as totalities which are in themselves manifold" (ibid.). Heidegger calls this in advance pro-posing of time and space "the formative self-giving of that which gives itself" (ibid.). Note the self-relating: the self-giving of that which gives itself. Because what is "given" here cannot be a present being, as per the *Anthropology*, it belongs to imagination, but of course, a pure, transcendental imagination. Technically, the look of time as a purely intuited manifold totality is "synoptic," according to Kant's conception of synopsis as the temporal intuition of the whole of time as succession. As the self-giving of that which gives itself, this synopsis is formative intuition—which "is only possible in the transcendental power of imagination, and that is all the more so as this [transcendental power of imagination] is in general the origin of all that is 'synthetic'" (p. 100). The co-implication of time—synopsis—and the *a priori* synthesis at the heart of knowledge draws closer, but via the transcendental imagination (p. 101).

Which means that "that which gives itself" is an "*ens imaginarium*," not in the sense of an imaginary being, but in the sense of a "some-thing," which cannot be a present object (ibid.). Call it the non-sensuous sensuous thing, the thing of time itself: time as *the ekstatikon par excellence* (*Being and Time*). This is what the discussion of iridescent imagination in the *Anthropology* could not encompass.

How to conceive the self-giving of the *ens imaginarium*? Returning to the transcendental apperception, the "I think" that accompanies all thought, Heidegger looks at the status of the "I." The *ego* of the *cogito* as concept forming, as pure understanding, is a "representing, forming spontaneity." This pure thinking as "representing, self-orienting-toward" clearly is not judging in Kant's usual sense, but is "thinking in the sense of the free, forming and projecting conceiving of something" (1990, p. 106)—a something which is not objectively present. This is the thinking of the *ens imaginarium*. In a startling statement, Heidegger says: "This original 'thinking' is pure imagining" (ibid.). Spontaneity, however, "constitutes but one moment of the transcendental power of imagination" (p. 107). As pure intuition, it is also receptive. "And it is receptive, moreover, not just apart from its spontaneity. Rather it is the original unity of receptivity and spontaneity" (ibid.). This is the transcendental, i.e., ontological, justification of the iridescence of the imagination, as *per* the *Anthropology*. Heidegger had asked if it was an "accident" that Kant had introduced the transcendental imagination as that of which "we are seldom conscious even once." He is now alleging that as the "iridescent seam," the foreign home, of the *CPR*, the transcendental imagination cannot belong to Kantian consciousness, to the *ego* of the *cogito*. Rather, this "I" itself can only be thought in relation to the transcendental imagination: "original 'thinking' is pure imagining."

All of this permits a summary statement:

> This original, essential constitution of humankind, "rooted" in the transcendental power of imagination, is the "unknown" into which Kant must have looked if he spoke of the "root unknown to us," for the unknown is not that of which we simply know nothing. Rather, it is what pushes against us as something disquieting in what is known. And yet, Kant did not carry through with the more original interpretation of the transcendental power of imagination… On the contrary: Kant shrank back from this unknown root.
>
> *(p. 112)*

Heidegger here is describing something like philosophical disavowal: the registration and repudiation of the disquieting in the known, the disquieting that pushes against the known, that which makes the known other than what we think it is. This is the structure Freud discovered in fetishism, such that the fetish itself is a "monument" to what it apparently repudiates. For Heidegger, the Kantian *cogito* is a "monument" to the transcendental imagination.

Can one go further in this direction? Here I must return to the question of the "unsaid" in Freud's theory of fetishism. Just as Heidegger gains access to the unsaid via a contradiction in Kant—two or three transcendental faculties?—so I have insistently tried to gain access to the unsaid via a contradiction in Freud. He says that the reality the fetish repudiates is the reality of castration. If Freud contends that the fetish disavows reality by using fantasy as a "patch" over that reality, then the contradiction is flagrant: castration is itself a fantasy. Freud does not notice that his own theory implies that the entire fantasy structure of phallic monism—sexual difference equals phallic or castrated—is the "patch" over the reality of sexual difference. And just as Heidegger contends that the transcendental-ontological questions are always at work in the empirical ones, so I have contended that something of that order is at work within the disavowal of empirical sexual difference. Likewise, I wondered previously if Freud's singular mention of "originally unconscious thought" could have anything to do with Heidegger's contention that the origin of Kantian thought is in a faculty of which we are not conscious even once. We will have to follow the rest of Heidegger's argument about the *CPR*, and what Kant had to disavow—shrink back from—to pursue this question.

Heidegger examines the differences between the A and B editions of the *CPR* in the treatment of the transcendental imagination to strengthen his point about Kant's recoil. He summarizes:

> Will not the *Critique of Pure Reason* have deprived itself of its own theme if pure reason reverts to the transcendental power of imagination? Does not this ground-laying lead us to an abyss?In the radicalism of his questions, Kant brought the "possibility" of metaphysics to this abyss. He saw the unknown. He had to shrink back. It was not just that the transcendental power of imagination frightened him, but rather that in between [the two editions] pure reason as reason drew him increasingly under its spell... The problematic of a pure reason amplified in this way must push aside the power of imagination, and with that it really first conceals its transcendental essence.
>
> *(1990, pp. 117–118)*

What is the transcendental essence that pure reason must push aside? If this has to be an ontological question, then of course it must be a question of time. Heidegger reframes his entire effort to this point. As the common root, the transcendental imagination must do the following:

> [M]ake possible something like a pure, sensible reason. Pure sensibility, however, namely in the universal meaning according to which it must come to be grasped in the laying of the ground for metaphysics, is time.Should time as pure sensibility stand in an original unity with the "I think" of pure apperception? Should the pure I, which according to the generally prevailing interpretation Kant placed outside of all temporality and all time be taken as temporal? And all this on the grounds of the transcendental power of imagination? How in general is this related to time?
>
> *(p. 121)*

One could insert all of *Being and Time* at this point. Suffice it to say that Heidegger demonstrates that the pure intuition of time cannot be confined to the current now, but must concern the sequence of nows such that each now looks ahead and looks back—synopsis. Recall the temporality of care, and recall "the self giving of that which gives itself," the non-sensuous sensuous of the *ens imaginarium*. Heidegger says: "In pure intuition, the self-giving which takes things in stride is in principle not related to something which is only a presence and is related least of all to a being which is at hand" (p. 122). Rather, he wants to demonstrate how the transcendental imagination allows time as the sequence of nows to "spring forth," and "as this springing forth" is "original time" (p. 123).

The demonstration is quite detailed. It winds up at the question of time as both the subjectivity of the subject and as that wherein all connections are made—the possibility of synthesis itself (1990, p. 131). If, as Kant says, space and time as *a priori* intuitions always "affect" the representation of an object, then as the pure internal sense, time itself is to affect us. But affection implies a relation to something at hand, something outside. How, then, can time affect us?

> Time is only pure intuition to the extent that it prepares the look of succession from out of itself... This pure intuition activates itself with the intuited which was formed in it, i.e. which was formed without the aid of experience. According to its essence, time is pure affection of itself... As pure self-affection, time is not an acting affection that strikes a self which is at hand. Instead, as pure it forms the essence of something like self-activating. However, if it belongs to the essence of the finite subject to be able to be activated as a self, then time as pure self-affection forms the essential structure of subjectivity.
>
> *(p. 132)*

Being and Time: time temporalizing itself *is* care; care is being-in-the-world as the relation to things. *Kant and the Problem of Metaphysics:* time as pure self-affection *is* the transcendental imagination; the pure intuition of the transcendental imagination is the intuition of the *ens imaginarium*. The idea that pure intuition is pure auto-affection is actually derived from Kant. Heidegger says that the following passage from the transcendental aesthetic can only be understood in the light of everything that he has said so far. Kant writes:

> Now that which... can be antecedent to every act of thinking anything, is intuition, and if it contains nothing but relations, it is the form of intuition. Since this form represents nothing except insofar as something is posited in the mind, it can be nothing other than the way the mind, through its own activity... comes to be affected through itself.
>
> *(cited, 1990, p. 133)*

Freud: originally unconscious thought, the "antecedent" to secondary process, conscious verbal thought, is the tension-raising binding, synthesis, of *relations* between memory traces of "objects." What are such memory traces? They express what Freud understands to be a basic property of the unconscious: to be permanently *affected* without the participation of consciousness. To be affected is to be differentiated. One must add to this conception something like a Freudian conception of "care." Freud himself says in the "Two Principles..." that the infant might look like a monadic "chick in the shell" because it appears unrelated to the maternal care that surrounds it (1911, p. 219). He does not pursue the question very far, but consistent with his conception of unconscious memory traces, particularly with his theory of the memory trace of being fed (the experience of satisfaction), the unconscious is always "affected," even if in traditional terms, it is not yet a subject related to objects. Is it stretching Freud too far to read his idea about unconscious binding of the relations between memory traces of "objects" to mean traces of relation, relation before a subject–object structure? Traces of the relation to "the self giving of that which gives itself" (the "breast" of the experience of satisfaction)? If the infant is not a subject and the breast not an object, is this a relation to an *ens imaginarium?* And thus, an intuition of "pure" relation, of "mind" acting upon *itself* in relation to that which gives *itself*? And if so, does this have any relation to time—*the ekstatikon*? Does it bring the Freudian unconscious close to Heidegger's iridescent transcendental imagination?

Considering "mind" itself, Heidegger says:

> [T]ime as pure self-affection is not found "in the mind" "along with" pure apperception. Rather, as the ground for the possibility of selfhood, time already lies within pure apperception, and so it first makes the mind into the mind... Time and the "I think" no longer stand incompatibly and incomparably at odds; they are the same.
>
> *(1990, p. 134)*

Thus, despite Kant's stated intent, there can be no timelessness of the *cogito.*

This conclusion is what led Derrida to say in "Freud and the Scene of Writing" that one would have to read Freud's repeated statements about the timelessness of the unconscious the way Heidegger read Kant on the timelessness of the *cogito.* I have previously examined Freud's own step in this direction in *Beyond the Pleasure Principle.* In another unusual passage, he momentarily wonders about the possibility of an unconscious time that would challenge Kant's conceptions of time and space (1920, p. 28). Significantly, Freud situates this possibility in the context of his reconsideration of trauma, and even wonders whether conscious time, the time in relation to which the unconscious is "time-less," might itself be the defensive response, the "stimulus barrier," to a traumatic unconscious time (ibid.). Trauma in Freud always means raised tension levels. In fact, in *Beyond...* the unconscious possibility of trauma leads Freud to envisage a "before" of the pleasure principle. This "before" is itself the binding of tension—especially the too much tension of trauma (1920, p. 61). Such binding is a prerequisite for the regular functioning of the pleasure principle. And at the very end of *Beyond...*, Freud wonders whether binding itself has to be understood as a tension poised between pleasure and unpleasure in relation to "units of time" (1920, p. 62).

In "Two Principles...," Freud envisaged binding as unconscious thought. Is there any possible relation between Freud on binding, unconscious time, and unconscious thought, and Heidegger's deconstructed Kant, for whom auto-affective time and mind acting upon itself are the possibilities of relation to the thing?

Heidegger has already established that a finite creature *needs* a play-space, a *Spielraum*, for any possible relation to a thing. In the discussion of the play-space previously, we said that Heidegger would come back to it once the self-undermining role of the transcendental imagination as time was established. It is now clear that "Original time makes possible the transcendental power of imagination which in itself is essentially spontaneous receptivity and receptive spontaneity" (1990, p. 137). In other words, "iridescence" is the joint unity and separation of active and passive. This has to be a quality of any auto-affective process, in which there is no subject–object structure, no opposition between action and acted upon. An auto-affective process has to have within it the *Raum*, the room, the space, for the play of iridescence. Heidegger writes:

> Kant wants to say: the encountering of the being itself occurs for a finite creature in a representing whose pure representations of objectivity as such have *played* up to one another [*auf einander eingespielt*]. This Being-*played*-up [*Eingespieltsein*] is... determined in advance in such a way that in general it can be *played* out in a *play*-space [*in einem Spiel-Raum abspielen kann*]. This [play-space] is formed through pure determinations of the inner sense. The pure inner sense is pure self-affection, i.e. original time.
>
> *(pp. 138–139)*

Hence, Heidegger can put "play" at the heart of the Kantian architectonic. If auto-affective time is the activating process of the finite self, it has to be spatial: "like time, space in a certain sense also belongs to the self as something finite... this [self], on the grounds of original time to be sure, is essentially spatial" (1990, p. 140). As in *Being and Time*, existential space *is* existential time. *Ekstasis*, time temporalizing itself, *is* the *ekstatikon par excellence,* and the space for play intrinsic to the auto-affection of *KPM*. The "I," the self, is as much the time-space of the *ens imaginarium* as the *ens imaginarium* is the thing, the space, of time. The space-time of the self-giving of that which gives itself.

At the end of his life, as we saw in Chapter 1, Freud mused that "'The breast is part of me. I am the breast.' Only later: 'I have it'—that is, 'I am not it'" (1923, p. 299). Can one read this ontologically? Certainly, Freud had always said that in the oral phase, the libidinal relation to the object is incorporative, identificatory: one is what one loves. But when he distinguishes "being" from "having," Freud also implies that the breast is not initially something one can possess, is not yet an object. The baby is the breast in that it is related to it before a subject–object structure. Previously, we asked about this relation in terms of Freud's passing thought about originally unconscious thought, and in terms of the self-giving of that which gives itself, the *ens imaginarium*.

It is now necessary to answer these questions, via Freud's explicit examination of the auto-affective structure at the heart of his theory of sexuality. This is the relation of Freud's theory to *KPM* on the transcendental imagination that I began to examine in *Interpretation and Difference* (2006, pp. 77–83). In "Instincts and Their Vicissitudes," Freud takes up an essential point in his theory of infantile sexuality. The "component drives," i.e., the sexual impulses of infancy, before their organization under the dominance of the genitals, are always pairs of opposites, an active and passive version of the same drive. For example, sadism and masochism are the active and passive versions of enjoyment of pain. When Freud examines voyeurism (scopophilia) and exhibitionism, he expects to find the same structure, but does not. To summarize a complicated development: sadism, which is always active, itself is not originally sexual. The task is to show how it becomes sexual, which, for Freud, is a consequence of what he calls turning around upon oneself. Voyeurism, also always active for Freud (the exhibitionist is passive, looked at), unlike sadism, is originally sexual. But infantile sexuality is essentially auto-erotic. This is why Freud says, "the scopophilic instinct is auto-erotic; it has indeed an object, but that object is part of the subject's own body" (1915, p. 130). Freud calls this a "preliminary stage" of voyeurism, which is "the source of *both* the situations represented in the resulting pair of opposites" (ibid.). In the preliminary stage, "oneself looking at a sexual organ" equals "a sexual organ being looked at by oneself" (ibid.). The first half of the equation ("oneself looking") becomes active looking at "an extraneous object" (the voyeuristic subject); the second half ("at a sexual organ"), becomes a part of oneself passively being looked at by an "extraneous person" (the exhibitionistic object) (ibid.). In the preliminary stage of scopophilia, the distinctions subject–object and active–passive do not hold. For this reason, Freud calls it intermediate. He is describing an auto-affective process.

Remarkably, this intermediate auto-affective process has a clear relation to the temporality, the historicity, of sexuality. Sexuality itself was the key to the unconscious history of the individual, the history at work in the formation of neurotic symptoms. Looking at this history, Freud found not only that the component drives of infantile sexuality occur as pairs of opposites, but that the active version of the drive could always turn into the passive version, and *vice versa*. To account for this possibility, Freud postulates the intermediate, active–passive, subjective-objective source of the drive. Speaking specifically of scopophilia he says, "The only correct statement to make about the scopophilic instinct would be that all of the stages of its development, its auto-erotic, preliminary stage as well as its final active or passive form, co-exist alongside one another" (1915, pp. 130–131). One may be a voyeur for a period of time; for another period, an exhibitionist. These may appear to be distinct identities, but the fact that voyeurism can turn into exhibitionism is made possible by their common root. Freud concludes: "This reference to the developmental history of instincts and the permanence of their intermediate stages should make the development of instincts fairly intelligible to us" (1915, p. 131).

Freud uses a geological metaphor to describe this history. Each apparently distinct period of sexual activity is like a volcanic eruption, leaving behind lava. The accumulated strata of "successive eruptions of lava" give the history of the development of the drive. The primary, intermediate phase, though, has to "accompany" each eruption, because it makes it possible for each stratum to appear distinct, but to become the other (ibid.). To mix metaphors, the primary, intermediate phase is both the "volcano" itself and a Heideggerean "seam" that unites and separates active and passive. As an auto-affective, temporal, process it is never present. It is the non-sensuous sensuous of sexuality.

Heidegger had said that the more subjective time becomes in Kant, the more it expands the subject, opens it to the thing. Can one say something similar about Freud's "eruptive" intermediate drives? With interpretation, I believe so. The interpretation concerns "being the breast," a relation without a subject–object structure. It is a relation in which mind is affected—an unconscious memory trace is formed. The trace of a relation in which "mind" is the thing—which "gives itself." Which gives itself periodically, in "units of time," as per the conclusion of *Beyond the Pleasure Principle*. Which can be reconfigured in terms of primary scopophilia. If one *is* the breast, then oneself looking at the breast is the breast being looked at by oneself. The originally sexual mind is auto-affective in relation to the self-giving, temporal thing.

At the beginning of his work, accounting for unconscious memory, and the origin of dreams, Freud had to conceptualize the trace of the experience of satisfaction—the baby being fed. At the end, he spoke of "being the breast." In between, he postulated primary scopophilia, which in combined Freudian–Heideggerean language could be said to provide the "pure look" of the thing. An "iridescent" active–passive process opens the "play-space" of the relation to the thing.

Without noticing the connection, Freud hypothesized primal binding in relation to unconscious thought and unconscious time. Unconscious thought-raised tension levels and relations between memory traces are the possibility of the temporal delay of secondary process, conscious rationality. Unconscious time is potentially traumatic; conscious time is the protective barrier against it. As the possibility of secondary process, delayed gratification, unconscious thought is the tension of the "spacing" within the relations between memory traces. As the possibility of conscious time, the tension of unconscious time meets the mind's tendency to reduce tension. The least one can say is that Freud's usual descriptions of "the unconscious" as timeless primary process become much more complex. The unconscious iridescent auto-affective processes of the primary, intermediate phases of the drives open the relation to the thing. They are "eruptive-expansive," related to the tension of unconscious thought and unconscious time. All of this is very close to Heidegger's understanding of the transcendental imagination as auto-affective time—the blind faculty of which we are seldom conscious even once; the abyss of metaphysics, from which Kant had to recoil.

The possibility of fetishism in the usual sense, the universal capacity for worship of, or sexual arousal by, a thing, would then reside in the integration of unconscious thought, unconscious time, and primary scopophilia. That is, in the auto-affective unconscious process of "being the breast," i.e., mind acting on itself as the opening to the thing that it is. This is the temporal space of the *ens imaginarium*. The traditional motifs of the description of the fetish—its self-referentiality, its "unity of opposites" (protective or harmful, phallic or castrated, good or bad)—are the recoil from its conditions of possibility, and from what they say about both mind and thing. Self-referential conflation of indication and indicated is disavowal of the auto-affective processes that constitute mind and thing. The "reality effect" of oscillation between opposites is disavowal of "iridescence." Apparently objective opposites are the conscious, closed versions of the unconscious opening of the relation to the thing. The non-symbolic, non-referential fetish is not exactly not yet a transcendental god, or an abstract sign. Rather, its complex structure of opening and closure shows why open and closed structures, auto-affection and self-reference, always co-exist. Auto-affection is the possibility of self-reference.

Returning to fetishism in *Being and Time*: Heidegger could not follow through on his idea that what the fetish apparently is *not* could indeed yield a formal conception of being-in-the-world larger than the one based on the sign structure of useful things. Perhaps Heidegger evaded another aspect of everyday *Dasein,* which can always make the thing into a god or a sexual object. Freud, on the other hand, sees the opening to a general structure in sexual fetishism. But could he have rethought unconscious processes in terms of the relatedness of mind and thing, i.e., in terms of unconscious time and unconscious thought? These are the processes that are the unsaid of the transcendental imagination. Such processes themselves are the reality of the *ens imaginarium*, mind and thing in their auto-affective relatedness. This is the reality that is the "foreign home" of reality conflated with objectivity. It is the reality of uncanniness. Freud, then, is somewhat like Kant in Heidegger's reading. He does not pursue possibilities he envisages, possibilities that undermine some of his basic ideas. But he is also somewhat like Heidegger himself, in that he does glimpse these possibilities: binding before the pleasure principle, unconscious thought, unconscious time, primary intermediacy.

Let us recall that Freud's own point of departure—how is it possible to have memories of which we are not conscious? What does defense say about mind?—is a question of mind acting upon itself. His most general answer is the theory of repression. And when he generalizes fetishism and disavowal at the end of his life he says that he is returning to his point of departure, to something both "old and familiar, and new and puzzling" (1940b, p. 274). I think that he did not see how large the puzzle was, the puzzle of the general structure of fetishism. To remain on the terrain of Heidegger and Freud, let us also recall that the perplexing knot of Heidegger's handkerchief in *Being and Time* can itself indicate Freud's most enduring questions: what is mind, what is conscious, what is unconscious, if I can always forget what I intend to remember? And then what is mind if fetishism is its most general condition? Both questions trench upon mind acting on itself and upon the relation to the thing, whether as memory-aid, or as religious or sexual object.

A knot binds. This binding is a synthesis of mind and thing. When the apparent reference is forgotten—really disavowed—and the knot, like a broken tool, appears just to be there, like the fetish—and *contra* Heidegger—the binding of mind and thing is "indicated." But indicated the way one indicates that which cannot be indicated: the iridescence of the *ens imaginarium*. The uncanniness of auto-affective process.

In the paper on "Fetishism," Freud says that he will surely disappoint in saying that the fetish is a substitute for the penis. He then goes on to say that it is a substitute for the fantasized maternal phallus, the antidote to the possibility of castration (1927, p. 154). Similarly, I might surely disappoint by saying that the possibility of fetishism is the relation to the breast. However, I am claiming that this is a relation to an *ens imaginarium* in Heidegger's sense. I am also claiming that the possibility of the memory of the experience of satisfaction, of the opening of the unconscious, its capacity to be affected, is the auto-affective structure of mind "acting upon itself" in relation to an auto-affective, self-giving thing. This is why in both *Difference and Disavowal* (2000) and *Interpretation and Difference* (2006), I attempted to revise the basic theory of unconscious process to include "registration," tracing, of non-objectively present reality—summarized under the rubric of the reality of differentiating process.

It is essential to remember that the origin of fantasy in Freud's sense is the hallucinatory revival of the experience of satisfaction. In other words, the prior condition of fantasy is the registration of the *ens imaginarium*. One can understand fantasy in this sense as imaginary in the way Heidegger read Kant on imagination in the *Anthropology*—the bringing forth of the "look" of something without its actual presence. To which Freud of course would add that this bringing forth can be hallucinatory, such that there is an effect of actual presence without actual presence. But one would have to add to this Heidegger's understanding of the *transcendental* imagination, in which imagination itself is auto-affective time in its paradoxical synthetic capacity. Empirical imagination can be responsible for apparent self-reference, but the transcendental imagination is its condition of possibility—auto-affection. To circle back to our constant theme: auto-affection as the opening to the thing, and as the possibility of symbolism, always co-exists with self-reference as the apparent closure of the possibility of symbolism. But co-exists in a structure of disavowal: paradoxically differentiating auto-affection is the uncanny, tension raising home of concrete self-reference.

In *KPM*, Heidegger increasingly emphasizes the play-space of auto-affection. It fulfills the transcendental *need* of a finite creature for the relation to the thing. In *Being and Time*, care is ecstatic time. "Care" itself always implies finitude and need, opening, relation to what is other than oneself. In Freudian terms, the need for care is the obvious empirical fact of the helplessness of the human infant, but it also has a more "transcendental–ontological" status in the theory of the drives. All of my previous work not only attempts to explore the import of Freud's generalization of fetishism, but also to rethink the question of therapeutic care in relation to Freud on need and drive. This is what led him to postulate the life-drive, Eros. To recapitulate quickly: In *Beyond the Pleasure Principle*, Freud corrected his previous assumption of inherent conflict between self-preservation and libido, the mainspring of the original theory of repression. While there is such a conflict in neurosis, this is no longer a general condition of mind. Rather, one must think of a combined libidinal-self-preservative drive, a life drive. This drive combines three functions, all of which relate to everything we have seen in *KPM*: it synthesizes mind with environment, binds energy, and "introduces fresh vital differences" into the psyche (1920, p. 55). Because it raises tension levels, Eros itself has to be in conflict with the tendency of mind to reduce tension, the pleasure principle hypostasized into the death drive (ibid.). Again, Freud postulates a primacy of binding, and again does not notice the connections to his other postulations of a primacy of binding. Nor does he see any connection to primary intermediate scopophilia, or to the question of "being the breast." Both the latter concern the question of care.

Eros as care is both self-preservative and libidinal. What does this have to do with fetishism? The libidinal aspect of the fetish, the thing, clarifies why it can always be an object of sexual arousal or worship. In psychoanalytic terms, it is actually both, in that the sexualized thing is venerated, and the venerated thing sexualized. This raises the very large question of idealization, Freud's point of departure for his discussion of fetishism in the *Three Essays* (1905). But idealization can always be reversed, as consistently pointed out in the history of discourse on fetishism: the replacement of the maternal phallus with the thing is a monument to the horror of castration; the worshiped thing can be harmful, persecutory. In Chapter 1, we saw Freud attribute uncanny doubling to primary narcissism. In the same essay, he also says that

> the quality of uncanniness can only come from the fact of the 'double' being a creation dating back to a very early mental stage, long since surmounted—a stage, incidentally, at which it wore a more friendly aspect. The 'double' has become a thing of terror, just as, after the collapse of their religion, the gods turned into demons.
>
> *(1917, p. 235)*

Each side of the equation can be taken as concretely real, as the result of the disavowal of the auto-affective process of Eros in its differentiating-synthetic function. The fetish then oscillates between apparent opposites: sexuality and destructiveness, phallic and castrated, idealized and persecutory, "friendly" and "terrifying."

In *Analysis Terminable and Interminable,* Freud offers an explanation of how this can come about. There, he said that "In the real world transitional and intermediate stages are far more common than sharply differentiated opposite states" (1937, p. 228). He is saying that apparent opposition is less "real" than one usually thinks. Later in the paper, he uses his old theory of universal bisexuality as an example. He wonders about a clinical issue. While bisexuality itself is part of "normal mental life," some people experience it as "irreconcilable conflict" (1937, p. 243). Why? Not for the reason one might expect: the castration complex. Rather, conflict over normal bisexuality illustrates an independent "tendency to conflict… [which] can scarcely be attributed to anything but the intervention of an element of free aggressiveness" (ibid.), the death drive in action. And Freud goes on to compare the life and death drives to Empedocles' *philia* (love) and *neikos* (strife) (1937, p. 244). The implication is clear: intermediate, "iridescent" bisexuality becomes an apparently irreconcilable conflict over hetero- and homo-sexuality because of the destructive, tension reducing, dedifferentiating aspects of the death drive. Intermediate, universal bisexuality is an aspect of *philia*, Eros, care.

This conception can be generalized. Eros "begins" with "being the breast," a binding, tension-raising, auto-affective-differentiating process, a relation to an *ens imaginarium*. It encounters two other aspects of unconscious process: the capacity to form memory traces that can be revived with hallucinatory intensity and the concomitant tendency toward tension reduction. When this occurs, objective presence is conflated with tension relief: what I see now is supposed to rid me of pain, while I am unaware that this objective presence is the *trace* of the *ens imaginarium*. In other words, the structure of wish fulfillment is the disavowal of "being the breast." One must not confine this operation to the oral phase. Whenever mind "affects itself" with differentiating process, it is always possible that mind will "attack itself," with the result that the trace of differentiating process is disavowed via objective presence. This is the point at which intermediacy becomes opposition, such that opposite states appear discrete, but can turn into each other. Again: the fetish as phallus and castration, the breast as idealized and persecutory. Overall *philia* and *neikos* interact. In *Group Psychology and the Analysis of the Ego*, Freud briefly noted a primal tendency to respond to differentiation with aggression, but said he could not explain it. This is the explanation.

This attack of the mind on itself—a kind of auto-immune response—would result in the closure of the *Spielraum*, the temporal play-space of auto-affective process. In psychoanalytic terms, it would be the closure of Winnicott's "transitional space," the origin of play. Winnicott famously calls transitionality a "third area of experiencing" between the subjective and the objective (1975, p. 230). The present participle, experienc*ing*, can remind us of Heidegger's reading of Kant's highest synthetic principle—the condition of possibility of experience in general. Heidegger had said that when Kant claims that this condition is *at the same time* the condition of possibility of the object of experience, the *simultaneity* of experience and object itself expresses exactly what Kant had to recoil from—the *Spielraum*. Winnicott himself says that because playing occurs on the "theoretical line" between the subjective and the objective, it is "precarious" (1971, p. 50). This precariousness may lead to a "high degree of anxiety" (1971, p. 52). "Games and their rules" are then part of "an attempt to forestall the frightening aspect of playing" (1971, p. 50). Heidegger makes a similar point about Kant. The *Spielraum* is what a finite creature *needs* for any possible relation to a thing (1990, p. 50). But Kant grants supremacy to the faculty of rules (pp. 52–53)—in Heidegger's reading, the inevitable recoil from the auto-affective temporality of the *Spielraum*.

Winnicott in general has not much use for Freud's death drive. Clearly, though, the "high degree of anxiety" of the intermediate experiencing of play can produce rule bound activity, which controls the "precariousness" of what is on "the theoretical line" between subjective and objective. In the context of Heidegger on Kant, of the *Spielraum* as the "abyss of metaphysics," Winnicott's sense of the anxiety of play requires a closer look at "transitional phenomena" themselves. He does not attend to Freud's "being the breast" or primary scopophilia, which are entirely relevant to his conception. But he comes close when he says that "two babies are feeding at the breast. One is feeding on the self, since the breast and the baby have not yet become... separate phenomena. The other is feeding from an other-than-me source" (1971, p. 89). This division of the baby is an expression of differentiation within auto-affection: the baby *is* the breast, but the breast is also a thing that is not an object. (The memory trace of the experience of satisfaction is the trace of the *ens imaginarium.*) This division within the baby is the "third area of experiencing." For Winnicott, this is why all babies at some point make use of a *thing* that is "not part of the infant's body," yet is "not recognized as belonging to external reality" (1971, p. 2). The baby moves from auto-affection of the body—"fist, fingers, thumbs" in the mouth—to attachment to a thing, typically soft and pliable. But while this thing comes from without for the observer, it does not for the baby. As intermediate, the transitional thing is akin to the division of the baby, both itself (feeding on itself) and not itself (other than me).

This auto-affective, differentiating process is the origin of play in terms of space and time. "*Playing has a place* and a time. It is not *inside* by any use of the word... Nor is it *outside,* that is to say, it is not a part of... that which the individual has decided to recognize as truly external" (1971, p. 41). This is the "first use of a symbol and the first experience of play" (1971, p. 96). Winnicott expands on symbol, time, space, union, separation:

> The object is a symbol of the union of the baby and the mother... This symbol can be located. It is at the place in space and time where and when the mother is in transition from being (in the baby's mind) merged in with the infant and alternatively being experienced as an object to be perceived... The use of an object symbolizes the union of two now separate things, baby and mother, *at the point in time and space of the initiation of their state of separateness.*
>
> *(1971, pp. 96–97)*

Rephrased: the space-time of transition, of play, of the relation to the thing, is the origin of symbolism as union–separation.

Winnicott says that the transitional object is the "substance of illusion," in a strong sense: it is the "stuff" out of which all cultural activity, all art, science, and religious experience, emerges. But it can be delusion, or even madness, to insist on the objective reality of illusory, or play, experience: the communicant must always know that the wafer is not literally the body of Christ (1975, pp. 230–231). If not, one has Hume's error of objective presence, magnified into possible insanity if one insists that others accept the reality of one's delusion. And one also has the possibility of a fetish, which Winnicott typically sees as an indication of environmental failure (1975, p. 240). He contends that "good enough" maternal care allows the extension of the transitional object onto the "entire cultural field." The fate of the transitional object is not to be lost or mourned, but to fade away (1975, p. 232). However, absent good enough environmental provision, the transitional object can become an infantile fetish, an object that always has to be present, that cannot fade away (1975, p. 233).

This is perhaps the point at which Winnicott's failure to consider the death drive is important. I have no dispute with his theory of environmental impingement, the impact of not good enough care. However, he does not take into account that in the situation in which the baby *is* the breast–mother, pain, or even trauma, is also auto-affective. Differentiation is then *neikos*. The play-space of transitionality becomes mandatory objective presence, or the threat of its absence. There is a Kleinian idealized good breast and persecutory bad breast. In fact, one could say that the Kleinian good and bad breasts are the fetishism of the oral phase, the disavowal of the differentiating "transitional" breast—again the *ens imaginarium*.

The distinction between transitional thing and fantasy object is critical here. Freud's brief account of *philia* and *neikos* potentially explains how intermediate thingliness *becomes* oppositional fantasy—with the proviso that each side of the opposition can become the other. This is why Freud and Klein, in their respective ways, theorize both splitting of, and oscillation between, phallic and castration, idealized and persecutory. The very possibility of this splitting–oscillation is something like a Heideggerean iridescent seam. The transitional "object"—and here I think that "thing," or even Winnicott's "phenomenon," are the preferable words—is itself a "symbol" of transition. The mother and the baby are in transition from union to separateness; the breast that one is becomes the breast that one has. Transition itself is the *Spielraum*, the play of time and space, that is both union and separateness, being and having. As union and separateness are themselves differentiated, transitionality is "subjectivized." One becomes a separate subject in relation to a present or absent external object; the breast that one has can also be the breast one does not have. The potential anxiety related to any play on the border of the subjective and the objective becomes the destructiveness directed against tension-raising intermediacy. The "rule bound" game of closed reference, of the conflation of fantasy and objective presence, apparently dominates. But it is always "haunted" by the auto-affective transitionality of oneself as thing. If this is so, then an integration of Winnicott on transitionality and Freud on primary intermediacy takes the theory of the unconscious further in the direction of Heidegger's conception of the transcendental imagination.

Sensation, thinging, fourfold

Heidegger returns to the *CPR* in *What is a Thing?* There is a kind of *mea culpa* to *What is a Thing?* Heidegger says that his aim is make up for what *KPM* lacked (1967, p. 125), namely the significance of the mathematization of physics (Newton) for the delineation of the *a priori* synthesis. As in *KPM*, Heidegger begins with the question of the "quiddity," the thingness of the thing, and observes that every thing is "this particular" thing. (Recall the supposed singularity of the fetish.) But this is precisely what Kant is not interested in; for him the thing is an object of mathematical–physical science (1967, p. 128). The thing is an object of experience to the extent that it is knowable according to axiomatic rules. Hence, Kant has "disregarded what is manifest (*das Offenbare*). He does not inquire into and determine in its own essence that which encounters us prior to an objectification into an object of experience" (1967, p. 141). The manifest is what has come into the open. Heidegger's consistent point is that the singular, *particular* thing is not an "object of experience," but rather an "experience" of what cannot be objectified, what cannot be conceptualized according to mathematical science: opening itself. What he called the *Spielraum* in *KPM*, he here calls the *Zeitraum*, the time-space of opening, of non-objectifying encounter with the thing.

As in *Being and Time* and *KPM*, Heidegger seeks the inner relation between the immediate, non-objectifying encounter with the thing via sensory reception and *Zeitraum*. Sensation, he says, "occupies a peculiar intermediate position between things and human beings, between object and subject" (1967, p. 208), and "reflects the uncertainty of the relation between man and thing" (1967, p. 211). Intermediacy and uncertainty: what rules cannot govern.

In *KPM*, Heidegger used the transcendental imagination in its relation to intuition and time as the lever to deconstruct the Kantian architectonic; here he uses Kant on "intensive magnitude" in a similar way. "Extensive magnitude" is the understanding of space as everywhere uniform, and so, measurable: this is Newton. Again, this is why the principles of mathematical physics are the condition of possibility for objects of experience: all objects are extended and measurable. "Intensive magnitude," however, concerns the "quantity of quality": how brightly does the moon shine? Kant himself says that all appearances are extensive magnitudes as intuitions, and intensive magnitudes as sensations (1967, p. 222). But, says Heidegger, this means that all sensory perception contains an "anticipation," a "reaching out" that makes it possible for sensation to be a "receivable, encountering this and that" (1967, p. 220)—i.e., a *particular, qualitative* encounter. Kant's discovery of anticipation in perception, says Heidegger, is "astonishing" in light of the role of mathematical physics in the *a priori* synthesis, because it puts the particular and the qualitative into sensory reception *a priori*.

Because Kant says that all appearances themselves are subject *a priori* to rules determining their relation in time (1967, p. 228), Heidegger can use non-rule bound intensive magnitude, and its relation to time, to delineate another aspect of the "unsaid" in Kant. Time, says Heidegger, is the "connection" in which *a priori* rules themselves have anticipatory power (1967, p. 229). Here, Heidegger enters into another detailed examination of aspects of the *CPR*, of what Kant says about time in relation to the analogies of experience. The latter are the *rules* that indicate the temporality of experience of an object (permanence, cause and effect, reciprocity) (1967, p. 235). But Kant has also posited quantity, quality, relation, and modality as the categories of thought—and quality, he has said, is a function of intensive magnitude (1967, p. 236). Hence, if there has to be a unity of pure conceptions of understanding (which has to be governed by rules), with space and time as forms of intuition (with space itself presupposing intensive magnitude), then there is a "circle" in which the "rulable" and the "non-rulable" turn into each other. (Recall the relation between the *Spielraum* and the faculty of rules in *KPM*.) This circularity is the essence of experience: "Experience is in itself a circular happening through which what lies within the circle becomes exposed (*eroffnet*). This open (*Offene*), however, is nothing other than the between (*Zwischen*)—between us and the thing" (1967, p. 242).

Undermining Kant's stated intent as usual, Heidegger now says that we cannot understand the *CPR* from the scientific viewpoint. The "between" itself "is not like a rope stretching from the thing to man," but is an "anticipation" that "reaches beyond the thing and similarly back behind us" (1967, p. 243). He concludes:

> Kant's questioning about the thing asks about intuition and thought, about experience and its principles, i.e. it asks about man. The question "What is a thing?" is the question "Who is man?" That does not mean that things become a human product (*Gemächte*), but on the contrary, it means that man is to be understood as he who always already leaps beyond things, but in such a way that this leaping-beyond is possible only while things encounter and so precisely remain themselves—while they send us back behind ourselves and our surface. A dimension is opened up in Kant's question about the thing which lies between the thing and man, which reaches out beyond things and back behind man.
>
> *(1967, p. 244)*

That the question "what is a thing?" is the question "who is man?" means that "who" and "what" are in a circular relation.[2] They are open to each other, opening itself being the intermediacy—the transitionality—that "links" (binds) them. But binds them not as a rope ties together two pre-existing objects, but as a structural futurity, an "anticipation," which again means that the who is a who by means of its relation to a what. This anticipation takes us back to particularity: things remain themselves. *This thing* is not encountered according to any rule (*Spielraum* as opening to the thing). Such an encounter sends "us back behind ourselves and our surface." What does that mean? If our surface is our consciousness, then the encounter is "behind" it. Can one hear a reference to that of which we are not conscious, even once? To a non-conscious, non-rule-bound play (Winnicott) of a relatedness to the thing (the "what") that I (the "who") am? A play in which particularity cannot be abstracted away, leapt beyond? In other words, a play in which "my" singularity *is* the particularity of the thing?

Throughout the history of discourse on fetishism, particularity is the spoke in the wheel of reason. For Kant fetishism is the veneration of the "trifling" with no sense of the sublime (see Chapter 2). This includes any sort of "fetish faith" in which "clericalism" prescribes "certain formalities" as the means to have God satisfy one's wishes, tantamount to dismissing all recourse to an "in itself" (1960, p. 181). But such dismissal would also dismiss any understanding of a non-deterministic, non-conscious process in which particularity *is* transitionality or intermediacy. Or in which the "object of experience" is made possible by the relation to a thing which is not an object, a relation that itself is "behind ourselves and our surface."

Heidegger's own dismissal of fetishism in *Being and Time*, then, sounds as Kantian as it is Hegelian. The fetish is only understood in terms of the conflation of indication and indicated, excluding it from the freedom of the sign structure. For Kant, reason and moral law also are the guarantors of a certain freedom. But this freedom rests upon rule-bound "leaping beyond" the thing, i.e., encountering the thing as an *object* of experience. Paradoxically, this is why there is always a "Kantian" aspect to fetishism. As Mauss made clear, a fetish never exists without reference to coded rules. And as Freud made clear, the fetish itself is an "object of experience," in that its "reality effect," as in dreams and hallucinations, depends upon the objectification of time and space (perceptual identity and temporal immediacy). Which is also why Freud himself had so many difficulties with the role of reality testing in his theory, especially in the theory of fetishism. (What is the reality disavowed by the fetishist?) But this would also explain why the fetishist as "Kantian" supports Heidegger's reading of Kant: rule bound objective reality is a disavowal of the play of intermediacy, which relates man and thing—behind ourselves and our surface. And relates them via singularity and sensation (intensive magnitude). But this also explains the disavowal structure of Heidegger's treatment of fetishism in *Being and Time.* He envisages a possible opening to being-in-the-world in fetishism, and then repudiates this possibility. He could not see that fetishism itself is possible because of the encounter with the thing in its sensation and singularity. But one must always recall Mauss' point about the coded nature of the fetish. Fetishism then would be precisely where singularity and the rule turn into each other—Heidegger's circle of experience in which the rulable and the non-rulable turn into each other.

When Heidegger describes "experience as a circular happening through which what lies within the circle becomes exposed" the reader familiar with *Being and Time* will recall what he says there about the hermeneutic circle. Countering the usual understanding of it as a vicious circle—the project of interpretation presumes interpretability itself, so has no foundation—he says that the question is how to enter the circle in the right way (1996, p. 143). Similarly, in the concluding remarks of *What is a Thing?* he is saying that Kantian "experience" unwittingly presumes a circular "happening," which Kant himself could not enter in the right way. Circularity can be another way of describing auto-affection: concept and intuition, rules and play, have to move around each other, revealing the opening to the thing. Experience as this circular moving around becomes a circular mirror play in "The Thing."

Heidegger contends that things "have never yet at all been able to appear to thinking as things" (1971, p. 171). In other words, a thinking that does not participate in the forgetting of being, a non-metaphysical thinking, would be able to let the thing appear as thing, in its particularity. Quickly summarizing his understanding of the history of metaphysics, Heidegger says that this means that the thing would appear as neither Latin *res*, nor medieval *ens,* nor modern object of representation (ibid.).

His example is a jug (*Krug*). The jug, he says, is a hollow vessel that holds liquid. It holds by taking in what is poured and keeping it. The pouring in and the holding are joined by outpouring from the jug: "The holding of the vessel occurs in the giving of the outpouring... the poured gift" (1971, p. 172). The gift of the outpouring is "drink for mortals," but may also be a "libation poured out for the immortal gods" (ibid.). The drink itself—say, wine—is the meeting of earth (what is grown) and sky (sun and rain).

> Mortals and gods, earth and sky dwell in the gift of the outpouring. In the gift of the outpouring earth and sky, divinities and mortals dwell *together all at once.* These four, at one because of what they themselves are, belong together. Preceding everything that is present, they are enfolded into a single fourfold... This manifold-simple gathering is the jug's presencing. Our language denotes what a gathering *is* by an ancient word. That word is thing (*ding*). The jug's presencing is the pure, giving gathering of the one-fold fourfold into a single time-space... The jug presences as a thing... But how does the thing presence? The thing things (*Das ding bedingt*). Thinging gathers. Appropriating the fourfold, it gathers the fourfold's stay, its while... We are now thinking this word [thing] by way of the gathering-appropriating staying of the fourfold.
>
> *(1971, pp. 173–174)*

The "gathering-appropriating," is not simply unification. Rather, "thinging" brings the remoteness of earth and sky, mortals and divinities, near to one another, but near in a way that preserves their distance (1971, p. 178). As always for Heidegger, relatedness is union–separation. This is why each of the four *is* itself because it reflects the other in a play of mirrors:

> Each of the four [earth and sky, mortals and divinities] mirrors in its own way the presence of the others... Mirroring in this appropriating-lightening way, each of the four *plays* to each of the others. The appropriative mirroring sets each of the four free into its own, but it *binds* these free ones into the simplicity of their essential being toward one another. The *mirroring that binds into freedom is the play* that betroths each of the four to each... None of the four insists on its own separate particularity. Rather each is expropriated, within their mutual appropriation, into its own being. This expropriative appropriating is the mirror *play* of the fourfold... This appropriating mirror-play... we call the world. The world presences by worlding... the inexplicable and unfathomable character of the world's worlding lies in this, that causes and grounds remain unsuitable for the world's worlding... The thing stays—gathers and unites—the fourfold. The thing things world... we let ourselves be concerned by the thing's worlding being. Thinking in this way, we are called by the thing as the thing. In the strict sense of the German word *bedingt,* we

> are the be-thinged, the conditioned ones. We have left behind us the presumption of all unconditionedness.
>
> *(1971, pp. 178–181,* passim*; my emphases)*

A passage like this can call for infinite commentary. I will pick out elements relevant to my argument so far. "Lightening" for Heidegger is opening that permits what one might call ontological seeing: the "light" required for "vision" of what is never objectively seen. This is the possibility of reception of the "non-sensuous sensuous," a kind of "experience free" intuition. Like the transcendental imagination in relation to time, this lightening is auto-affective: mirroring. But a mirroring of what is always simultaneously itself and other. Hence, it *binds* each to the other in such a way that each remains itself, in its particularity, *as* the relation to the other. Particularity *is* relation. This is a non-Kantian "freedom," because it is *play* (*Spielraum*). In other words, it is an *a priori* synthesis without rules, without cause or even ground. Hence, the deliberately paradoxical "mirroring that binds into freedom." The things that were the point of departure for the analysis of being-in-the-world in *Being and Time* now have "a life of their own," a "freedom" perhaps greater than the freedom of the referential sign-structure. Rather, things are the auto-affective structure of world itself: the thing "things world." *Das ding bedingt.* To be in the world, then, to be oneself *as* bound to things, is to be auto-affected by the auto-affective thing. *Bedingen* means "to be conditioned"—to be affected; to be differentiated. To be in the world is to be conditioned *a priori*. To be conditioned is particularity, singularity. There is no possible "unconditionedness," no possibility of not being auto-affected by the auto-affective thing: the world.

Is this not a description of the possibility of fetishism as being the breast, as being the thing *a priori*, before subject and object, in an originally conditioning, differentiating, auto-affective play?

The play of the fourfold in "The Thing" cannot be divorced from Heidegger's contemporaneous delineation of the fourfold play of time *as* space. The title of his late essay, *On Time and Being*, itself indicates the relation to *Being and Time.* Returning to his earlier sense of ecstatic time as the reaching out to each other of the past, present, and future, and meditating on the givenness of time and space, that there is being (*Es gibt Sein*) and there is time (*Es gibt Zeit*), Heidegger says that past, present, and future are inter-related, as:

> the presencing that is given in them. With this presencing there opens up what we call time-space… Time-space now is the name for the openness which opens up in the mutual self-extending of futural approach, past and present. This openness exclusively and primarily provides the space in which space as we usually know it can unfold… the unity of time's three dimensions consists in the *interplay* of each toward each. This *interplay* proves to be the true extending, *playing* in the very heart of time, the fourth dimension. True time is four dimensional.
>
> *(1972, pp. 14–15; my emphases)*

The play of the world as fourfold mirror play of the thing *is* the play of four-dimensional time. The spatial thing, the extended thing, the particular thing, can only "bething" if it is temporal. The fourth dimension of time, opening, *is* space. Time as thing, the *ekstatikon* of *Being and Time*, is four-dimensional play. This is world itself as time-space. Derrida has commented on this passage:

> Whether it is a matter of Being, of time, or of their deployment in presence (*Anwesen*), the *es gibt* plays (*spielt*) says Heidegger… The *play* (*Zuspiel*) also marks, works on, manifests the unity of the three dimensions of time, which is to say a fourth dimension: The "giving" of the *es gibt Zeit* belongs to the play of this "quadridimensionality"… The fourth dimension, as Heidegger makes clear, is not a figure, it is not a manner of speaking… *it is said of the thing itself.*
>
> *(1992, p. 22; my emphasis)*

That the thing itself *is* four-dimensional time also means that as auto-affective mirror play, the thing itself must be iridescent.

For Heidegger, it is critical that before Plato, Heraclitus characterized time as play with a thing. Heraclitus' enigmatic Fragment 52 is given by Heidegger as "Time is a child that plays, shifting the pawns" (cited Schurmann, 1990, p. 42). The more literal translation is "Time is a boy playing, playing *pessoi,* kingship belongs to the boy" (Kurke, 1966, p. 265). Scholars do not know exactly what *pessoi* was, but from references in Homer and Plato, it seems to have been a game in which pieces were moved around, probably on a board. Some scholars think that "kingship" refers to a king piece in the game. For Heidegger, it is the movement of the thing, the "shifting of the pawns" by a playing child that characterizes time. Heraclitus is also the thinker of iridescence, the shifting of opposites (day and night, the living and the dead, the young and the old). In Fragment 52, he is specifically concerned with day and night as One, *Hen*—a one that is famously in difference with itself in and of itself, the *hen heautoi diapherein.* Heidegger says that there is no explanation, no reason *why* "the great child of the world-play seen by Heraclitus" plays (Schurmann, 1990, p. 42). Commenting on this play as time Schurmann writes:

> *Hen* … in the sense of… the oneness of day and night… [is the] "originary form of the difference"… time is the simultaneity of *phuein* and *kruptesthai,* of breaking forth into presence and of retreating from the sunlight… This agonistic play… designates the intrinsic motility of the One… [T]he temporality of presencing-absencing, understood as a play, means that the One founds nothing. It is "without why,""only play".
>
> *(pp. 178–179)*

One can wonder whether Heidegger was too eager to ignore the possibility that Heraclitus' child was playing a game with rules, a game in which there is a king piece, perhaps like checkers or chess. Giving the fragment a psychoanalytic, or Winnicottian gloss, one can also wonder whether the pieces in the game are themselves the fetishes of transitional time, time as the iridescent *hen heautoi diaphereien*, the seam of presencing-absencing. In other words, the rules of a game that disavow the anxiety of what is on Winnicott's "theoretical line" between the subjective and the objective, the anxiety of the one in difference from itself in which the rulable and non-rulable turn into each other. Schurmann wrote that in general for Heidegger the "step back" to thinking presenc*ing* as the open and the between is quasi-traumatic. Such thinking "is abrupt since the resistances may suddenly vanish by which the 'rational animal,' the metaphysical animal, defends itself against polymorphous presencing as against its death" (1987, p. 42). Such "resistances" themselves have the disavowal structure that Heidegger attributed to Kant's recoil from the "abyss of metaphysics," the unsaid, or the unknown, that structures his work.

For one can also think that Winnicott's divided baby, feeding from itself and something other than itself, is a version of the one in difference from itself. And in a Freudian sense, structured by a different version of a fourfold mirror play. What is the experience of satisfaction? The experience of four elements, each of which reflects the other: self-preservation, erotic arousal, feeding from oneself, and feeding from the other. (The splitting of self-preservation and arousal, as discussed previously, account for the fetish as religious or sexual object.) In a Heideggerian–Freudian–Winnicottian sense, this auto-affective play is "perceived" in the passive-active sense of the relation to the thing in primary scopophilia. It conditions, "bethings," is traced in the "*a priori* synthesis" of originally unconscious thought and the inevitable tension of unconscious time as binding. Precisely because this is so, there will always be primal anxiety and recoil from this non-objective, non-rule-bound transitional reality. *Philia* meets *neikos.* In the auto-immune response to oneself as *bedingt*, objectification becomes the economical rule of tension relief. The iridescent thing becomes an idealized presence or a threatening absence.

Which is why one can ask what might appear to be an absurd question: is Heidegger's jug a breast? He does choose a thing that holds and gives liquid to describe the fourfold mirror play of the thing. Heidegger did not read Freud carefully enough to notice where auto-affection and other ways of thinking time entered his work. And Freud did not read Heidegger, particularly *KPM,* such that he could understand why his claim that psychoanalysis was not metaphysics, could not simply be a claim that psychoanalysis was science in the Kantian sense—precisely because that science was a defensive response to transitional, auto-affective time-space. And neither saw that the unavoidable question of fetishism has to be understood in these terms.

Notes

1 This harkens back to our introduction, to the question of "immediate pre-reflective experience," as raised, for example, by Merleau-Ponty. To be pursued in Chapter 5.

2 On the question of the "who" as a "what," particularly in *Being and Time*, the essential reference is Stiegler, *Technics and Time 1.*

4

THE SIGNATURE OF THE TRANSCENDENTAL IMAGINATION[1]

The title of this chapter is a slight deformation of an expression of Kant's. The reference to the transcendental imagination presumes knowledge of the previous chapter.

Fetishism and signature

I am taking my cue from a question Derrida asks in *Signéponge* (*Signsponge*), his reading of the work of Francis Ponge. The thrust of that reading is the role of Ponge's "signature" as the *thing* of his work, focusing on *éponge,* sponge. Toward the conclusion of *Signéponge*, Derrida asks: what if all of this were a scientific reading of the effect of fetishism (1984, p. 107)? To answer this question, Derrida refers to his analysis of fetishism in *Glas*. There he had analyzed—deconstructed—the opposition of the fetish to what it replaces. That opposition, he had said, is a constant throughout the history of discourse on fetishism. A possible scientific reading of fetishism, then, would have to integrate the fetish as replacement, substitute (e.g., the maternal phallus for Freud), with the main themes of *Signéponge*—the signature and the thing. This reading will take us back to the transcendental imagination.

Derrida distinguishes three "modalities" of the signature. 1. Not only signing one's name, but authenticating that one is signing, as when a signature has to be notarized. 2. What he calls the "confused and banal metaphor" of the first sense: the idiomatic marks left in a work of art by its creator, i.e., the creator's idiomatic style, which has nothing to do with his name itself. 3. The most complicated sense: "one can call a general signature, or signature of the signature, the fold of the *mise en abyme* when, contrary to the usual sense of signature, writing designates itself, describes and inscribes itself as act (action and archive), signs itself before the end by giving something to be read: I refer to myself, this is writing, I am writing, which excludes *nothing* because, when the *mise en abyme* succeeds, it is the other, the thing as other who signs" (1984, p. 55).

I hope to clarify what the general signature means as we proceed. For now, let us note that Derrida relates it to the signature of what he calls "the thing as other." It is not obvious how the thing as other emerges from the self-reflexivity of the *mise en abyme*.[2] Let us attempt a brief, initial clarification. For Derrida, the signature combines the paradoxical qualities of uniqueness and iterability: it has to be singular, it has to be repeatable. And to sign one's name is to signify oneself in the insignificant—beyond sense and concept. One's name (e.g., Ponge) designates one but has no meaning. What Derrida calls "the law of thing" is "singularity and difference" (1984, p. 15); each thing is this thing. This is the ancient theme of *haeccitas*: the uniqueness of each thing, which cannot be grasped in any concept. Heidegger called this "quiddity," the particularity of each thing that cannot be a Kantian *object* of experience. In *What is a Thing?* this is the encounter with the singular and qualitative. The question about the relation between the thing and the signature (p. 19) can be understood as a re-edition of the question of non-conceptual singularity.

There is clear link between Heidegger and Derrida on the question of non-conceptual singularity, but also a difference. Again: for a signature to function as signature it has to be simultaneously unique and repeatable, iterable. Derrida is integrating the uniqueness and *iterability* of the signature with the singularity and difference of the thing. In *Signéponge*, this is the relation between Ponge and sponge (*éponge*): the singularity and difference of a sponge; the uniqueness, iterability, and insignificance of the name Ponge. (*Signéponge* can simultaneously mean "sign and Ponge [*signe et Ponge*]," "sign is Ponge [*signe est Ponge*]," "signed Ponge [*signé Ponge*]," "sign hates Ponge [*signe hait Ponge*]," and "sign sponge [*signe éponge*].") This exemplifies the general signature: the *éponge*, a singular thing, each time designates Ponge in his texts. This relation between a thing and a signature is the "contamination of the proper name (*nom propre*) in contact with a common noun (*nom commun*)" (1984, p. 73): a self-reflexive, *mise en abyme* effect. Derrida says that the sponge itself "overflows with activity," but an "entirely receptive activity" (p. 81).

The question of receptive activity is the question of the transcendental imagination. Derrida knows this, even if he does not mention it here. So, a scientific reading of fetishism as the relation of signature and thing, is a question of receptive activity. Strangely enough, there is an analogy between the signature and the transcendental imagination in *The Critique of Pure Reason*.

Kant's monogram and the general signature

We are in the chapter of the *Critique of Pure Reason* about which Kant famously remarked that "even Herr Beck cannot find his way within" (cited in *KPM*—Heidegger, 1990, p. 80), the chapter on the transcendental schematism. Kant is asking how it is possible for categories—call them the general organizing principles of thought—to be applied to appearances. In other words, how is it possible to get beyond *haeccitas,* singularity? How do I know that *this* animal is a dog or that *this* shape is a triangle (Kant's examples)? Something has to mediate between the category and the appearance, so that the category can be applied to the appearance. This mediating something must share the attributes of both: like the category it must be pure in Kant's sense, i.e., non-empirical; like the appearance it must be sensory, i.e., empirical. Kant calls such a mediating representation a transcendental schematism (1998, p. 272).

Based on everything that precedes this point, Kant says that this mediating representation is time. Why? As that which *connects all* representations, time *a priori*, i.e., purely, non-empirically, contains their multiplicity, their manifold. As we know from the transcendental aesthetic, time itself is what we sense, what we intuit, *a priori*—purely, non-empirically. This is why Heidegger had said that Kant for the first time achieves a conception of a non-empirical sensory perception, the justification for a transcendental aesthetic. One must always note the paradox: time and space are both sensory, intuitable, and non-sensory, transcendental. Derrida will call this the non-sensuous sensuous, borrowing an expression of Hegel's that will also be used by Marx in his analysis of commodity fetishism.

We know that for Kant, time is the pure internal sense, and space is the pure external sense. What this means is that insofar as I think, or in Kant's terms, I judge, i.e., insofar as my mind is capable of understanding things it has not created, I have to synthesize external things I sense in space with my internal, temporal sense of my mind. Ultimately, this is the question of the possibility of *a priori* synthetic judgments, the very possibility of integrating what I sense with what I conceptualize, the central question of the *CPR*. Without the transcendental schematism there can be no *a priori* synthetic judgments, because the schematism *is* the mediating, synthetic representation between category and appearance. Which is why time is the possibility of the transcendental schematism. As pure intuition, the pure internal sense, time connects the multiplicity, the manifold of *all* representations. As this pure intuition, time is "homogenous" with appearance, as it is contained in every empirical representation. Time shares properties with both category and appearance. "By means of the transcendental time determination" (1998, p. 272) we can know that *all* of certain animals are dogs, *all* of certain shapes are triangles.

Like Herr Beck, I am not sure I understand exactly what this means. But we know that Heidegger finds in time the lever for his deconstruction of Kant. And the role of time in the transcendental schematism will produce the analogy with the signature. Pressing on: Kant says that to connect category and appearance is to synthesize them. The faculty of mind responsible for synthesis itself is imagination. Hence as synthetic, the schematism is a product of the imagination (1998, p. 273). If the schematism allows us to know all these are dogs, all these are triangles, it obviously cannot be a particular image. For example, five points are an image of the number five. But number itself is a way to represent "a multitude with a concept" (ibid.). As it is an overall question of the application of category to appearance, the schematism is the "general procedure of the imagination for providing a concept with its image" (ibid.).

One must understand imagination here in the Kantian sense: the mediating faculty between sensory perception and concept formation. When Kant says that imagination provides a concept with its image, such an image, again, clearly cannot be an empirical one, as when I picture a dog, a triangle, five points. The image of a concept is then, an image that is not an image. Recall that time itself is a transcendental form of sensory perception, the non-sensuous sensuous. The non-image image is a form of the non-sensuous sensuous. Hence the schematism is a transcendental function of time and imagination, which no particular image can be.

Which leads to the fundamental problem: "This schematism of our understanding with regard to appearances and their mere form is a hidden art in the depths of the human soul, whose true operations we can divine from nature and lay unveiled before our eyes only with difficulty" (ibid.). This sentence is akin to others in which Kant refers to pure, *a priori* imagination as "blind but indispensable," something of which "we are seldom conscious, even once." It is an art in the nature of our souls, but an art we can only infer, because its very nature is to be hidden, unavailable to consciousness.

Kant does not back off from the difficulties into which his own thought leads. Thus, he is reticent about his own necessary attempt to "divine from nature" and "unveil" the workings of the "hidden art." He begins the next sentence: "We can say only this much" (*So viel können wir nur sagen*): The rest of the sentence contains the analogy with the signature: "We can say only this much: the image is a product of the empirical faculty of productive imagination, the schema of sensible concepts (such as figures in space) is a product and as it were a *monogram* (*Monogramm* [my emphasis]) of pure a priori imagination, through which and in accordance with which the images first become possible, but which must be connected with the concept, to which they are in themselves never fully congruent, always only by means of the schema they designate" (1998, pp. 273–274).

I will attempt to paraphrase. Because it is so difficult to divine, to unveil, the hidden art that produces the schematism, we must cautiously indicate whatever we can. An image of a dog or a triangle is empirical. It is not a direct perception of a dog or a triangle, but something in our minds, an abstraction from a perception; thus, it must be produced by empirical imagination. The schemata that produce the rules which tell us these are dogs, these are triangles, which mediate between appearance and category, must also be products of imagination, but are not images in the usual sense. If they are produced by imagination, it must be by pure, *a priori,* transcendental imagination. Any particular image, say of a triangle, has to be connected to the concept triangle, but does not coincide with this concept. Rather, it *designates* the possibility of mediating between image and concept; it designates the working of the faculty of mediation, pure *a priori* imagination. Schemata, then, designate, bear the mark, the monogram, the signature of the transcendental imagination. We can say something about the possibility of the hidden art that produces schemata, even if it is not much, because the transcendental imagination signs off on them, leaves the stamp of its initials, its monogram, on them.

We already know the name monogrammed on the transcendental schematism: time. Time mediates between category and appearance because it has attributes of both. Kant makes the point again: "The schema of a pure concept of the understanding… is something that can never be brought to an image at all, but is rather only the pure synthesis… which the category expresses, and is a transcendental product of the imagination, which concerns the determination of the inner sense in general, in accordance with conditions of its form (time) in regard to all representations, insofar as these are to be connected together a priori in one concept" (1998, p. 274). Paraphrase: a schematism is a rule that cannot be an image. It is made possible by time. Therefore, it has to be congruent with what Kant calls the rules of time.

The rules of time are a function of the categories. For Kant, these are quantity, quality, modality, and relation; how much, in what way, by what means, and how connected. As the transcendental schematism is a mediating rule between category and appearance via time, time itself has to have rules congruent with the categories. To wit: quantity, magnitude, is the rule of the succession of time, which Kant calls "the generation (synthesis) of time itself"; quality, the way in which we perceive things, is the rule of the "filling of time," the "synthesis of sensation (perception) with the representation of time"; relation is the rule that all perceptions can be connected according to the determinations of time; modality is "the determination of whether and how an object belongs to time" (1998, p. 274). In other words, schemata are "nothing but a priori time determinations in accordance with rules, and these concern, according to the order of the categories, the time-series, the content of time, the order of time, and finally the sum total of time in regard to all possible objects" (ibid.). The monogram, the signature, of the transcendental imagination, is time and its rules. Without its stamp, we could not distinguish dog from cat, triangle from square; we would not know what a number is. The transcendental imagination hides in the depths of the soul, but it leaves the mark of its name on our ability to know dogs and triangles in general. What kind of name is time, and what kind of mark can it leave?

Heidegger's analysis of the transcendental schematism in *Kant and the Problem of Metaphysics* pays no attention to the monogram. Why should it? For Kant, the monogram is a manner of speech, an analogy, "as it were," *gleichsam,* to how the transcendental imagination designates itself. But Heidegger does answer the question I have just asked about the mark of time. This he would have to do, given that his reading of the *CPR* is organized around time and the transcendental imagination. We must follow some of the tenets of his argument that we did not examine in the last chapter, along with some we did, to the point at which he comes to the transcendental schematism.

Basically, Heidegger integrates time as the opening of the subject with the transcendental schematism. We know that the schematism mediates between category and appearance. Examining the historically vexed question of categories, Heidegger reinterprets them as "ontological predicates" (1990, pp. 39–40), as ways of characterizing the being of beings. He does so to prepare his crucial interpretation of the synthesis of category and appearance.

Heidegger boldly calls Kant's description of all knowledge as the synthesis of sensory reception and concept formation "superficial" (1990, pp. 43–44). Why? Because it does not do justice to the role of time as pure sensory reception, the non-sensuous sensuous. In other words, the synthesis of perception and concept must take into account what Heidegger has already said about time as the pure internal sense: it *opens* the subject onto any possible relation to a being. It is also internal to the concept—categories are ontological predicates, time has ontological priority. Synthesis itself is the common denominator between perception and concept:

> This synthesis is neither a matter of intuition nor of thinking. Mediating between both, so to speak, it is related to both. Thus in general it must share the basic character of the two elements, i.e. it must be a representing. "Synthesis in general, as we shall hereafter see, is the mere result of the power of *imagination*, a blind but indispensable function of the soul without which we would have no knowledge whatever, but of which we are seldom conscious even once."
>
> *(p. 44)*

KPM lays out the consequences of this passage. Synthesis itself must be "unveiled" as the "ground for ontological knowledge"; synthesis has to do with time as non-empirical intuition; synthesis is a product of the blind, non-conscious, but indispensable faculty of the soul—imagination.

I am not giving a complete exposition of Heidegger's argument leading up to the transcendental schematism, but rather picking out certain points. As always, making Kantian knowledge (judging) ontological, Heidegger reminds us that a finite creature, man, who does not create what he encounters, can encounter anything at all only if it is in advance "recognized," i.e., non-theoretically known, as a being, as something which "stands against" (*Gegenstand*) him. Without the ontological possibility of openness to the being, we could not know anything at all. (And I add: nor would fetishism—a religious or sexual relation to a thing—be possible.) To cite again the crucial passage:

> But this implies: ontological knowledge, which here is always pre-ontological, is the condition for the possibility that in general something like a being can itself stand in opposition to a finite creature. Finite creatures *need* [my emphasis] this basic faculty of turning toward... which lets [something] stand in opposition. In this original turning-toward, the finite creature first allows a space for play [*Spielraum*] within which something can correspond to it. To hold oneself in advance in such a play-space, to form it originally, is none other than the transcendence which *marks* [my emphasis (*auszeichnet, Kant und das Problem...*, p. 70)] all finite comportment to being.
>
> *(Heidegger, 1990, p. 50)*

The *Spielraum,* we know, is the space of play without which I cannot encounter anything at all. I think that Heidegger introduces play here, because he knows that he is approaching the transcendental schematism governed by the *rules* of time, and Kant, of course, speaks of a faculty of rules. Rules master, rules control. On the next page, Heidegger says that "we are *not in control* [my emphasis] of the Being-at-hand of the being" (p. 51). This, again, is finitude: if we do not create, then we do not control beings. And yet we *need*, we are dependent upon, beings. Our access to what we need that we do not control, what opens us to what stands against us, then has to be in a non-rule bound space, a play-space. The relation to beings is a *mark* of the *Spielraum.*

What to do with the faculty of rules then? Ontologize it, of course. How? By recalling the essence of the Kantian rule: "it represents a connectedness which in advance rules all possible gathering together" (Heidegger, 1990, p. 52). Pure concepts of the understanding, then, have "ruling unities as their unique content. They serve not only as rule, but also, as pure representings, they give first of all and in advance something rulable" (ibid.).

Is the giving of the rulable, the being that stands against, itself rulable? To answer, a clarification is necessary. Recall the point that had to be hammered in at the beginning: Kant's statement in the transcendental aesthetic that all thought is in service to intuition—meaning the non-empirical intuitions of space and time. Heidegger now makes a complex argument, by setting up a straw man. If Kant says that the faculty of rules regulates the being in advance, has not the faculty of rules turned into the master of intuition, which it is supposed to serve? In other words, does the faculty of rules contradict Kant's statement that all thought is in service to intuition? Heidegger's answer is no, because what the rule rules in advance is empirical, not transcendental intuition: "Only insofar as the pure understanding, as understanding, is the servant of pure intuition can it remain master of empirical intuition" (1990, p. 53). Transcendental intuition, the pure relation to..., the opening of the space of standing against..., is itself the "master" served by understanding. But because it is not conceptual, it is not a rule. Rather it is the play-space that "reveals precisely the most original *neediness* [my emphasis] of the finite creature" (ibid.), the need for the being which we cannot control. There are indeed rules that allow us to know these are dogs, not cats. But as the opening to anything at all, time makes possible the rule, but is not—contra Kant—a rule: it is *play*. In other words, Heidegger has transformed Kant's rules of time into the play of time. As always, he spatializes time—the play-*space*. If the occupation of space is the basic sense of every empirical *thing*, then the non-empirical space of time, the play-space, extends the conception of the non-sensuous sensuous. Time is the non-sensuous sensuous thing, like "the *ekstatikon* par excellence" of *Being and Time.* Or, as we cited Derrida in the last chapter, the "*play* (*Zuspiel*) also *marks*, works on, manifests the unity of the three dimensions of time, which is to say a fourth dimension: The 'giving' of the *es gibt Zeit* belongs to the play of this 'quadridimensionality'... The fourth dimension, as Heidegger makes clear, is not a figure, it is not a manner of speaking... *it is said of the thing itself*" (1992, p. 22; my emphases. Heidegger again: "To hold oneself in advance in such a play-space, to form it originally, is none other than the transcendence which *marks* [my emphasis] all finite comportment to being" [1990, p. 50]).

Still working toward the transcendental schematism, and always attentive to time, Heidegger cites Kant introducing the transcendental deduction, i.e., "the elucidation of transcendence" (ibid.) itself. Kant says that "all modifications of the mind... are subject to time... as that in which they must all be ordered, connected, and brought into relation with one another" (1990, p. 57). Heidegger: "It might initially seem striking that in neither... way of [the transcendental deduction; there are two] does Kant discuss in more detail and explicitly the a priori essential relationship of the pure power of the imagination to time" (ibid.). But Kant does discuss pure imagination itself, indeed has to, because he has established that synthesis is a function of imagination; transcendence itself (the *a priori* unification of perception and concept as the possibility of knowledge), is synthetic.

Kant remarks that the role of imagination in the transcendental deduction "is indeed strange, based solely on what is clearly obvious from what we have seen so far" (1990, p. 58). Essentially, Heidegger will compound the strangeness via the relation of time to the transcendental imagination.

Heidegger introduces the analysis of the transcendental schematism with a discussion of images [*Bilden*; imagination is *Einbildung*]. We know that Kant distinguishes between empirical and non-empirical images, *Bilden*. Commenting on Kant's sense of image, Heidegger says that he uses it in three ways: as the *immediate* look of a being; as the at hand *likeness* of a being; and as the look of something *in general* (1990, p. 65; my emphases). He illustrates. The first sense is the empirical perception of a being: I see something, for example, a dead body. The second sense is a transcription of what I see, for example, a photograph of the dead body. Or a death mask can give the image of the dead face. The third sense, the look of something in general, resides in the possibility of producing "a copy (photograph)... from such a likeness, [a photograph] of a death mask for example" (p. 66). Here Taft appends a translator's note: Heidegger's word for copy is *Nachbild*, i.e., an *after* image, as distinguished from *Abbild*, a copy that is an image *from* (p. 227, n.33). The death mask is the *Abbild*; the photograph of the death mask the *Nachbild*.

Heidegger is going into these details because he is approaching the question of what a look, an image, means in general. He says:

> The photograph of the death mask, as copy of a likeness, is itself an image—but this is only because it gives the "image" of the dead person, shows how the dead person appears, or rather how it appeared. According to the meaning of the expression "image"... making-sensible means on the one hand the manner of immediate, empirical intuiting, but on the other hand it also means the manner of immediate contemplation of a likeness in which the look of a being presents itself.
> *(ibid.)*

In other words, the "immediate contemplation of a likeness in which the look of a being presents itself," the photograph of a death mask, the copy of the copy, illuminates any possibility of having the image of a being: the look of something in general.

Heidegger expands the point:

> Now the photograph, however, can also show how something like a death mask appears in general. In turn, the death mask can show in general how something like the face of a dead human being appears. But an individual corpse can also show this. And similarly, the mask itself can also show how a death mask in general appears, just as the photograph shows not only how what is photographed [appears], but also how a photograph in general appears.
>
> *(ibid.)*

Every specific likeness implies the general question of likeness itself. This is the transition from the second sense of image (transcription) to the third (the look of the look, image in general).

Let us pause at the photograph of the death mask. As the likeness of a likeness, the transcription of a transcription, it says "I am a transcription," and shows how a "photograph in general appears." What is a transcription that says it is a transcription? Is it the Platonic copy of a copy, like the painting of a bed at third remove from the ideal form of a bed? Is Heidegger elliptically referring to Plato when he asks, "what do these 'looks' (images in the broadest sense) of this corpse, this mask, this photograph, etc. now show? Which 'appearance' (*eidos, idea* [note the Greek]) do they now give?" (ibid.). Kant's third sense of "look"—the non-empirical "look of the look"—has to be something of which no empirical copy can be made. As for Plato, no image of a bed can provide the concept, the *eidos*, of a bed. But unlike Plato, it seems that Heidegger introduces the question of the Kantian "pure look" via the copy of the copy, the copy that shows what a copy in general, an image in general, might be. The photograph that self referentially says I am a photograph is saying something general about images—and their relation to time as the *Spielraum* that *marks* (Heidegger, Derrida) all relations to things.

Because we are circling around the signature of the transcendental imagination, let us recall Derrida's third sense of signature: the writing that refers to itself, designates itself, that says, I am writing, the writing in which the thing as other signs. But let us also recall what might make this juxtaposition unjustifiable. The question of the signature as the question of the thing is for Derrida the question of the thing as singular and different. For Kant, this could only be a non-conceptual, empirical thing. Heidegger, however, is analyzing Kant on the "look" in general. Has Heidegger introduced the question of the Kantian look in general via something like the signature in general? Let us not forget the example. A photograph of a death mask is not only a copy of a copy, that is, a copy of a copy that indicates that it is a copy. It can also be read as a statement about the copy as a haunting image: a *Nachbild*, an after image in general. To know that a dog is a dog, or a triangle a triangle, the transcendental schematism must be a haunting after image. But here, the "after" is *a priori*.

What kind of thing is the haunting image of a thing that says something general about the image? It does refer to itself. We already know from *Being and Time* that time temporalizes itself, and from *KPM* that the more internal time is to the subject, the more it opens the subject to the being. Derrida: the *mise en abyme* as general signature is the signature of the other as thing. The photograph that says I am a photograph, and particularly the one that says I am a photograph of a haunting likeness of a thing, does imply the *mise en abyme* effect. What kind of image-thing is it?

I think it is what Heidegger calls the *ens imaginarium*. In other words, the photograph of a likeness, the copy of a copy, illustrates why a pure look, an "image thing," has to be "imaginary" in the transcendental sense. Given what we know about the *ens imaginarium* and the transcendental imagination, can we return to Derrida on the sponge that "overflows... with an entirely receptive activity"? If receptive activity is time itself, if the the *ens imaginarium* is the thing of time, and if it is the "general signature," does this give added weight to Kant's "monogram" of the transcendental imagination? Or to Heidegger's and Derrida's "mark" of the *Spielraum*? Does the sponge then have the "iridescence," which Heidegger attributes to the (transcendental) imagination?

We have already seen Kant say: "The pure image... of all objects of sense in general... is time" (cited Heidegger, 1990, p. 73). What is time for Kant? On the one hand, the pure succession of now points that is always there, permanence. Time is "immutable and lasting" (cited, p. 76). But, on the other, as every now always becomes another now, time is also the "image of pure change in what lasts" (ibid.). Pure permanence, pure change as the pure internal sense, giving the "pure image," which for Heidegger opens the subject to what stands outside it: transcendence itself, which makes possible any empirical perception of a thing. And for Heidegger, time is the "pure self giving," *das rein sich Gebende*, which "makes perceivable to a finite creature the 'Being-in-opposition-to' of objectivity" (pp. 76–77). This is what he calls "pure discernibility"—the *Spielraum,* the play-space of self-giving time, as the opening of the relation to the thing. Kant used the analogy to the "monogram" because the transcendental imagination, as non-conscious, cannot be directly known. It leaves the trace of its operation in accordance with the rules of time. Time designates itself, signs itself, in the transcendental schematism as the functioning of the transcendental imagination. Derrida's allusion to the receptive spontaneity of the general signature concerns thing and name: sponge and Ponge in their singularity and iterability, their "iridescence." For Heidegger, time as self-giving auto-affection is the relatedness of subject and thing. Recall Heidegger's citation of Kant on mind acting upon itself, justifying his statement that auto-affection is what first makes mind into mind. When Derrida says that the question of the general signature, the success of the *mise en abîme* in which the other signs, is also a "scientific reading" of the fetish effect, is he not accounting for the opening to the thing as mark, signature, monogram? To pursue our most important theme, if fetishism is the general structure of psychopathology for Freud, and an irreducible, universal aspect of what we call "mind," then Derrida is expanding Heidegger's conception of the transcendental imagination as the foundation of the theory of unconscious processes. When Derrida said in "Freud and the Scene of Writing" that we should read Freud the way Heidegger read Kant (1978, p. 215), i.e., that the unconscious can no more be atemporal than the Kantian *cogito*, there are at least two implications. Unconscious time would have to be related to auto-affective time; "the unconscious" would have to be akin to Heidegger on the transcendental imagination.

Fetishism: the relation of mind and thing. Heidegger: auto-affection as the opening of the play-space of pure discernibility, the pure relation to the thing. Derrida: a scientific reading of the fetish effect concerns the signature and the thing. In *Glas,* as cited previously, Derrida had examined one motif in the traditional discourse on fetishism: the opposition of the fetish to the thing it replaces. For the moment, I am purposely choosing two other motifs: the fetish appears to be non-conceptual, to have no relation to an abstraction, to refer only to itself; the fetish combines opposite properties, is beneficent or persecutory, an expression of castration or non-castration. To translate these motifs into the ideas just developed: the fetish is a thing that is mine—my rock god, my erotized shoe—which designates me, is my signature (signature as non-conceptual, signifying in the insignificant; the law of the thing as singularity and difference). The fetish is iridescent in that it always oscillates between apparent opposites. The hypothesis, then, is that the synthesis of self-reference and iridescence is made possible by the trace of the primary, active–passive, auto-affective "look of the thing": Freud's primary scopophilia.

Derrida had said that when the *mise en abyme succeeds*, the thing as other signs. What would it mean for the *mise en abyme* to fail? What could this have to do with a scientific, or non-scientific, reading of fetishism? In *Glas*, Derrida had distinguished between restricted and general fetishism. Restricted fetishism is fetishism as conceived throughout the history of metaphysics, the assumption that the fetish, as substitute, is secondary to what it substitutes for. The fetish effect, then, maintains the opposition of the fetish to the thing itself—the real thing. But, the fetish effect, as consistently noted throughout its history, and particularly as analyzed by Freud, is always oscillation between apparent opposites, such that one can become the other. In other words, there is irreducible substitutability in the effect of fetishism. This is the substitutability Freud finds in the primary, intermediate organizations of the drive, in which passive and active can become each other. I think that this is what Derrida calls general fetishism. In other words, the auto-affective, passive–active nature of time in Heidegger's sense, time as the *ens imaginarium,* contains substitutability within itself. This is the substitutability of the general look of the thing as the paradoxically *a priori Nachbild*, the copy of the copy.

Perhaps the *failure* of the *mise en abyme* would be the failure to understand this passive–active, iridescent, substitutability as the opening to being affected by the thing. In that case, the fetish's oscillation between opposite properties becomes the closed self-reference of mind projecting its irrational ideas or fantasies onto things. In the history of discourse on fetishism, this is usually understood as the attempt to *control* uncontrollable nature that characterizes so-called primitive religion.

For Heidegger, this is not only an aspect of primitive religion, but of the metaphysics of *rules.* This is why he emphasizes that we are not in control of the Being-at-hand of the things that we need. His contention that Kant had to "recoil" from the "abyss of metaphysics," the transcendental imagination as auto-affective time, would then be the recoil from play to rule, from the uncontrollable to the controllable.

Because the play-space opens us to the non-rulable "being at hand" of the thing, Heidegger has called it "pure discernibility." Derrida calls pure discernibility "differential quality." Analyzing the *mise en abyme* effect practiced by Ponge, he says that "the structure of the *mise en abyme*... appears to me to repeat each time..., but each time in a necessarily idiomatic way, the 'differential quality' affecting even the form of the signature, the latter remaining that *of the other*... [A] return of the signature no longer linked to a single proper name, but to the atheological and modern multiplicity of a new *signatura rerum*" (1984, p. 51). *Signatura rerum*: the signature of divine creation in all things, most highly elaborated in Böhme's Christian mysticism. For Kant, only God possesses creative intuition—but he does not legibly sign his creations (e.g., a certain plant is created to resemble a part of the body, indicating its curative power for that part of the body, as per Böhme). But, man's finite knowledge of what he does not create demands a transcendental schematism to mediate between intuition and concept, which, in turn, demands the passive–active synthetic property of the transcendental imagination. The hidden art of the transcendental imagination as it were, *gleichsam*, does leave its signature, its monogram, its mark. Derrida's sponge-thing overflowing with receptive activity is an atheological way of rethinking the *signatura rerum*. As the signature of the transcendental imagination, it becomes the signature of the thing of time as the pure discernibility, the idiomatic *repetition* of the "differential quality." In Freudian terms, this is the repetition of the non-sensuous sensuous of the primary, intermediate phase of the drive, which, in primary scopophilia, gives the "pure look" of the thing. Fetishism itself, then is the oscillation between the *general* registration of this differential quality and its *restricted* repudiation—disavowal.

In "Freud and the Scene of Writing," Derrida had characterized Freud's conception of non-conscious memory traces, the unconscious itself, as the "opening to the effraction of the trace" (1978, p. 201). The unconscious is differentiable. Derrida had also said about the sponge that it is "open, welcoming... ready to receive all impressions" (1984, p. 81). As the general signature, the signature of the signature, the "sponge" *signs itself*, leaves a trace of itself, the monogram of auto-affection. This is why Derrida transforms Heidegger, and always says that auto-affection is "auto-hetero-affection." Auto-affection is the opening to the trace of the differential quality of the thing as other—the success of the *mise en abyme*. This atheological *signatura rerum* is the "scientific reading" of the general effect of fetishism. And when Heidegger, in "The Thing," envisages a *mirror play* of the fourfold in which each element mirrors the other, is he not also understanding the opening to the thing as a kind of *mise en abîme?* Would this not account for the *mise en abîme* effect that Assoun found in the history of generalizations of fetishism?

The non-scientific failure of the *mise en abyme* effect would confine fetishism to its restricted form. (Heidegger would speak of the thing as rulable *object*.) This is the reduction of the differential quality of auto-hetero-affection to self-referential closure: auto-affection as conventionally understood, enclosure in a narcissistic monad, which then *apparently* encloses the thing in its projections. The fetish as the expression of an irrationally projective theology becomes the mystification characteristic either of capitalism (Marx) or of the castration complex (Freud). Derrida asks about Ponge's sponge: "Name or thing, would the sponge-cloth form a kind of fetish (of merchandise or the penis), that would be interpreted according to a conventional reading of Marx or Freud?" This sentence precedes our point of departure: "Perhaps, why not, if all of this were not also a reading, a scientific reading, of the effect of fetishism?" (1984, p. 107).

Derrida is clearly saying that no matter how essential their contributions, neither Marx nor Freud has given a completely scientific account of fetishism. Derrida says that what interrupts the conventional readings of the effect of fetishism is Ponge's "diabolization" of his signature. A proper name is aleatory, and should have no meaning itself. It is to signify oneself in the insignificant, non-conceptually. But when the signature becomes significant via its "contamination" by a common noun, when it becomes a thing, which can only be a non-deterministic effect of chance, it "enters into the frameworks of a general science mastering the effects of the *alea*" (1984, p. 119). This is the general science of undecidability. The undecidability of the generalized fetish effect.

To summarize: for Heidegger, the pure discernibility of the thing is the effect of the play-space of time, making the Kantian rule an effect of chance. This is the "abyss" of metaphysics, or even the *mise en abyme* of metaphysics. It is the transcendental imagination as the play-space of auto-hetero-affective time, whose monogram is pure discernibility, the differential quality of the thing. The auto-hetero-affective monogram—as the thing itself signs. The signature as sponge, which not only overflows with receptive activity, but which is also "open, welcoming... ready to receive all impressions" (1984, p. 81). The differentiable unconscious open to the trace, the signature of the thing. The unconscious reconceived as the signature of the transcendental imagination.

Derrida and Heidegger's Kant

To expand the previous analysis, I now want to chart the profound influence of *KPM* on Derrida, particularly as concerns Freud, eventually working back to Marx on fetishism. This section can be considered as an extended footnote to the previous one, important for my overall effort to integrate the reading of the transcendental imagination with the theory of fetishism.

In his famous 1968 text, "*Différance*," I hear an allusion to *KPM* when Derrida says that philosophy perhaps began by dividing the middle voice—the voice of auto-affection—into an opposition of passive and active (p. 9). The definition of *différance* as the becoming-time of space and the becoming-space of time owes something to Heidegger on the play-space of the *Zeit-* or *Spiel-raum*.

"*Différance*" was delivered in 1968, as a kind of programmatic summary of what Derrida had already worked out. "Freud and the Scene of Writing" was originally published in 1965. The essay is a *compte rendu* of one of three lectures Derrida presented in André Green's seminar at the Paris Psychoanalytic Institute. He introduces it with a list of topics from the previous lectures, one topic being auto-affection and *différance* (1978, p. 197). Auto-affection and *différance*: passive–active and active–passive; time becoming space, space becoming time. Heidegger and Freud radicalized by Derrida.

The juxtaposition of Heidegger and Freud is explicit in the essay itself. Its topic is Freud's concept of the unconscious memory trace, of writing as both psychic content and the structure of the psychic apparatus. For Freud, from the beginning, the unconscious is the part of the mind that can store memory traces permanently, and is differentiable. This also means that repressed memory traces are timeless, preserved intact, not worn away by the passage of time. From the very beginning, Freud also said that this is why such traces can have a deferred—temporally differentiated—effect. His reasoning was that when the force of repression against memory traces diminishes, the intactly preserved past, the repressed, returns. This is why an adult neurosis has its roots in childhood.

Deferral itself is the temporal sense of *différance*. Derrida's deconstruction of metaphysics, like Heidegger's, targets the privilege of the present. Unlike Heidegger, however, Derrida links the privilege of the present to the privilege of spoken models of language—speech as the presence of language, presence as consciousness. Freud is compelling for Derrida precisely because his challenge to the privilege of consciousness is inseparable from a theory of unconscious trace and deferred effect.

But there are unexamined metaphysical assumptions in Freud. A particularly important one is the timelessness of the unconscious memory trace. For Derrida, it would be a contradiction in terms to link trace and timelessness, because trace as differentiating has deferral "built into" it. Hence, Derrida's already cited statement: "The timelessness of the unconscious is no doubt determined only in opposition to a common concept of time, a traditional concept, the metaphysical concept: the time of mechanics or the time of consciousness. We ought perhaps to read Freud the way Heidegger read Kant: like the *cogito*, the unconscious is no doubt timeless only from the standpoint of a certain vulgar conception of time" (1978, p. 215).

This is a clear reference to *KPM* in relation to psychoanalysis. If we are to read Freud on the timelessness of the unconscious the way Heidegger read Kant, all of *KPM* would have to be integrated with all of Freud—critically. One would have to think about the Freudian unconscious in terms of the transcendental imagination and the auto-affective nature of time. One would have to think about the non-conscious art hidden in the depths of the soul in relation to unconscious memory trace and deferred effect. What effect would this have on Freud's conception of the entire psychic apparatus?

"Freud and the Scene..." is known for its analysis of Freud's little 1925 text on the *Wunderblock*, the "mystic writing pad"—the "magic slate," as we call it. Freud found in the *Wunderblock*, a material analogy to the psychic apparatus. It has a conscious surface always available to fresh reception of perceptual stimuli (the middle layer of the slate), which also can be lifted to make traces disappear (repression); a stimulus barrier that protects against traumatic over-stimulation that could "tear" the middle layer (the uppermost layer); and an unconscious surface (the bottom wax layer) on which traces are stored permanently when the middle level is lifted. Freud's text also contains remarks about time as the periodic rhythm of inscription and erasure of traces. So we might ask: where are auto-affective time and the transcendental imagination in the *Wunderblock*? Is Derrida's mention of auto-affection and *différance* an elliptical allusion to this question? Is the necessary stimulus barrier, the protection against too much sensory input (against trauma), possibly akin to Kant's having to shrink back from the abyss of metaphysics (the transcendental imagination as time)? Derrida says that the stimulus barrier of the *Wunderblock* implies that all inscription, writing, has to protect against itself (1978, p. 224). This is an early version of what he was later to call auto-immunity.

Here I must return yet again to the passage in *Beyond the Pleasure Principle* in which Freud began to read *himself* on the timelessness of the unconscious the way Heidegger read Kant, and did so in relation to trauma and time. After postulating that the essence of trauma is a breach in the stimulus barrier, due to an unexpected inrush of external energy (e.g., a bomb unexpectedly explodes in the trenches of the First World War), Freud says that there is no such stimulus barrier against internal energy. He then abruptly says that this might be a way to rethink Kant on time and space as *a priori* forms of perception. To call the unconscious timeless, says Freud, is simply to contrast it with conscious time, Kantian time. Derrida: "the unconscious is no doubt timeless only from the standpoint of a certain vulgar conception of time." Perhaps, Freud says, there is an unconscious time, against which conscious time serves as a protection. He notes that these remarks sound obscure, and then drops the topic (1920, p. 28).

To my knowledge, there is no extended analysis of this passage by Derrida, but he does make a significant comment about it elsewhere. In "To Speculate—On 'Freud,'" his monograph on *Beyond the Pleasure Principle*, Derrida writes: "Does not everything that Freud ventures on the subject of time in these environs have to be related to the auto-affective structure of time (that which there gives itself to receive is no present-being) such as it is described in Husserl's *Lectures on Internal Time Consciousness* or Heidegger's *Kantbuch*?" (1987, p. 359). I am focusing on the *Kantbuch*. Derrida's parenthetical remark speaks of that which gives itself. Heidegger: time as *das rein sich Gebende*, the pure giving of itself. Derrida links that which gives itself to reception. Heidegger: time as reception, intuition—but "pure" reception of the non-sensuous sensuous. Derrida: that which both gives itself and receives—time as pure giving of itself, time as "pure intuition"—is no present-being.

Derrida puts Freud's name between quotation marks in the title of his monograph. The entire title, "To Speculate—On 'Freud'"—speaks of speculation about Freud and speculation on Freud's name. It is not clear from the title who is speculating—Derrida? Freud himself? Whatever Derrida or Freud might mean by speculation, the word itself implies self-reflection, the mirror—*speculum*. There is already a *mise en abîme* effect in the title, an effect which Derrida will pursue throughout the monograph. He will do so, as in *Signéponge*, four years earlier, via reflection on a name and a thing. Or, on reflection of the name in the thing. (Derrida presented much of this material over three years in a seminar at Yale on "The Thing," whose trajectory was Heidegger/Ponge, Heidegger/Blanchot, Heidegger/Freud; *Signsponge,* 1984, p. ix).

The thing in *Beyond...* is the famous spool used by Freud's grandson Ernst in his game of *fort:da*. In a complex analysis, Derrida reads Freud on Ernst's repetition of the *fort:da* as a mirror of the writing of *Beyond...*; Derrida is struck by the way in which Freud distances the pleasure principle, which the title says he is going beyond, only to bring it back: *fort:da* of the pleasure principle. In French, the abbreviation for pleasure principle, pronounced *pé-pé*, is also the affectionate term for grandfather. Derrida alleges that the distancing and return of the spool as the *pp*, is a distancing and return of "grandpa" Freud himself in his text. It is his signature in his text, and the role his name plays in the history of psychoanalysis (1984, pp. 309ff.). Thing and signature reflecting each other: Ponge and the sponge, the *mise en abyme*.

Just before asking whether everything Freud says about time in *Beyond...* should be related to the auto-affective structure of time, Derrida speaks of "the automobile auto-affection of the *fort:da*" (1987, p. 359). Freud's interpretation of the *fort:da* is that his grandson, in his mother's absence, is playing at her departure and return. This is the prototype of restricted fetishism. One attempts to control the uncontrollable via manipulation of a thing that can be absent or present. In the general sense, this use of a thing is made possible by the "pure look of the thing" in primary scopophilia: the auto-hetero-affective trace, signature, of the mother as "other thing."

Derrida notes that Freud characterizes his grandson's play with the spool as a *selbstgeschaffene Spiel*: a self-invented game (1987, p. 301). There are several implications here. The "auto-mobile auto-affection of a *fort:da*" refers to the self-invented game with a thing. As this concerns auto-affection, and everything Heidegger said about the auto-affective structure of time, we are justified in asking whether this is Derrida's interpretation of time as "self activation"—in relation to a thing. A thing which is *this thing*. Ernst is not playing with spools, but with *this* spool. The uniqueness of his mother, her repetitive departures and returns, going back to the repetitive departures and returns of the breast, the other thing that signs, are repetitively, auto-hetero-affectively, enacted with the unique spool. Unique and iterable: the signature-thing.

Freud does not relate his analysis of the self-invented game to his remarks about the possibility of unconscious time. But when Derrida asks whether everything Freud says here about time should be related to the "auto-mobile auto-affection of a *fort:da*" he is clearly making the connection. If conscious time, in Freud's remark, is the stimulus barrier against unconscious time; if the stimulus barrier itself, in Derrida's reading, implies that all writing, especially the unconscious trace, calls for protection against itself; if the *fort:da* is the repetitive play of absence and presence generated by an "auto-mobile auto-affection;" then the entire process implies the "monogram of the transcendental imagination"—the "success" of the *mise en abyme,* the signature of the other thing as generalized fetish effect.

Further, Derrida is also saying that psychoanalysis itself is for Freud a *selbstgeschaffene Spiel*. The "auto-mobile auto-affection of a *fort:da*" concerns Freud's distancing and bringing back of himself (his *pp*, himself as *pp*) in his text and in the history of psychoanalysis. A history, Derrida reminds us, like none other, in that it is irreducibly linked to a self-analysis (1987, p. 305). Which is why Derrida says that Freud is elaborating the science of his proper name (1987, p. 332) via the "the auto-mobile auto-affection of the *fort:da.*" Freud is speculating on himself, on "Freud." The reflection of his theory in the *fort:da* is *also* a signature in the general sense. The name is the thing: Freud is the spool. The monogram of the transcendental imagination, the temporal mark of the non-conscious art hidden in the depths of the soul, is the possibility of psychoanalysis itself.

Is this empty formalism? I think not, because it illuminates something essential about psychoanalysis. In *Signéponge*, Derrida says that every philosopher, as philosopher, denies the idiom of his name (1986, p. 33). Kant, or even Heidegger, may reflect upon the nature and possibility of reflection, but it is not part of such reflection to reflect upon itself, to reflect upon its own idiom, its own writing as writing. Starting with the relation between Freud's self-analysis and his *selbstgeschaffene Spiel,* Derrida is saying it is entirely different for psychoanalysis. Whatever the evident limitations of a self-analysis—think of the old joke about the problem with self-analysis: counter-transference—Freud found it mandatory to undertake one as the foundation of his discipline. Thereby, he inscribed what Derrida calls an "unreplaceable idiom" (1986, p. 129) into it.

All analysis, in the last analysis, is self-analysis. The function of the analyst is to initiate and safeguard a process in which the patient's mind changes itself. If what we call mind was not capable of relating to itself (Kant), or if it did not become mind through auto-affection (Heidegger on Kant), no modification of mind through a relation to another (Derrida: auto-hetero-affection) would be possible. What Derrida calls the unreplaceable idiom is an auto-affective signature that "necessarily passes through the affect of the other, the affect which affects itself with the other" (ibid.). With the analyst as other *thing*. For Derrida, Ernst reflects himself as reflection of his mother in the spool of the "auto-mobile auto-affection of a *fort:da*"; Freud reflects himself writing *Beyond...* in his reflection of himself in Ernst's game. I am alleging that this is the structure of analysis itself, the relation of analyst and patient.

Freud was fond of Fechner's expression, *das andere Schauplatz,* the *other* stage or scene. He thought it captured the sense of the unconscious as the other place in the mind, the place from which consciousness recoils. To name only two other elaborations of this idea: Lacan—the unconscious is the discourse of the other; Laplanche—the unconscious as the place of implantation of otherness, the other's other, i.e., the mother's unconscious desire directed toward the baby. As important as these two conceptions are, I do not think that they come to grips with the rethinking of time and thing as auto-hetero-affection, as signature of the transcendental imagination; or with the implications of Freud's own generalization of fetishism; or with the question of restricted and general fetishism.

To explain what I mean, I must say more about the primary, intermediate phases of the drives, their relation to fetishism, and to "recoil." Recall the constants in the history of fetishism: the fetish has opposite properties; the fetish is self-referential; the fetish substitutes control of a thing for an uncontrollable *reality*. Freud repeats this history in saying that a man's sexual fetish embodies the fantasy of the mother's phallus as a substitute for the "*reality* of castration." Freud is to a certain extent right here, and to a certain extent wrong, as I have long alleged. Right, in that the male fetishist does indeed seem to move back and forth between convictions that the woman is castrated and the woman is phallic. Wrong, in that there is no "reality" in this description: Freud is describing oscillation between two fantasies. It is clear that this description of the fetish replicates the little boy's fantasy theory of phallic monism: everyone has to have had a penis; those who do not have been castrated. Everyone is just like me—narcissism, in the usual sense. There is no sexual difference. The fantasy of the castrated woman is then a form of phallic control. Control of what? Of the reality of sexual difference. Why would sexual difference have to be controlled?

Freud calls sexual difference one of the three great polarities of life. Each polarity corresponds to a phase of psychosexual development. These are the polarity of self and other from the oral phase; of passive and active in the anal phase; of male and female—meaning phallic and castrated—in the phallic, Oedipal phase (1923, p. 144). Freud consistently said that for the boy, femaleness, sexual otherness, is a product of adolescence, and that for the girl, it practically never occurs. The woman spends her life dealing with the inevitable result of the "reality of castration": penis envy. We have seen that as concerns the first two polarities—self and other, active and passive—Freud postulated their primary, intermediate, auto-affectively *temporalizing* common root. A self-differentiating common root, out of which the presumption of self-other, active–passive polarities, oppositions, emerge. Is Freud's statement that self and other, active and passive, are polar *opposites* his "recoil" from the reality of the common root?

The common root is never empirically present; as self-differentiating *and* auto-affective, it *is* the non-sensuous sensuous. The other thing non-consciously intuited in pre-reflective experience, which potentially disrupts the conscious senses of reality and time. The conscious senses of reality and time are then the protection against such disruption, from which there has to be protection, as against trauma. In Heidegger's terms, recoil. In Freudian terms, disavowal. Freud's entrenched conviction of the polarity of phallic and castrated would then be the recoil from, the disavowal of, sexual difference as such a self-differentiating, auto-affective common root.

To put this in drive terms, it would be the disavowal of the bisexuality that Freud always thought was constitutive of sexuality. Previously, we saw that in *Analysis Terminable and Interminable*, Freud wondered why bisexuality is a source of conflict for some people, and not for others. His surprising answer was that constitutive bisexuality is a manifestation of Eros, the life drive, whose antagonist is always the death drive. Conflict over bisexuality is the "free aggressiveness" of the death drive in action. When Freud equates sexual difference with the polarity of phallic and castrated, making castration into *reality*, one sees the "free aggressiveness" of the death drive in action in his theory construction. Particularly because he had stated earlier that "in the real world transitional and intermediate stages are far more common than sharply differentiated opposite states" (1937, p. 228). *Reality* as transitional and intermediate: conflict over bisexuality as recoil from, disavowal of transitional, intermediate reality. As the common root of phallic and castrated, then, bisexuality is self-differentiating and auto-affective, like the primary, intermediate phases of the drives. Recoil from it, disavowal of it, produces restricted fetishism. Self-differentiation becomes opposition; auto-affective time becomes conscious time.

The clinical implication is that if Freud is right that fetishism is the general model for psychopathology, then effective analysis as self-analysis is a process of moving from restricted to general fetishism. In other words, the fact that unconscious processes are structured by the differentiating trace of the non-sensuous sensuous means that there is in everyone a monogram, an idiom, a unique and iterable signature-thing, general fetishism, which is disavowed. The result is the conflict between what appear to be polar opposites, which are actually the objectifying, projective, self-referential defense against the general fetish effect of the signature-thing. The general fetish effect as self-differentiating, auto-affective opening. Apparently closed, self-referential, restricted fetishism is made possible by, is haunted by, the "pure discernibility" of the transcendental schematism (Heidegger) or the "differential quality" (Derrida) of the general signature. The monogram of the transcendental imagination.

I cannot spell out here how this would have to change what interpretation means in psychoanalysis. I have tried to do so in my previous work. This is a more theoretical expansion of how and why every analysis has to be a self-analysis, which always requires an other, what I have called the promise of transference (2006, p. 186). (Freud knew this in a way: see his letters to Fliess at the time of his self-analysis: "I can barely do without the other—and you are the only other, the alter…" [1985, p.73]; "I cannot do without you as the representative of the other" [1985, p. 374].) In a larger sense, Derrida wants us to think of this as Freud's signature, which opens psychoanalysis to everything implied by the philosophical denial of the idiom, the idiom of the proper name as differential quality. Which would open psychoanalysis to all the disciplines of the aleatory and the undecidable, which Derrida also analyzed in "My Chances/*Mes chances*" (2007a).

In a relatively early text, "Ousia and Gramme: Note on a Note in *Being and Time*" (1982b), Derrida challenges Heidegger on several key points. One is the distinction between vulgar and primordial time (1982b, p. 63). This can come as a surprise given Derrida's statement in "Freud and the Scene…" that the timelessness of the unconscious is determined in relation to a vulgar conception of time. His point is that the concept of time as presence *is* metaphysics, such that "another concept of time cannot be opposed to it" (ibid.). However, Derrida is also looking at the concept of the "non-sensuous sensuous." He daringly challenges Heidegger's contention that Kant was the first to achieve a conception of a "non-empirical sensibility," the non-sensuous sensuous.

In the long footnote from *Being and Time* that Derrida is analyzing, Aristotle, Hegel, and Bergson are Heidegger's examples of the vulgar conception of time. Derrida looks at Aristotle's *Physics IV*, the text cited by Heidegger. Time, for Aristotle, neither belongs to beings themselves, nor is a determination of them. To use Kantian terms, time is neither phenomenal—knowable by the senses—nor noumenal—knowable by reason. (The two stems of knowledge.) Hence, says Derrida, Aristotle had to conceive time as "a pure form of sensibility (the non-sensuous sensuous)" (1982b, p. 48). In other words, Kant was not the first to develop such a conception.

Derrida is pointing out that in giving Kant what Derrida calls the "generous repetition" in *KPM*, Heidegger is overlooking something about the history of the metaphysics of time. If time and movement are sensed together for Aristotle, even in the absence of any body that affects us (as when we are in the dark), then time "is the form of that which can occur only *en tei psukhei*. The form of inner sense is also the form of all phenomena in general" (1982b, p. 49). If Aristotle has anticipated the concept of the non-sensuous sensuous, then he "furnishes the premises of a thought of time no longer dominated simply by the present... Whatever elements of the transcendental imagination that seem to escape the domination of the present... doubtless have been foreshadowed by *Physics IV*" (ibid.). Not that Heidegger is simply wrong about Aristotle's conception of time and presence. "What Aristotle has set down, then, is both traditional metaphysical security, and, in its inaugural ambiguity, the critique of this security" (ibid.). Extrapolating: Aristotle's conception of *psukhei*, anticipating the "elements of the transcendental imagination that seem to escape the domination of the present," also anticipates the way unconscious time structures conscious time. Or, since Derrida challenges the idea of a concept of time that is not metaphysical, one would have to say that Freud's intimation of unconscious time is also an example of the "inaugural ambiguity" of metaphysics. The overall point is that time as presence is always "haunted" by a thinking of the non-sensuous sensuous that exceeds consciousness, like the *Nachbild* which *a priori* "haunts" every thing. Hence, Derrida can say that Aristotle's *psukhei* anticipates certain aspects of the transcendental imagination, or even of a reconfiguring of the Freudian unconscious.

Derrida makes a similar point about Hegel, specifically via *KPM*, in "The Pit and the Pyramid," an essay on Hegel's semiology (1982c). Because Hegel's conception of the sign is rooted in his aesthetics, and because "productive imagination" is its "fundamental concept," Derrida says:

> [T]he productive imagination... has a site and a status analogous to those of the transcendental imagination. Because it is also a kind of natural art—"an art concealed in the depths of the human soul," a "productive imagination," Kant says too. But above all because the transcendental schematism

> of imagination, the intermediary between sensibility and understanding, the "third term" homogenous with the category and the phenomenon, carries along with it the contradictory predicates of receptive passivity and productive spontaneity. Finally, the movement of the transcendental imagination is the movement of temporalization.
>
> *(1982c, p. 79)*

At the first mention of "productive imagination," Derrida appends a footnote that cites the passage from the *CPR* on the transcendental schematism as the monogram of pure *a priori* imagination (ibid.). My sense is that at that time, Derrida had not yet thought about the signature in depth, so he did not say anything about the monogram. Nor did he refer here to what he had said about Aristotle, and the inaugural ambiguity of the metaphysical treatment of time. However, the point is implied in the comparison of Kant and Hegel on imagination, especially as Derrida alleges that the relation between the Hegelian imagination and the Hegelian sign makes the sign "production *and* intuition... the place where all contradictory characteristics intersect" (ibid.).

There is another comparison to the transcendental imagination along these lines in "Plato's Pharmacy." That essay is about Plato on writing as *pharmakon*—both remedy and poison. Derrida at that time was much concerned with examples of the inevitable contradictions found in the philosophical treatment of writing, expressed in the blind use of words with contradictory double meanings to characterize writing itself (e.g., remedy–poison). Double meanings, opposite properties—writing, the fetish, the transcendental imagination. About the remedy–poison Derrida writes:

> The "essence" of the *pharmakon* lies in the way in which, having no stable essence, no "proper" characteristics, it is not, in any sense... of the word... a *substance*. The *pharmakon* has no ideal identity, it is aneidetic, firstly because it is not monoeidetic (in the sense in which the *Phaedo* speaks of the *eidos* as something simple: *monoeidos*). This "medicine" is not a simple thing. But neither is it a composite, a sensible or empirical *suntheton* partaking of several simple essences. It is rather the *prior milieu in which differentiation in general* [my emphasis], and the opposition between the *eidos* and its other, is produced; this milieu is *analogous* to the one that will, subsequent to and according to the decision of philosophy, be reserved for the transcendental imagination, that "art hidden in the depths of the soul," which belongs neither simply to the sensible nor simply to the intelligible, neither simply to passivity nor simply to activity.
>
> *(1981a, pp. 125–126)*[3]

Writing as *pharmakon*, *pharmakon* and the transcendental imagination. Referring to the previous passage on Hegel, this is a clear juxtaposition of the transcendental schematism and writing. The "prior milieu," the "place" of differentiation in general: Heidegger on the transcendental schematism and pure discernibility; Derrida on the general signature, the general fetish effect, the differential quality, and the differentiability of the unconscious.

All of this clarifies both the profound influence of *KPM* on Derrida, and its importance for the theory of general fetishism as auto-hetero-affection.

Commodity fetishism and spectrality

Marx is one of the great theoreticians of fetishism before Freud. At the conclusion of *Specters of Marx*, Derrida brings Marx and Freud together in relation to the non-sensuous sensuous, the transcendental imagination, and what he calls spectrality. In doing so, he will refer to Heidegger on Kant, and to Hegel; the previous remarks about Plato and Aristotle are implicit.

"Spectrality," for Derrida, is an extension of his thinking about the thing, the non-sensuous sensuous, and repetition. A ghost is by definition something that returns, a revenant (in both French and English; from *revenir*: to come back), whose substance is insubstantial. It is often called a "thing." Derrida makes much of the first scene in *Hamlet*, in which the question about the ghost is: "Has this thing come back again tonight?" (1994, pp. 9–11). Marx used the image of the ghost; think of the "specter… haunting Europe, the specter of communism." The very large question will be about the role of spectrality in the analysis of commodity fetishism.

Leading up to this question, Derrida writes about Marx's critique of Stirner in *The German Ideology*. It was Stirner who had said, "*Menschen, es spukt in deiner Kopf*." Derrida will have much to say about the phrase "*es spukt*." For now, let us attend to his introductory contextualization of the theme of the specter in the nineteenth century. In a note, Derrida speaks of Kant, "not only the Kant interested in Swedenborg, but the thinker of the transcendental imagination and thus of all the conceptual third terms that the fantastic introduced between the sensible and the intelligible, which are so many propitious places for spectrality" (1994, p. 190, n. 13). If one were not aware of all Derrida's previous references to *KPM*, one might not see the implicit reference to Heidegger here. And one might not pick up the implication that Heidegger's integration of the theme of the non-sensuous sensuous and the transcendental imagination could make him into a thinker of spectrality. Derrida will return to this possibility as he proceeds through his analysis of Marx, and his return to Freud.

We must begin with terminology. In *Capital*, Marx calls "commodity fetishism" the attachment of monetary value to an ordinary "use object," for example, a table, for purposes of exchange. When a price is attached to the table, making it exchangeable against other things that have prices, Marx says that an "ordinary sensuous thing" is transfigured into something supernatural. This is what will lead him to coin the term "commodity fetishism" (1977, pp. 163ff). Marx knew some main aspects of the history of the concept of fetishism; in an early article, he referred to de Brosses on gold as the fetish of the Spanish. Marx is using the anthropological-religious analysis of fetishism—in sum, primitive magic—to make a critical point about capitalism. The belief that there can literally be a monetary value of things, the belief that sustains all exchange of commodities, is religious, in the sense that *all* religion is a form of primitive magic. The exchangeable commodity is a mystified idealization of an ordinary object of use (the table).

The important point for Derrida is that Marx uses a conception of the non-sensuous sensuous to explain commodity fetishism. Marx says about the transformation of the table into something supernatural: "*verwandelt er sich in ein sinnlich übersinnliches Ding*" (cited 1994, p. 150). Derrida comments: "Marx does not say sensuous *and* non-sensuous, or sensuous *but* non-sensuous; he says sensuous non-sensuous, sensuously super-sensible [*ein sinnlich übersinnliches Ding*]. Transcendence, the movement of *super-*, the step beyond (*epekeina tes ousias*), is made sensuous in that very excess. It renders the non-sensuous sensuous" (1994, p. 151). Heidegger, of course, had emphasized Kant's transcendental conception of the sensuous. Derrida himself had often used the Greek phrase *epekeina tes ousias* in his earlier work. It means the "beyond of being, of substance," i.e., in Plato, the realm of ideal, transcendental forms. Derrida's point about Marx's use of *übersinnlich*—over, beyond, the sensory—is subtle. To make the non-sensory sensory, is to make the thing an idea, the idea a thing, to introduce something akin to transcendentality—the quasi-transcendental—into the relation of idea and thing.

If the non-sensuous is already in the sensuous, we are on the terrain of Kantian "pure intuition." Here, it means that the ordinary sensuous thing, Marx's table as an everyday object of use, is always "haunted" by the possibility of exchange value. The fetishism of exchange value *is* the idea as thing, the thing as idea—the non-sensuous sensuous. Given everything we have seen about *KPM*—time as the non-sensuous sensuous that is the relation to the thing—one can anticipate that the question of time will have to inhabit the question of exchange value. Derrida had set up this question earlier in *Specters of Marx*. The question of time as non-sensuous sensuous had already been posed with reference to the ghost, the returning "thing," and to Hamlet's famous line about "time out of joint." Anyone familiar with *Capital* knows that the secret of commodity fetishism is labor time. How will these be brought together?

For Marx, commodity fetishism is a mystification. This is why he says that when the table becomes a commodity, it seems to take on an existence of its own, to become alive, to "dance," and to enter into conversation with other commodities. It is "possessed." Derrida uses a Freudian vocabulary to describe this process. Because the "magical transmutation" of a use object into a commodity fetish seems to take place "in a glance… through the omnipotence of a thought, we might also be tempted to describe it as the projection of an animism or a spiritism. The wood comes alive and is peopled with spirits: credulity, occultism, obscurantism, lack of maturity before Enlightenment" (1994, p. 151). "Omnipotence of thought," "projection," "animism": these are all the terms used by Freud in *Totem and Taboo* to describe primitive magic. Before Freud, these were the basic categories of the traditional discourse on fetishism. Derrida sees that Marx's use of such terms carries this history with it, and that Freud's analysis of magic depends upon similar thinking. Marx and Freud are both speaking in the name of the Kantian inheritance: scientific enlightenment, demystification.

Marxist enlightenment reveals what fetishistic magic conceals. The real values hidden in commodity fetishism are social relations, the social relations structured by labor time. (This is what the capitalist wants to keep the worker, and society at large, mystified about.) For Marx, social relations throughout history have been structured by labor time. This time is what creates the (apparent) social relations of commodities to each other in capitalism. As time is the very form of the social bond, and, hence, of commodity fetishism (the "spectralization of the thing"), there is reason to think of the relation of the commodity as non-sensuous sensuous to time as non-sensuous sensuous (1994, p. 154).

Derrida thus comes back to the original definition of the commodity fetish, and synthesizes it with the question of time in Hegel and Kant:

> In question is the formula that, at the opening of *Capital*, defines exchange-value and determines the table as "non-sensuous sensuous thing," sensuously supersensible. This formula literally recalls… the definition of time—of time as well as of space—in Hegel's *Encyclopedia*… Hegel subjects the Kantian definition to a dialectical interpretation, that is, to the *Aufhebung*. He analyzes time as that which is first of all abstract or ideal (*ein Ideelles*) since it is the negative unity of being-outside-itself (like space of which it is the truth). (*This ideality of time is obviously the condition of any idealization and consequently of any ideologization and any fetishization* [my emphasis], whatever difference one must respect between these two processes.) Now, it is in order to make explicit the movement of *Aufhebung* as temporalization of abstract and ideal time that Hegel adds this remark: "As space, time is a pure form of sensibility or of the act of intuition, the non-sensuous sensuous [*das unsinnliche Sinnliche*]".
>
> *(1994, p. 155)*

In "*Ousia* and *Gramme*," Derrida had alleged that Aristotle already prepared Kant's conception of time as non-sensuous sensuous. Here, he is looking at Hegel's rethinking of Kant on the same topic. Hegel's phrase, *unsinnliche Sinnliche*, literally non-sensuous sensuous, then, repeats the "inaugural ambiguity" of Aristotle's definition. Hegel specifies that time is an "ideal." Derrida had already spoken about Marx's *übersinnliche sinnlich Ding*—idea as thing, thing as idea. Inflecting Hegel on the non-sensuous sensuous as ideal, Derrida now says that the ideal character of time is the possibility of any idealization whatsoever, and hence of any "ideologization" or "fetishization." In other words, time as the non-sensuous sensuous is the possibility of both idealization *and* of belief in "abstraction" as materially real. In economic terms, this is the belief that there is an intrinsic relation between the table and its price. But Marx has established that the "secret" of commodity fetishism as non-sensuous sensuous is labor time. *All time, including labor time, is the auto-hetero-affective reality of the non-sensuous sensuous, of spectrality itself.* This is another reason why fetishization, exchange value, always "haunts" use value. Exchangeable or not, there is no table without time. Marx may want to describe the fetish effect as "phantasmagoria," but for "the thing as well as for the worker in his relation to time, socialization or the becoming-social passes by way of spectralization" (1994, p. 156).

Is Derrida now reading Marx the way Heidegger read Kant? He links Hegel on Kant on the non-sensuous sensuous to Marx on the non-sensuous sensuous. He had already spoken of Kant as "the thinker of the transcendental imagination and thus of all the conceptual third terms that the fantastic introduced between the sensible and the intelligible, which are so many propitious places for spectrality" (1994, p. 190, n. 13). The key question, then, is whether spectrality is ontological. In other words, does the role of time in Marx's analysis of fetishism require the same kind of rethinking of time that Derrida earlier demanded of Freud (Heidegger–Kant, auto-affection)? The answer is both yes and no. Yes, in that to "haunt does not mean to be present" (1994, p. 161): spectrality is the out-of-jointness of time itself that undermines the privilege of the present. No, in that "it is necessary to introduce haunting into the very construction of a concept. Of every concept, beginning with the concepts of being and time. That is what we are calling here a hauntology" (ibid.). In other words, spectrality as time itself, "time out of joint," is a larger conception than being or time, although inherent to them as the non-sensuous sensuous. Hence, Derrida's previous reference to Kant on the transcendental imagination and "all the conceptual third terms that... are so many propitious places for spectrality" (1994, p. 190, n. 13)

Derrida uses the idea of "conjuration," "conjuring up" the ghost only to exorcise it, as a way of describing how images of spectrality arise whenever it is a question of being or time, but are then dismissed as mystifications—as Marx does in his analysis of fetishism. This is the "inaugural ambiguity" of metaphysics. It is the inaugural ambiguity that Derrida first found in his analyses of the role of writing in traditional discourse on language. In "Freud and the Scene...," he called it a metaphor that "haunts" metaphysics (1978, p. 197): whenever the question of difference in language comes up, scriptural terms are inevitable, only to be dismissed as the threat to the living presence of language. But, like the fetish, these scriptural terms have double meanings. Thus, Plato's *pharmakon* as an iridescent third term linked to the transcendental imagination and spectrality. This would open Freud's entire thinking of unconscious and trace to the "hauntological."

To put this in other, related terms: what is the relation between commodity fetishism and general fetishism? Is Marx, like de Brosses, Comte, Freud, and Derrida himself, a moment in the history of the generalization of fetishism? Let us return to Derrida on Marx, leading to his re-introduction of Freud. Derrida has established that spectrality as the non-sensuous sensuous already inhabits the table, the thing, as use value. He says of spectrality:

> [H]aving hollowed out in use-value... the repetition (therefore substitution, exchangeability, iterability, the loss of singularity as the experience of singularity itself... without which a use could never even be determined). This haunting is not an empirical hypothesis. Without it, one could not even form the concept of either of use-value, or of value in general, or inform any

> matter whatsoever, or determine any table, whether a wooden table—useful or saleable—or a table of categories.
>
> *(1994, p. 161)*

What is Derrida saying? To know that a table is a table is to have an idea of it, a repeatable, iterable sense of table that distinguishes it from a chair. One hears the echo of the transcendental schematism, to Heidegger's reading of it in terms of pure discernibility, an echo enhanced by iterability. Once a table is a table, then *this* table, *this thing*, can be exchanged for an identical table: both are the same table. Hence, this singular thing can be itself only because it is not singular: "the loss of singularity as the experience of singularity itself." Uniqueness and iterability: the signature, the thing. "This is not an empirical hypothesis": is it then a Kantian transcendental hypothesis? It is larger than that, because it makes possible not only a table, but also a table of categories. Whether a table of categories is the basic way to "in-form" any matter whatsoever, or whether, as Heidegger reads Kant, it is a set of ontological predicates, it is a signature in the general sense.

The general signature-thing is the differential quality. It is the monogram of the transcendental imagination, itself so propitious for spectrality:

> [O]nce the limits of phantasmagorization can no longer be controlled or fixed by the simple opposition of presence and absence, actuality and inactuality, sensuous and supersensible, *another* approach to differences must structure ("conceptually" and "really") the field that has thus been re-opened. Far from effacing differences and analytic determinations, this other logic calls for other concepts. One may hope it will allow for a more refined and more rigorous restructuration… this de-limitation will also affect discourse on religion, ideology and fetishism. But one has to realize that the ghost is there… *before its first apparition:* the latter had announced itself, from the first it will have come second. *Two times at the same time,* originary iterability, irreducible virtuality of this space and this time.
>
> *(1994, p. 162)*

Derrida had already said that time as the non-sensuous sensuous is the possibility of any ideologization or fetishization whatsoever. He now adds religion—inevitable not only in the context of Marx's use of the term fetish, but because of the entire theological–anthropological history of fetishism. Every thing, every fetish is haunted by itself as singular and iterable. Spectral time as non-sensuous sensuous is "there," if the table is a table; Heidegger's *a priori Nachblid*, as that which "from the first comes second." Spectral time is "there," if it is possible to form ideologies or religions. They require a thinking of original difference, the question de Brosses had already encountered, however incoherently. But the thinking of original difference, of a reality that is "irreducibly virtual," is the *mise en abîme* as the abyss of metaphysics. There will have to be recoil, disavowal. Or in Derrida's terms here, conjuration: calling up the ghost and exorcising it.

Marx performs such an exorcism, says Derrida, with his presumption of the "disappearance to come of the ghost, the fetish, and religion as cloudy apparitions" (1994, p. 164). The "ghost," the fetish, and religion will disappear with the disappearance of commodity production, capitalism itself. One has to be cautious here. Derrida is not simply dismissing the Marxist analysis of capitalism, of commodity fetishism, any more than he simply dismissed Freud's analysis of fetishism. It is rather that the question of fetishism is also always linked "to the question of phantomatic spectrality" (1994, p. 167). This means that religion itself is not "just one ideological phenomenon or phantomatic production among others" (1994, p. 165).

Why? Because, Derrida says, Marx grounds his critique or exorcism of the spectral simulacrum in a pre-deconstructive ontology of the possibility of dissipating the phantom, of conjuring it away as representative consciousness of a subject, of bringing this representation back to the world of labor, production, and exchange: the mystification of fetishism as substitute for the real thing. "Pre-deconstructive here does not mean false, unnecessary, or illusory. Rather it characterizes a relatively stabilized knowledge that calls for questions more radical than the critique itself and than the ontology that grounds the critique" (1994, p. 170). The same can be said of Freud. His ontological presumptions about reality as absence and presence, his conviction that the reality disavowed in fetishism is the reality of an absence, prevented him from seeing what his own theory implies: sexual fetishism is the disavowal of sexual difference as spectral, in the sense that the auto-affective primary intermediate phases of the drives, like primary bisexuality, always come back, but are never actually present: virtual. The real, but virtual, unconscious process that makes general *and* restricted fetishism inevitable.

To elaborate the "other logic," the "other approach" to differences that must "conceptually" and "really" re-elaborate, for example, the question of fetishism and its relation to spectrality, Derrida returns to the expression *es spukt* used by Stirner and criticized by Marx. It is untranslatable, literally meaning "it ghosts." *Es spukt* describes "the absolute proximity of a stranger whose power is singular *and* anonymous (*es spukt*), an unnameable and neutral power, that is undecidable, *neither active nor passive*, an an-identity that, without doing anything, invisibly occupies places belonging finally neither to us nor to it" (1994, p. 172; my emphasis). *Es*: it, singular, anonymous, neutral. *Spuken*: to ghost, the coming back by itself of the non-sensuous sensuous. Because it comes back by itself it is auto-affective, neither active nor passive. Undecidable, constitutively oscillating. The iridescent signature-thing of the transcendental imagination.

Es spukt. I hear Heidegger's late meditation on the *es gibt* of *es gibt Sein, es gibt Zeit*. (The German for "there is" is *es gibt*: literally, "it gives.") In *KPM*, Heidegger had already characterized auto-affective time as "*das rein sich Gebende*," pure self-giving. Derrida says that it is necessary to introduce the specter into every concept, starting with being and time. To introduce *es spukt* into *es gibt Sein, es gibt Zeit* is to expand the thinking of being and time into the undecidable and the irreducibly virtual.

It is just at this point that Derrida returns to Freud on the uncanny. Here, a reminder is necessary: Derrida's first reference to Freud on the uncanny was in

"The Double Session," which he said was a re-reading of "*Das Unheimliche*" in relation to Mallarmé and Gödel on undecidability (1981b, p. 219). In *Specters…*, Derrida calls the phrase *es spukt* undecidable. Now he notes that Freud uses the expression *es spukt* toward the conclusion of "*Das Unheimliche.*" In what Derrida calls "an unbelievable paragraph," Freud says that he did not begin where he should have begun, with *es spukt* as the "strongest example" of *Unheimlichkeit*. Derrida comments: "if he had to begin not where he could have or should have begun, it is because with the thing in question (the strongest example of *Unheimlichkeit*, the *es spukt*, ghosts, and apparitions) one scares oneself too much… One confuses what is *heimliche-Unheimliche*, in a contradictory, undecidable fashion" (1994, p. 172). Derrida then says that all of this has to be crossed with the frequent, decisive, organizing use Heidegger makes of *Unheimlichkeit*, in *Being and Time* and elsewhere. "In both discourses, that of Freud and that of Heidegger, this recourse makes possible fundamental projects or trajectories. But it does so while destabilizing permanently and in a more or less subterranean fashion, the order of conceptual distinctions that are put to work" (1994, p. 174). Derrida is now reading Freud and Heidegger the way Heidegger read Kant. For Heidegger, the necessity of the transcendental imagination in the *CPR* takes Kant to the abyss of metaphysics that undermines his entire architectonic. For Derrida, *Unheimlichkeit* in Freud *and* Heidegger has a similar function.

The double meaning of *Unheimliche*—simultaneously the unfamiliar and the familiar, the unfamiliar that always resides at the heart of the familiar—clearly makes it undecidable, and related to the pattern of words with double meanings that characterize writing. One grasps immediately why Derrida would be fascinated by Freud's speaking of *Unheimlichkeit* as the "doubling and dividing" of the self. But there is an aspect of Freud on the uncanny that is almost always forgotten, including by Derrida, namely Freud's attribution of the origin of uncanniness to primary narcissism, as already discussed in Chapter 1. Freud grasps that in primary narcissism, the relation to a thing is the relation to oneself. Thus, the eventual individual "self," the subject, emerges out of a structurally uncanny situation. I have attempted to integrate this idea with the idea of primary scopophilia—the active, passive, auto-affective look—and with the memory trace of the breast. This is Derrida's auto-hetero-affection.

In *Being and Time*, Heidegger speaks of an ontological self individuated in uncanniness, a self foreign to the usual subjectivist self (1996, p. 255). Heidegger there is speaking of a primordially anxious and uncanny self related to being-toward-death. One might say that Freud's originally uncanny self in primary narcissism is being-toward-life. It expresses the essential uncanniness of the life drive itself, of self-preservation and libido as auto-hetero-affective trace, as the signature of the other thing—the origin of the general fetish effect.

If so, then there is another reason why religion itself is not simply one phantomatic effect among others. In a deconstructive–psychoanalytic rethinking of the history of fetishism as theological–sexual, the origin of religion would be irreducible general fetishism. (This casts an essential retrospective light on de Brosses' universalization of fetishism as the origin of religion.) Freud notes that the original self-preservative breast becomes the god that can also be a demon. The beneficent and the persecutory emerge from a common source. The inevitable recoil from, and disavowal of, the common source can then make beneficent and persecutory, relieving presence and threatening absence, seem to be objective, essential opposites. They then seem to be real in the conventional sense, because they seem to be effects only of conscious perception and the immediacy of the present. But these opposites also always strangely reside in the same thing: restricted fetishism. Restricted fetishism then becomes the fetishism to be demystified by philosophical, economic, or psychoanalytic reason. But if its secret is the irreducible virtuality of difference and time, the non-sensuous sensuous, the demystification always contradicts itself, and winds up with another generalization of fetishism.

Intuition of spectral space

I have been tracing this argument via the influence of *KPM* on Derrida. So far, I have given too little attention to Kant's other form of *a priori* perception: space. The traditional definition of the thing is not only that it is always *this* thing. It is also always that it is extended in space, occupies space, has a measure. Descartes speaks of *res extensa,* Kant of the pure external sense. Hegel subjects the Kantian definition to a dialectical interpretation, that is, to the *Aufhebung,* and conceives space as the unity of being-outside-self. Heidegger, deconstructing Kant, introduced the idea of the *Zeitraum*, the space of time as a play-space. We have seen how Derrida introduces the idea of spectrality into the conception of time as non-sensuous. As "hauntology" demands that spectrality be introduced into every concept, how might it produce a rethinking of space? If the ghost is a thing, is it extended in space? What is its measure?

In *Le toucher—Jean-Luc Nancy*, Derrida closely reads Nancy's analysis of Freud's elliptical note about space from the very end of his life: *Psyche ist ausgedehnt: weiss nichts davon.* "Psyche is extended: knows nothing about it" (1941, p. 299). Derrida comments on Freud's comment: psyche "is extension: name and attribute. To put in his own language what would have made Descartes turn in his grave, extension would be the essence, the essential substance or attribute of that soul which answers to the name of Psyche" (2000, p. 22). In other words, Freud is reversing Descartes, and the entire tradition of the externality of space. If the tradition says that extension is precisely that which is not *psyche*, soul, *Seele*, if mind itself is precisely not an extended thing, Freud is saying that it is. This immediately raises a question. As space, extension has substance, is measurable, can be touched. Common sense says that I can only touch an extended thing, what we call a body, a material body (2000, p. 28). If Freud is asking us to conceive of psyche itself as extended, then he is asking us to *imagine* an extension that cannot be touched. (Here, one can already wonder about the spatiality of the *ens imaginarium*; or the substantiality of the spectral thing.) The only possible way to imagine an untouchable extension, says Derrida, is to put it in terms of some kind of non-sensuous sensuous—which immediately raises all the questions about the transcendental aesthetic and the transcendental imagination. Thus, Derrida writes:

> The conceptual passage… between the extension of a body (easy to apprehend for common sense, essential attribute of corporeal substance for Descartes…) and the extension of psyche (a paradoxical extension, rebellious to intuition, perception, consciousness)… goes through a thinking of *place*, and of a place which here is reduced neither to extension nor to objective space. This place must be a *spacing* before being a space, it must open an opening, if you will, an interval, that is an apparently incorporeal extension. Which is nonetheless neither sensory nor intelligible.
>
> *(2000, pp. 36–37)*

Spacing, the opening of an interval, which as non-sensuous sensuous belongs to neither of the two stems of knowledge, can only be imagined—transcendentally, in the way that Heidegger reads Kant. And in the way that Derrida reconfigures Heidegger, making this interval, this opening, spectral. Recall what Derrida had early on said about Freud's conception of the unconscious. As differentiable, it is the *opening* to the effraction of the trace.

In a kind of psychoanalytic expansion of the question of psyche as unmeasurably extended, as opening, Nancy interprets it as the opening of the mouth, the space between the lips. The space opened by the cry, by the mouth closed around the breast and then detaching itself from the breast, by the first smile (cited, 2000 p. 34). My own sense is that one must also include here the unconscious memory trace: the mouth open to the breast *as* the opening to the trace of the breast. The breast of auto-affective looking, the originally spectral breast. Derrida describes something like this, commenting on Nancy's conception that the self, the *ego*, emerges out of this opening as place, and therefore:

> [Of] space itself, the primary spatiality of a veritable *trace* within which, and within which alone, *ego* can come to be, and to trace itself, and to think itself… I do not think that such an opening of *self*… signifies autonomy or auto-affection. The non-space of this space is also opened by the other. Simultaneously auto-affected and hetero-affected, uniting the two affections, like two lips, it lets itself be opened.
>
> *(2000, pp. 40–42,* passim*; Derrida's emphases)*

The breast as other thing of auto-hetero-affection, the breast as that which comes back auto-hetero-affectively: the breast as the original spectral thing, the extended thing without substance. Common sense might retort that anyone who has watched a baby being nursed has seen it palpate the breast. Is the baby not touching a substantial thing in the everyday sense? In the everyday sense, yes; but in the psychoanalytic-deconstructive sense, the answer is no: the baby is not only looking at the breast auto-affectively, it is touching the breast auto-affectively. Here one necessarily refers to Winnicott on the "two babies," one "feeding from itself" and the other from an "other than me source."

This original touching of the "spectral revenant," says Derrida, *is* the spacing of an auto-affective trace. In Freudian terms, this is the memory trace of the breast for a differentiable unconscious in an organization of primary narcissism. As non-sensuous sensuous, virtual place, it inevitably becomes the place that is replaced by something else—Derrida says by the "technical prosthesis" (2000, p. 48), to which I would add the fetish. The actual fetish or prosthesis is material, substantial—spatial in the usual sense. But this spatiality would "belong to an irreducible *spacing*, a spacing heterogeneous to the extending of an *extensio* from which, however, it should not be dissociated" (ibid.).

All of this comes out of Freud's note on the psyche's spatiality. The entire note reads: "Space may be the projection of the extension of the psychical apparatus. No other derivation is probable. Instead of Kant's a priori determinants of our psychical apparatus. Psyche is extended; knows nothing about it" (1941, p. 299). What are the consequences of Freud's mention of Kant? Reading Freud's use of "projection," Derrida says that the "spatiality of space… its *exteriority* would only be a projection outward of an *internal* and *purely psychic* extension" (2000, p. 57). This looks like an extreme "psychologism"—even that which is usually considered to be purely external is derived from the internal, from the psyche (ibid.). But one has to ask whether the affirmation of a psychic extension that is not yet spatial—i.e., "before" projection—is still psychologistic. "What is an internal extension? What could a non-spatial extension be, an extension without exteriority, a psychic extension from which one would derive space *via projection?*" (ibid.).

Perhaps, says Derrida, the word "apparatus," used twice by Freud, bears the weight of the argument (2000, p. 58). (*Seeleapparat* is the deliberately oxymoronic expression Freud always uses for psychic apparatus: the theory of the unconscious demands a "mechanics" of the soul, a theory of its automatic, non-conscious, complex operations.) But, Derrida continues, when Freud says, "no other derivation likely," nothing seems more unlikely, more contrary to common sense, than a derivation of exteriority from the projection of a psychic interiority. Further, how could one even speak of projection where there is not yet external space? "In truth, nothing is more paradoxical or more unbelievable" (ibid.)

And Freud is opposing all this to Kant on space. At this point, Derrida explicates Freud, and brings us back to the question of the transcendental aesthetic:

> Is this really an opposition? What if Freud, far from opposing himself to Kant, only wanted to refine the Kantian model, substituting for it, but from within the same logic, a kind of improved formalization?… Freud writes "instead of" (*Anstatt*): "Instead of Kant's *a priori* conditions, the psychic apparatus. Psyche is extended. Knows nothing about it." According to this reading (that of a more adequate or consistent substitution, but from within the *same* perspective), a transcendental psychologism, more precisely a transcendental psychoanalysis, or better still a psychoanalytic transcendental aesthetic would

> account for spatiality on the basis of a psychic apparatus which indeed would have to be extended in order to carry within it, of the two pure forms of sensory intuition, an *a priori* form of the external sense. And when Kant… in the *Critique of Pure Reason*… states that "the representation of space… cannot be drawn, from experience, out of the relations of external phenomena, but [on the contrary] this external experience is itself possible, before all else, only thanks to this thought representation. Space is a necessary *a priori* representation which serves as the foundation for all external intuitions," is he not, in effect, announcing a certain Freudian argumentation?… Does not Freud confirm that the "pure intuition [here, of space] has to be found in us *a priori*," that is before all perception of an "object," and "consequently it must be a pure and non-empirical intuition"? Therefore, a kind of pure sensibility, the non-sensuous sensuous whose motif will reappear in Hegel and in Marx?
>
> *(2000, pp. 58–59)*

Having made this point, it is inevitable that Derrida comes back to *KPM*:

> If one kept to a more consistent elaboration of this Kantian given, one would have to return to the (metaphysical and transcendental) exposition of the concept of time. One would have to return not only to the place where time is the form of the internal sense, but is "the formal *a priori* condition of *all* phenomena," whether internal or external. And there we would find, on the traces… of *Kant and the Problem of Metaphysics* the great question of pure auto-affection, of a pure "touching oneself," in the movement of temporalization. It is there, around Psyche (*peri psykhes*), that is, around the great question of a "pure" touching oneself and of a pre-empirical auto-affection that doctors Kant, Husserl, Freud, Heidegger, Merleau-Ponty, and so many others… would be holding what one calls a consultation. No doubt they would call upon their ancestor Aristotle. Or they should in any case. To follow him and to leave him.
>
> *(p. 61)*

Peri psykhes: Aristotle's *De Anima*, on the soul. We have already seen Derrida cite Aristotle's *Physics IV* on the anticipation of time as the non-sensuous sensuous: the inaugural ambiguity of metaphysics. We know that in *KPM*, Heidegger "hammers in" Kant's points that all thought is in service to intuition; that time is the formal *a priori* condition of all phenomena; that the transcendental imagination leaves its mark (monogram) on the transcendental schematism according to the rules of time; that time *is* the transcendental imagination in that both are auto-affective, simultaneously receptive and spontaneous. So, Derrida is taking Freud's enigmatic saying about space, and showing how it links up with the entire tradition of investigation of the non-sensuous sensuous, with special reference to *KPM*.

What Derrida does not do here, is to link Freud on Kantian space to the earlier statement about Kantian time from *Beyond the Pleasure Principle*. (Neither does

Freud himself.) At very least, the two remarks show Freud wanting to replace Kant on time and space with a theory of the unconscious origins of *a priori* perception, or, as Derrida says, with a kind of psychoanalytic transcendental aesthetic. This is why Derrida can say that Freud is putting his theory in the place of Kant's from within the same perspective. Perhaps this is the inaugural ambiguity of Freud's work. On one hand, he seems to accept Kant's conceptions of time and space, but wants to give a psychoanalytic account of them, an account based on the primacy of mind as unconscious. Heidegger might say here that there is no explicit challenge to the privilege of the present or to reality as objectivity in Freud. Derrida himself had said that all of Freud's concepts are marked by metaphysics (1978, p. 197). Yet, Derrida also found openings to non-metaphysical thinking in Freud, starting with the differentiability of the unconscious as a theory of the mark, the trace. Thus, on the other hand, when Freud envisages an unconscious version of time, a time not determined in opposition to conscious time—to Kantian time—he also envisages it as trauma, against which conscious time serves as a stimulus barrier. Derrida, like Heidegger in *KPM*, is saying that one can extend Kant on time as the *a priori* condition of all phenomena to what Freud says about space here; the "common denominator" is the non-sensuous sensuous. Hence, Drs. Kant, Heidegger, and Freud are in consultation about auto-affection, and about *Seele,* soul, psyche, mind, and should be calling in Dr. Aristotle.

Joining the consultation, Dr. Derrida is saying that the art hidden in the depths of the soul of which we are never conscious, but whose workings can be divined from nature, is a crossing of Heidegger's version of the transcendental imagination with Freud's unconscious. This makes Freud's unconscious not only an abyss from which metaphysics would have to recoil, but the explanation of why mind has to recoil from itself. Disavow irreducible virtuality, the spectral, the non-sensuous sensuous, auto-hetero-affective primary intermediacy. Disavow the general fetish effect of the signature of the transcendental imagination, creating restricted fetishism.

Coming back to the point of departure: fetishism, general or restricted, concerns mind and thing, let us now say an unconscious mind crossed with the transcendental imagination and a thing crossed with the *ens imaginarium*, spectrality. I join the consultation, around the question of the *projection* of a (non-sensuous sensuous) psychic extension. Freud's remark contains another puzzle: what does it mean for a psyche to project an extension it knows nothing about? Does projection not imply not only a pre-existing external space, as Derrida says, but some kind of knowledge? As a defense mechanism, projection is traditionally a way of dealing with unwanted knowledge, conscious or unconscious. As the explanation of animism and magic, it is similarly the means of endowing external things with one's wishes in order to control them, implying that at some level one knows, but wishes one did not, that they are uncontrollable. In either case, one has a version of knowing and not knowing, the process of disavowal or splitting that, for Freud, became the model of defense with his generalization of fetishism.

Just as Freud's generalization of fetishism has gone largely unexplored, so has his rethinking of projection. I wrote about this long ago (1992), but bring it back now.

In 1922, Freud wrote a paper on "Some Neurotic Mechanisms in Homosexuality, Jealousy, and Paranoia." The paranoid, always the model of projection, he said, never simply projects "into the blue." Rather, the paranoid has intuitive, unconscious knowledge of someone else's *unconscious wishes.* Thus, the man who unjustifiably accuses his wife of infidelity, to defend against his own homosexual wishes, might be literally wrong, but right about his wife's unconscious wishes (1922a, pp. 225–226). The paranoid, then, is not simply transposing his unwanted wishes outward; rather he is, as Freud says, "switching" (*Schalten*) them. That is, switching them *into* (*Einschaltung*) a place that he knows unconsciously, even if there is no conscious justification for this (1922a, pp. 226–227). (The man's wife has not been unfaithful: hence his apparently irrational jealousy.)

Freud did not only use this revision of the theory of projection to revise his thinking on paranoia. The 1922 paper was written at the same time as his first paper on telepathy (1922b). Freud used the same idea to explain some supposedly miraculous predictions made by fortune tellers and the like. He did not think that anyone could really tell the future. He did think that when a medium amazed someone by making a prediction that had some truth to it, it was because he or she was using intuitive knowledge of the subject's unconscious: switching. Thus, the famous example of the prediction made to a patient of Freud's that his brother-in-law would die of shellfish poisoning; the brother-in-law had, in fact, almost died of shell-fish poisoning the year before. Freud contends that his patient's hostile wishes against his brother-in-law were active in his mind during the consultation with the fortune teller, who did not even know how she came to make this prediction.

In *Difference and Disavowal*, I examined Hans Loewald's last paper (1988), "Psychoanalysis in Search of Nature: Some Thoughts on Metapsychology, Metaphysics, Projection" (2000, pp. 135–145). Loewald did not specifically pick up on Freud's revision of projection, but he did see that the 1922 paper on "Some Neurotic Mechanisms..." could be extended to include not only knowledge of someone else's unconscious, but of what he called unconscious aspects of nature itself, of what is apparently simply external to mind. Unconscious knowledge of unconscious reality, like the paranoid's or the medium's knowledge, is intuitive, "telepathic" in a large sense. This is a sense in which one might understand Comte. In rejecting the traditional understanding of fetishism as projection of one's fancies or desires onto an external object, and instead insisting that fetishism yielded a kind of direct knowledge of things without metaphysical mediation, Comte was placing a kind of "switching" at the heart of his theory. His final theory of positivism as a neo-fetishistic "subjective synthesis" uniting poetry, philosophy, and mathematics, would then have to contain a place for something like telepathy.

Derrida wrote about Freud on telepathy, bringing us to our last reference to *KPM.* He closely examined Freud's rhetoric in the telepathy papers, Freud's cagy suspension of the question of whether he believed in telepathy or not. In "Dreams and Telepathy" (1922b), Freud rebaptized telepathy "thought transference," which is an extension of the idea of "switching." Looking at Freud on "thought transference," Derrida notices that he explains mediumistic predictions via the "receptivity" and "passivity" (1922b, p. 207) of the medium's unconscious. Derrida writes that when Freud "says 'receptive and passive' without raising any further questions, one regrets that he hasn't read a certain *Kantbuch* that was being written just at the time that he himself was changing his views on the possibility of telepathy " (2007b, p. 254). Receptivity and passivity of course refer to Kant on the transcendental aesthetic, in which Heidegger found the statement he said had to be "hammered in": all thought is in service to intuition, which eventually produced the rethinking of the transcendental imagination. So I read Derrida here to be saying that one can integrate Freud's thinking about telepathy as an inevitable aspect of the theory of unconscious processes with Heidegger on intuition and the transcendental imagination. To which I add that Comte's neo-fetishism, expressed in a self-referential, double, writing, a writing that says that it is writing, also trenches on something like the signature of the transcendental imagination.

Before his papers on telepathy, Freud had already elliptically linked it with the other great theme he shares with Heidegger: the uncanny. In that essay, where Freud derived doubling from primary narcissism, he said: "We must content ourselves with selecting those themes of uncanniness which are most prominent, and with seeing whether they too can fairly be traced back to infantile sources. These themes are all concerned with the phenomenon of the 'double,' which appears in every shape and in every degree of development. Thus we have characters who are to be considered identical because they look alike. This relation is accentuated by mental processes leaping from one of these characters to another—by what we should call telepathy" (1919, p. 233).[4]

Notes

1 This chapter is based upon "The Signature of the Transcendental Imagination" by Alan Bass and is reproduced from *The Undecidable Unconscious: A Journal of Deconstruction and Psychoanalysis*, vol. 1, 2014, with permission from the University of Nebraska Press. © 2015.

2 In the Introduction, we saw Assoun use the term "*mise en abîme*" in relation to the self-reflexivity of the fetish and the pattern of generalizations of fetishism.

3 My thanks to Geofrrey Bennington for pointing out this passage to me.

4 Telepathy will also come up in the chapter on Merleau-Ponty.

5

"EVERY HISTORICAL OBJECT..."

In the Introduction, I cited Pietz:

> Certain structured relationships—some conscious, others unconscious—are established, constituting the phenomenological fabric (the "flesh" in Merleau-Ponty's sense in *The Visible and the Invisible*) of immediate pre-reflective experience... If the fetish, as theorized out of the entire history of the term itself, can be taken as a name for the total collective material object, *at once social and personal*, then Merleau-Ponty is right in saying that "*tout objet historique est fétiche*" [every historical object is a fetish].
>
> *(1987, pp. 13–14; my emphasis)*

The Visible and the Invisible is an incomplete manuscript and set of working notes interrupted by Merleau-Ponty's death. Its conception of the "flesh"—the materiality of "immediate pre-reflective experience"—synthesizes ontological, psychoanalytic, and scientific principles. All these principles are built into the remark about the fetish character of every historical object, which comes at the end of the manuscript.

For Merleau-Ponty, the "science of the body" is the "relation to the other" (1968, p. 9). But to elaborate a "science of the body" in terms of the relation to the other, Merleau-Ponty discusses a well-known idea from physics, *ontologically*. He says that physics now recognizes "relations between observer and observed" (p. 15). He is referring to Heisenberg's discovery that the conditions for observation of subatomic particles affect what is observed. Merleau-Ponty immediately clarifies the possible misunderstanding of this discovery, a misunderstanding that persists. He says that the change in physics, the dislodging of the assumption that science observes the "Great Object," does *not* relegate "all the truths of physics to the side of the 'subjective'—a move that would maintain the rights of the idea of an inaccessible 'objectivity'—but they should contest the very principle of this cleavage and make the contact between the observer and the observed enter into the definition of the real" (p. 16). To clarify: the choices made by a given physicist for the use of an apparatus to observe subatomic processes affect the observation itself. This is not the direct effect of the observer's mind, but rather the result of interactions of matter (between the observing apparatus and the particles observed) as a consequence of the observer's choices. Heisenberg found that these interactions make it impossible to observe the position and momentum of an electron simultaneously.

Because the position and momentum of a moving body *can* be calculated simultaneously in classical physics, its initial state allows an accurate prediction of its trajectory. Position and momentum can be *determined*. Heisenberg called his discovery the "uncertainty principle" to describe its not strictly deterministic nature: one *cannot* predict the position and momentum of an electron from its initial state. The physics underlying the uncertainty principle is Planck's discovery of the "quantum of action," i.e., the non-continuous, not strictly deterministic, emission of electrons from a "black body." The implication, again, is *not*, as sometimes popularly believed, that there are no causal physical rules, but rather that deterministic *and* non-deterministic processes are part of "nature." Merleau-Ponty's idea is that the "science of the body" requires an "integration of science [i.e., principles from physics] with the meaning of being" (ibid.).

When Merleau-Ponty says "the meaning of being," I presume that he is referring to Heidegger. We know that for Heidegger man's *being* opens him to *things*, a relation not conceivable as subject to object; we know that this opening is a "play-space" that introduces the non-deterministic process into Kantian rules. Heideggerian "opening" challenges the presumption that truth is the adequation of a subject's representations and an object—what Merleau-Ponty calls the "Great Object," i.e., a deterministic externality. He clarifies that "classical ontology" assumes that "what is, is not *that upon which we have an openness,* but only *that upon which we can operate*" (1968, p. 17). This again sounds very much like Heidegger on technology as the "end of metaphysics": the extreme objectification of nature such that the "real" is the calculable. Merleau-Ponty says that to assume that the world is "that upon which we can operate" is to "impose upon the world in advance the conditions for our control of it" (p. 39), recalling the Heidegger of *KPM,* who said that man is not in control of the thing that he needs. Hence, Merleau-Ponty's "science of the body" is an ontological version of the principles from physics that undermine the strict determinism that equates objectivity with control. Recall the understanding of animism and fetishism as forms of magical control of uncontrollable processes.

On the whole, Freud shared the assumptions of "classical ontology" and "classical physics," which is why he wanted to guarantee the scientificity of psychoanalysis in terms of *unconscious* determinism. But the ideas of auto-affective primary, intermediate drive organizations, reconceived as auto-hetero-affection, and of the unconscious *open* to the effraction of the trace, put non-deterministic process at the heart of unconscious determinism. This is why the kind of thinking demanded by the quantum theory is "ontological" in a way necessary for psychoanalysis, as Merleau-Ponty demonstrates throughout.

He is clear that the ontological reality of openness has to include its "occultation" (1968, p. 28). The task of philosophy is to "tell us how there is openness, and... how the occultation remains at each instant possible" (ibid.). This is what Heidegger, in a late text, called the "task of thinking," which is neither traditional science nor traditional metaphysics (1972). Throughout Heidegger there is always a version of the way in which truth as disclosure, unconcealment, has to include its concealment—whether as *Dasein's* inevitable flight from itself into a subject–object structure, as Kant's inevitable "recoil" from the abyss of metaphysics built into the *CPR*, or as metaphysics itself, which "knows nothing of the opening" (1972, p. 66). This is what Derrida early on characterized as writing's protection against itself, and later as the auto-immune response. For Freud, this is inevitable disavowal. For Merleau-Ponty, the task of thinking that shows how "occultation" is always possible, has to take "the changes it introduces into account" (1968, p. 38). "Philosophy" becomes "hyper-reflexion" (ibid.). In other words, philosophy must reflect on itself, on its own relation to opening, and to the "occultation" of opening.

Again, for Derrida, the writing that reflects on itself, the "general signature," is a "scientific reading" of the fetish effect. My hypothesis is that the pattern of self-reflexivity built into the history of discourse on fetishism, such that discourse on fetishism tends to become a discipline's reflection upon itself (see Pietz and Assoun in the Introduction), is the "registered and repudiated," "occulted," disavowed, expression of general fetishism, i.e., the substitutability, oscillation, and chance of the auto-hetero-affective opening to the *thing*. The non-objective, non-deterministic thing.

Merleau-Ponty puts it succinctly: "what we are finally as *naturata* we first are actively as *naturans*" (1968, p. 33). This sentence calls for explication. "We are," is an ontological predication. But "hyper-reflective," "autocritical" (p. 92) thought has to take into account that the "tendency toward statement in theses," "detach[es] thought from its ante-predicative context" (ibid.), that is, from immediate pre-reflective experience itself. Thus, "we first are actively as *naturans*" means that *a priori* we *are* nature as non-deterministic process. "Finally as *naturata*": as a result of the "occultation" of opening, we are subjects closed off from objects.[1] Furthermore, when Merleau-Ponty says "we are first actively," he does not mean "actively" in the usual sense. He says that there is no question of fitting together passivity before the transcendent with the activity of immanent thought. Rather, the task is to reconsider the interdependent notions of active and passive (1968, p. 43). This requires the "hyper-reflexion" that rethinks "a subjectivity situated in time and space" "in terms of facticity, and not essences" (p. 46).

What we are, our "facticity" as *naturans,* cannot be confined to the identity of essences. To presume essence is to presume the "pre-established" signification of *naturata,* which, again, would "impose upon the world in advance the conditions for our control of it" (1968, pp. 38–39). Metaphysics, restricted fetishism, and clinical concreteness, are attempts to control the uncontrollable, conceivable as the passive–active time-space of *naturans*. *Hyper*-reflexion is the "rediscovery" of "the pre-reflective zone of openness to Being," "free... of all the terms philosophy uses to distinguish me absolutely from things: representation, thought, image, subject, mind, Ego" (p. 51).

Merleau-Ponty explains why all this comes under the rubrics of the "visible" and the "invisible": "I will never be present to, will never directly witness, what will always be invisible to me: the difference which predestines the other to be a mirror of me as I am of him" (1968, p. 82). "Predestines" means that *a priori* there is otherness, difference, which is "me" as my reflection, my mirror: Freud's primary scopophilia, Heidegger's general look as "pure discernibility," Derrida's "differential quality." This mirroring difference is invisible, in that it cannot be "present," but is lodged within mirroring "perception." The mirroring perception of what is not present implies something very like Heidegger's transcendental intuition of the non-sensuous sensuous by the transcendental imagination. I am aligning it with Merleau-Ponty's "immediate pre-reflective experience."

Reacting to a major philosophical issue of the 1950s, "Being and Nothingness" (Sartre), Merleau-Ponty writes: "the relationship between the two terms [Being and Nothingness] covers a swarm of relations with double meaning, incompatible and yet necessary to one another (complementary, as the physicists say today)" (1968, p. 91). Again, ontology and physics. "Complementarity" was Bohr's term for the finding that light can be both wave and particle, both continuous and discontinuous. Its relation to the uncertainty principle is clear: continuous processes are generally deterministic, discontinuous processes generally are not. There are aspects of physical reality in which the opposition of essences, for example, wave and particle, continuity and discontinuity, do not hold.

Bohr himself expanded complementarity into the kind of general principle[2] Merleau-Ponty describes: it is a way of thinking physical reality itself as "a swarm of relations with double meaning, incompatible and yet necessary to one another." This is what I am calling the "iridescence" of the transcendental imagination. For Derrida, it is the inevitable double meanings of difference as trace, *différance*. For Freud, it is *Unheimlichkeit* and the reality of transitional, intermediate states. As Merleau-Ponty explains: "the words most charged with philosophy are not necessarily those that contain what they say, but rather those that most energetically open upon Being, because they more closely convey the life of the whole and make our habitual evidences vibrate until they disjoin" (1968, p. 102).

The vibration (oscillation, iridescence) of disjunction (difference), is what Merleau-Ponty means by "flesh": "Under the solidity of the essence and of the idea there is the fabric of experience, this flesh of time" (1968, p. 111). Flesh is the "spatial and temporal pulp where the individuals are formed by differentiation. The things—here, there, now, then—are no longer in themselves, in their own place, in their own time; they exist only at the end of those rays of spatiality and of temporality emitted in the secrecy of my flesh" (p. 114). This "non-coincidence, this differentiation... [has to] be also an openness upon the thing itself" (p. 124). It is "difference without contradiction" (p. 135)—another way of describing complementarity, as the kind of self-differentiating, auto-affective "root" of passive and active, intuition and concept. Hence, by way of Merleau-Ponty, I am also postulating a homology between complementarity and Heidegger on the transcendental imagination, all the places in Freud in which double meanings are irreducible (primary phases of the drive, uncanniness, fetishism), and, of course, Derrida (writing, *différance*, undecidability, etc.).

In the previous chapter, we saw Derrida invite Merleau-Ponty to the "consultation" *peri psykhes*, i.e., to the questions of the "extension" of psyche and of touch as auto-affection. From the beginning of his work, Merleau-Ponty was concerned with the touching–touched relation, with the body as that which in touching touches itself. Here, he takes up that question again, in relation to vision and the thing: "there is a fundamental narcissism of all vision... for the same reason, the vision [one] exercises, [one] also undergoes from the things... I feel myself looked at by the things, my activity is equally passivity—which is the second and more profound sense of narcissism" (1968, p. 139). In the Introduction, I cited Pietz on the "activity of thing," which "subverts the ideal of the autonomously determined self." To be "looked at by the things" explains this activity and transforms narcissism into precisely that which "subverts the ideal of the autonomously determined self." I read Merleau-Ponty's "second and more profound sense" of narcissism as a version of Freud's primary narcissism and primary scopophilia: the active–passive, auto-affective looking at, being looked at by, the thing. The integration of primary narcissism and primary scopophilia is the relation to the original "thing": the breast. Merleau-Ponty makes an analogous point: the "science of the body" becomes "a psychoanalysis of Nature: it is the flesh, the mother" (p. 267).

"To look at, be looked at" in terms of the mother as "flesh" is "to be seen by the outside, to exist within it, to emigrate into it, to be seduced, captivated, alienated by the phantom, so that the seer and the visible reciprocate one another" (1968, p. 139). Earlier, Merleau-Ponty had spoken of the occultation of openness to the thing as "the phantom of the unthought" (p. 30). One hears Derrida's spectrality in this statement, which explains why the "spiritualization" of the thing makes fetishism an ontological question. An ontological question linked to fundamental questions of physical reality. Physical in Merleau-Ponty's sense of "flesh" as uncertainty and complementarity, i.e., "flesh" as "matter" and "the flesh of time": the science of the body and the meaning of being.

Merleau-Ponty calls the "coiling over" of "our flesh in the flesh of things" "invagination" (1968, p. 152). Invagination is the structure of "experience" as chiasmatic: "we situate ourselves in ourselves *and* in the things, in ourselves *and* in the other, at the point where, by a sort of *chiasm*, we become the others and we become world" (p. 160). "Mother" as "flesh," "invagination," and "chiasm": difference itself is the "folding in" of ourselves and things such that the one becomes the other. What we call "mind" is the "chiasm in which leaving oneself is retiring into oneself" (p. 199).

Recall Heidegger's citation of Kant: "Now that which... can be antecedent to every act of thinking anything, is intuition, and if it contains nothing but relations, it is the form of intuition. Since this form represents nothing except insofar as something is posited in the mind, it can be nothing other than the way the mind, through its own activity... comes to be affected through itself" (cited 1990, p. 133). Heidegger interprets this statement to say that relation itself is the transcendental intuition of the non-sensuous sensuous, the auto-affective, "self relating" time of the transcendental imagination. It makes "mind" into "mind." This is why I propose to integrate Freud's "originally unconscious thought," which is the trace of a relation, but is not representational, with primary narcissism and primary scopophilia. Merleau-Ponty extends this kind of thinking to the body. He says that the "time that is space, [the] space that is time rediscovered via analysis of the visible and the flesh: Mind as *other side* of the body—no idea of a mind not *doubled* with body... chiasm of mind and body" (p. 259). To integrate Freud, Heidegger, Derrida, and Merleau-Ponty: the never conscious opening to the phantomatic "thing" is the "chiasm in which leaving oneself is retiring into oneself," mind doubled with body.

Psychoanalysis began with a doubling of mind and body via a newly historicized, temporalized sexuality. The unconscious, one might say, *is* the chiasm of mind and body. For Merleau-Ponty, this calls for further ontological transformation. The "unconscious is to be sought not at the bottom of ourselves, behind the back of our 'consciousness,' but in front of us, as articulations of our field. It is 'unconscious' by the fact that it is not an *object*, but it is that through which objects are possible" (1968, p. 180). Is Merleau-Ponty rethinking Kant's "highest synthetic principle": "the conditions for the *possibility of experience* in general are at the same time conditions for the *possibility of objects of experience*" (1998, p. 84)? For Heidegger, the crucial words were "at the same time," because synthesis itself is a temporal function of the transcendental imagination—of which we are never conscious. The generalization of fetishism as the disavowal of difference itself calls for a "surface unconscious" in which the "invisible" "flesh" of "pre-reflective experience" is registered, intuited, and repudiated, "traced" and "occulted." A surface unconscious which is open to, and closes itself off from, non-present, non-objectifiable reality.

This is why Merleau-Ponty says that perception, thought in terms of body–mind, is differentiation, and forgetting undifferentiation (1968, p. 197).[3] In other words, the surface unconscious "articulation of our field" is the "condition of possibility" of any "object of experience," the differentiation that is the opening to the thing. To assume that perception is "an object acting on a subject" (p. 23) is the "forgetting," the "undifferentiation," the "occultation," of pre-reflective, surface-unconscious, *experience*. This transforms Freud's conception of perception as a conscious, bodily activity that occurs on the "surface" of the mind, precisely in the traditional sense of "an object operating on a subject" (p. 23). Body–mind as the "flesh of time," the temporalized sexuality grounded in auto-affective, primary–intermediate drive organizations, integrates perception with the unconscious as "immediate, pre-reflective experience."

Because the theory of the unconscious is so concerned with time, history, the past, and childhood, childhood itself has to be submitted to the same kind of ontological transformation. We have "no right," Merleau-Ponty says, to understand the time and space of the child as the undifferentiation of *our* time, of *our* space:

> This is to reduce the child's experience to our own, at the very moment one is trying to understand the phenomena. For it is to think it as the *negation* of *our* differentiations. It would be necessary to go all the way to thinking it *positively*, unto phenomenology... Solution: recapture the child, the alter-ego, the unreflected within myself by a lateral, pre-analytic participation... When I perceive the child, he is given precisely in a certain divergence (*écart*) (*originating presentation of the unpresentable*) and the same for my perceptual lived experience for myself and the same for my alter ego, and the same for the pre-analytic thing. Here is the common tissue of which we are made.
>
> *(1968, p. 203)*

In this context, Merleau-Ponty contests "Piaget's logicism," the developmental account of the inevitable progression of the child from concreteness to abstraction. He calls it an "absolutization of our culture" (p. 204). We have seen earlier versions of this account in de Brosses (how to account for the progression from a concrete to an abstract deity?) and in Hume (the error of "real presence" characteristic of the child's mind). The usual account of the "pre-reflective" relation to the thing sees it as a primitive, infantile incapacity for abstraction, the negation of classical conceptions of time and space. Merleau-Ponty is criticizing Piaget along lines similar to Freud's statement in *Beyond the Pleasure Principle* that to call the unconscious "timeless" is to impose the conception of conscious, Kantian, time upon the unconscious. When Merleau-Ponty says that we have no right to impose upon the child the "differentiation" of our time and our space, he clearly means the traditional conceptions of time and space, taken by the "adult" as incontestable. This is actually the inevitable "occultation" of opening as the "blind spot of consciousness," which "in principle... disregards Being and prefers the object to it" (p. 248).

Hence, the "mind" of the child or the "primitive" will never be understood if it is seen *only* as not having reached the opposition of subject and object that informs the classical understanding of time and space. Whether one thinks of Winnicott's "double baby," feeding from both itself and an other than "me" "source," or of the differentiating trace of this process in auto-hetero-affective primary scopophilia, Merleau-Ponty is saying that this is Being as the "common tissue," the "flesh," "of which we are made." It is the relation to the thing. Which means that it is also inevitably "occulted" by the baby, the "primitive," the developmental psychologist (Piaget), the scientist, or the philosopher when it becomes the preferred "object," which provides the illusory control of "that upon which we can operate." This "occultation" always occurs because difference and opening are uncontrollable.

Remarkably, Merleau-Ponty relates all this to sexual difference as substitutability, one of the "ontological" characteristics of general fetishism. The I–other relation, he says, is "like the intersexual relation with its indefinite substitutions" (1968, p. 217). Masculine and feminine are "complementary." As light cannot be a wave without being a particle, so masculine and feminine are complementary in that "one... cannot be occupied without the other being also" (p. 220). Merleau-Ponty calls this the "carnal universe and its polymorphic matrix" (p. 221). In other words, the I–other difference and sexual difference as complementarity *are* a "polymorphic matrix." I think that this provides another way of thinking sexual difference in relation to Freud on the originally "polymorphously perverse" child. Freud's position was always that all sexuality, including apparently "non-perverse" heterosexuality, has to contain elements of original polymorphous perversity, due to sexuality's temporal mutability. Merleau-Ponty's point is that wherever one finds complementarity, whether in matter or "mind," one is dealing with "flesh," i.e., the thingliness of "difference without contradiction," "identity within difference" (p. 225), complementarity as the "union of incompossibles," the "male–female relation" in which "each is the possible of the other" (p. 228). This is an "Instability instituted by the organism itself, *fluctuation organized by it*, [the] vortex of temporal differentiation" (pp. 230–231). Hence, the "organism," the body that is male or female, but for which sexuality is temporalized, cannot exist as such without a fluctuating "polymorphic matrix."

This again requires the "critique of Freud's unconscious" (1968, p. 231). The "existentials" of "my personal history" are not "hidden," but are on "the surface of separation and union" (pp. 233–234), the invisible surface of the "differentiations of a spatio-temporal architectonics" (p. 232). As "flesh," this is the "body of the mind" (p. 253), not conceivable in the sense of the "unconscious" as "inaccessible representation" (p. 254).

As opposed to any attempt to create "an existential psychoanalysis," a project "in the air" in the 1950s, Merleau-Ponty proposes "an ontological psychoanalysis" (1968, p. 267). Consistent with the critique of causality from this perspective, Merleau-Ponty says that:

> [W]hat Freud wants to indicate are not chains of causality; it is... what is contact with the Being... investment of the openness to Being in an Entity—which, henceforth, takes place *through this Entity*. Hence the philosophy of Freud is not a philosophy of the body but of the flesh—The Id, the unconscious—and the Ego (correlative) to be understood on the basis of the flesh. The whole architecture of the notions of the psycho-logy... is suddenly clarified when one ceases to think all these terms as *positive*... but as *differentiations* of one sole and *massive* adhesion to Being which is the flesh... This in virtue of the "ontological difference."
>
> *(p. 270)*

"Investment of the openness to Being in an Entity," reconfiguration of "id" and "ego" "in virtue of the 'ontological difference.'" This is general fetishism as the complementarity of masculine and feminine, Freud's primary bisexuality and primary phases of the drive, the unconscious as "polymorphic matrix"—"in virtue of the 'ontological difference.'"

A few pages later, the manuscript ends. Contesting the "anthropological" vision of the early Marx influenced by Feuerbach, and again critiquing Sartrean existentialism, Merleau-Ponty writes: "Capital as a *thing* (not as a partial object of a partial empirical inquiry as Sartre presents it), as '*mystery*' of history, expressing the 'speculative mysteries' of the Hegelian logic. (The *Geheimnis* of merchandise as 'fetish') (every historical object is a fetish) / Worked-over-matter-men = *chiasm*" (p. 275).

I think that Merleau-Ponty is saying the following: For Marx, the *Geheimnis,* the secret, of capitalism is commodity fetishism. In the traditional sense, the fetish is always a mystified idealization of a thing that replaces the "real thing": for Marx, social relations and labor time. The mystification serves the interests of capitalism. As Derrida had said, this is a necessary analysis, but it is also "pre-deconstructive," i.e., elaborated without the tools of what Merleau-Ponty calls an ontological psychoanalysis, or what Derrida himself calls the "scientific reading of the general fetish effect." When Merleau-Ponty calls capital a "thing," I understand him to be saying that because it is a mystification, as Marx says, it is related to the general mysteries of Hegelian, *speculative* logic. What mysteries does Merleau-Ponty mean? "Speculative," of course, means "reflective." Along the lines of his entire argument, I think that Merleau-Ponty is taking "thing" here in his ontological sense, the "hyper-reflective" conception of the "thing," thing as the "flesh of *pre-reflective* experience," the experience of the "invisible," the non-sensuous sensuous of differentiating time-space.

Derrida has reminded us that when Marx described the table as "exchange value" he used the term "non-sensuous sensuous," which he took from Hegel; and that there is already a conception of the "non-sensuous sensuous" in Aristotle as "the inaugural ambiguity of metaphysics." Even if Heidegger was wrong to say that Kant was the *first* to achieve a non-empirical conception of the sensuous, his understanding of its relation to the transcendental imagination is essential to an "ontological psychoanalysis." When Merleau-Ponty writes, "Worked-over-matter-men = *chiasm*," I think that he is "ontologizing" Marx in a similar way. The table is worked over matter, whether as use- or exchange-value. "Chiasm" is "invagination": the possibility of working over matter depends upon the opening to the thing, my relation to myself and the thing as "differentiating mirror." "Every historical object is a fetish" in the "chiasmatic" sense that it is "personal and social" (Pietz).

Merleau-Ponty contends that this sense of history is "closer to Marx," and is "not a Sartrean type of ethics" (1968, p. 274). Again, he means the later Marx: "The *visible* is realized through man, but is not anthropology" (ibid.). The "visible" is what can be present, the "preference" for the object, the "occultation" of opening. Merleau-Ponty calls it "anthropology" because the "visible," the possibility of an object of experience, can *appear* to be a function of man's subjectivity, rather than as the not strictly human relations of time, space, difference, oscillation, to a non-subjective unconscious. To say that "every *historical* object is a fetish" is to make a statement about general fetishism. It is a "hyper-reflective" statement about history itself, history as temporality, and the "facticity" of history: "Time must *constitute itself*—be always seen from the point of view of someone who *is of it*" (p. 184): again, "the *visible* is realized through man, but is not anthropology." That one has a "personal history," an "anthropology," what is "visible," in one's history, is made possible in that one "is of" self-constituting time. This is the flesh of invisible "existentials," which are not "hidden," but are on the unconscious "surface of separation and union" (pp. 233–234). The unconscious surface of uncertainty and complementarity, the non-deterministic processes of the transcendental imagination.

What Merleau-Ponty calls the "interminable psychoanalysis of objective knowledge" "does not suppress the past or phantasms but transforms them from powers of death into poetic productivity" (1968, p. 116). The past or phantasms can become "powers of death" because of "the conviction of the algorithm as spiritual automaton" (ibid.). "Algorithm as spiritual automaton" is the assumption that mind, spirit, is a function of a brain regulated by axiomatic procedures, an automaton; in our day, this has become the analogy of the brain to a computer. I think that Merleau-Ponty is saying that it is indeed possible for the past or phantasm to operate algorithmically, in which case they do become a "power of death," because they *determine* the present and the future as their *undifferentiated* repetition. To generalize fetishism as the model of all psychopathology, but as the *disavowal of difference*, makes the same point. The great question of psychoanalytic therapy would be the transformation of the past or phantasm into *differentiated repetition*.

The problem of Freud's conception of mind is that his assumption of unconscious determinism does make the past or phantasm into a power of death, of undifferentiated repetition. This is one reason why he linked the repetition compulsion to the death drive. Restricted fetishism, manifest as clinical "concreteness," is itself the compulsion to repeat defenses against differentiation, producing an insistence on extreme objectification. When Merleau-Ponty says that every historical object is a fetish, and that the task is to transform the past and phantasm into "poetic productivity," he conceives the "thing" as substitution, oscillation, the chiasm of man and matter—the terms of general fetishism. Comte's general fetishism aimed to integrate poetry, philosophy, and mathematics, and produced a self-referential, "hyper-reflexive" text. And Comte did see fetishism as a check to human destructiveness, but in terms of fixity, excluding transformational processes from his account. If every historical object is a fetish, as the chiasmatic relation of man and matter, then thought "has to incorporate into itself attributes like transition, becoming, the possible. It oscillates between itself and these thoughts without being able to sacrifice one of them nor to unite them. It is ambivalence itself… that which always affirms or denies in the hypothesis what it denies or affirms in the thesis" (1968, p. 73). I think that Merleau-Ponty uses the phrase "ambivalence itself" in the strong sense of the "double values" of auto-affective process. The oscillating fetish, always "ontologically complementary," *embodies* the "flesh of time," conceivable only as "ambivalent" thought.

Generalizations of fetishism themselves, then, have always unwittingly described a chiasmatic body–mind. Merleau-Ponty, enlarging Freud, has emphasized the sexual body–mind, but it is necessary to include the "flesh" of the brain itself. Discussing the implications of Comtean neo-fetishism, I mentioned the neuro-physiologist

Gerald Edelman, for whom "the matter of the mind," the brain itself, operates auto-affectively with a "generator of diversity." Edelman shares with Merleau-Ponty the idea that the brain-mind is not an "algorithmic spiritual automaton."

Edelman dedicates *Bright Air, Brilliant Fire* to Darwin and Freud. His aim is to apply Darwinian ideas about populations to how mind emerges from the matter of the brain. His point of departure is that "mind is a process, not a stuff" (1992, p. 6), but that process itself is "matter":

> Modern scientific study indicates that extraordinary processes can arise from matter: indeed, matter itself may be regarded as arising from processes of energy exchange. In modern science, matter has been reconceived in terms of processes; mind has not been reconceived as a special form of matter. That mind is a special kind of process depending on special arrangements of matter is the fundamental position I will take in this book.
>
> *(pp. 6–7).*

Like Freud in the *Project*, the aspect of mind Edelman is most concerned with is memory. He says that even though the brain gets input from the sense organs, and produces output via its connection to muscles and glands, the major portion of the brain receives input from other parts of the brain, and gives output to other parts without direct connection to the external world. The brain is "in touch more with itself than with anything else" (1992, p. 19). The brain is primarily "a self-organizing system" (p. 25). The "matter of the mind interacts with itself at all times," and this is the possibility of memory (p. 29).

To explain memory on the basis of mind–matter interacting with itself, Edelman uses an elaborate comparison to the immune system. As a "recognition system," the immune system must have "memory" in order to function. The memory of the immune system is clearly not psychological, but cellular. Originally, the theory was that a foreign molecule transferred information about its shape and structure to the antibody molecule, and then removed itself, leaving a "cookie cutter" shape to which identical foreign molecules could bind. This apparently commonsensical theory turned out to be wrong, and was replaced by a much more counterintuitive theory. Roughly speaking, a foreign molecule encounters "a population of cells, each with a *different* [author's emphasis] antibody… It binds to those cells… having antibodies whose combining sites *happen* [my emphasis] to be more or less complementary to it. When a portion of an antigen binds to an antibody with a sufficiently close fit, it stimulates the cell… bearing that antibody *to divide repeatedly* [my emphasis]." These cells are clones, i.e., doubles. Hence, "the whole process is one of differential reproduction by clonal selection" (1992, p. 77). The cellular memory of the immune system depends upon a chance encounter in an originally differentiated population, division, doubling, repetition. (Can we call it cellular *Unheimlichkeit*?) As Edelman says, the immune system is a "molecular recognition system that is noncognitive… Like evolution it has a generator of diversity…, a means of perpetuating changes by a kind of heredity (clonal division)" (p. 78).

What does this have to do with the neurology of memory? Edelman thinks that memory itself is a "selective recognition system," working according to principles such as those of the immune system. As in the immune system, "diversity exists beforehand" in the matter of the brain (1992, pp. 79–80). This was Freud's point of departure for the explanation of unconscious memory in the *Project*: the (so-called) *psi* neurons were an "originally differentiated" "population" in that they offered varying levels of resistance to incoming stimuli, but were always "open to the effraction of the trace" (Derrida), accounting for the opening of different memory pathways, *Bahnungen*. Edelman's Darwinian emphasis on diversity within populations explains the "enormous variation," and "stochastic [i.e., probabilistic, statistical] fluctuation of cell movement, extension and death," which involves "not single neurons, but populations of them" (p. 83). During behavior, synaptic connections are strengthened or weakened biochemically. "This mechanism, which underlies memory... effectively 'carves out' a variety of functioning *circuits* [author's emphasis]" (pp. 83–85). Call it "biochemical *Bahnung*" in an originally differentiated population. Finally, via a process Edelman calls "reentry," neuronal groups receive stimuli and form "maps... connected by massively parallel and reciprocal connections" (p. 85). Edelman describe this connectivity in irreducibly complex language: "each cell contacts cells in its own group and in other groups... [producing] the dense intrinsic connectivity of groups... each cell therefore receives inputs from cells in its own group, from cells in other groups, and from extrinsic sources" (p. 88). The first two forms of connectivity—input from cells in its own group and from cells in other groups—describes the "self organizing" or auto-affective or self-referential functioning of the matter of the brain. The reentry or mapping process is like the clonal reproduction of the immune system, but it is also the link between non-cognitive and cognitive recognition. So, we have a non-cognitive, auto-affective, differentiated, doubling and dividing process as the possibility of cognitive memory. This non-cognitive, non-deterministic auto-affective differentiation is the "ontological" process of the body–mind, the "flesh of time" that makes "mind into mind."

For Freud, the question of memory is always linked to forgetting, to repression. Edelman agrees with Freud on this question:

> Freud's notion of repression is consistent with the model of consciousness presented here. The extended TNGS [theory of neuronal group selection] strongly implicates value-dependent systems in memory formation. *Self-nonself discrimination requires the participation of memory systems that are forever inaccessible to consciousness* [my emphasis]. Repression, the selective inability to recall would be subject to recategorizations that are strongly value-laden. And given the socially constructed nature of higher-order consciousness, it would be evolutionarily advantageous to have mechanisms to repress those recategorizations that threaten the efficacy of self concepts.
>
> *(1992, p. 145)*

Edelman's description of repression is consistent with what Freud called "secondary repression": the elimination from consciousness of mental contents in conflict with conscious, "value-laden" categorizations. But the great question Edelman does not examine is what Merleau-Ponty calls forgetting as undifferentiation, which I propose to integrate with Heidegger's inevitable forgetting of being, with the Kantian recoil from the "abyss of metaphysics," and with Freud's generalization of disavowal. When Edelman says that "*Self-nonself discrimination requires the participation of memory systems that are forever inaccessible to consciousness*," however, he is saying that there is a non-conscious form of memory as differentiation. If there is forgetting as undifferentiation, then it would have to be a non-conscious *process.* In Edelman's terms, this would be a process akin to the strong analogy between the functioning of the immune system and memory itself.

Derrida's description of the "auto-immune response" gains importance here. If defense against differentiation is the foundation of all defensive process, as *per* a revised understanding of Freud on disavowal, can one say that it is the inevitable unconscious response to mind–body auto-affective differentiation? This would be the response that would divorce the *process* of mind becoming mind from mind itself. "Mind" then appears to be independent of body, and as exclusively conscious, as in so much of the metaphysical tradition, or in the current tradition of a computer-like mind. Or it becomes the psychoanalytic version of a deterministic unconscious that produces fetishistic fantasies of absence and presence, idealization and persecution, castration and non-castration, projected onto things. Mind becomes the restricted fetishism of the general fetishism of the chiasmatic body–mind, the brain.

My hypothesis is that the universality of fetishism is the result of this process. In other words, the non-conscious auto-affective, differentiating, non-deterministic processes that make mind into mind are always subject to an auto-immune response that creates the self-referential ("concrete"), dedifferentiated, deterministic structure of restricted fetishism. This has always been the case, and explains the uniformity of descriptions of fetishism as projections of fantasies and desires onto things as a form of dedifferentiating control. The problem has always been that such descriptions stop at that level—even as they generalize fetishism.

In *The Emperor's New Mind*, Roger Penrose also offers a critique of a computer-like, algorithmically functioning brain–mind. (Edelman explicitly disagrees with Penrose's account of brain-mind interaction, although he appreciates the analogous stance on the brain.) Penrose is a fearless speculator. His book is a complicated voyage through mathematics, some of the further reaches of quantum theory, and brain research. We have already seen Merleau-Ponty argue for the ontological necessity of uncertainty and complementarity. Penrose takes the further step of integrating this kind of thinking with Gödel's undecidability, i.e., the proof that an axiomatic system, such as arithmetic, has to contain statements, which, if true, are false, and vice versa, making arithmetic "incomplete."

To link his critique of the "computer brain" to Gödel, Penrose goes back to the work of Alan Turing, the inventor of computers. Turing showed that it is impossible for computers, necessarily operating according to algorithms, to solve certain problems about computers themselves. Penrose reminds us that "Turing found his argument after studying the work Gödel" (1989, p. 111). Penrose also wants to explain how we can grasp this non-logic of logic. He says that we "*see* [author's emphasis] the validity of the Gödel proposition... though we cannot derive it from the axioms. The type of 'seeing' that is involved... requires a mathematical insight that is not the result of the purely algorithmic operations that could be coded into some mathematical formal system" (p. 110). Restated: "what was historically perhaps the most important part of [Gödel's] argument... [was] the 'undecidability' of the consistency of the axioms. My purpose... [is] to show that a specific Gödel proposition—neither provable nor disprovable using the axioms and rules of the formal system under consideration—is clearly *seen*... to be a *true* proposition" [author's emphases] (p. 116). "True" here means mathematically real; undecidability is a real quality of arithmetic. Gödel considered himself a Platonist because he did think that the possibility of numerical operations opens onto the transcendental, and Penrose agrees. But this is a Platonism of the undecidable, of a reality whose "truth" is *between* the usual senses of true and false, objectively real and not real. Recall Merleau-Ponty on the thinking that "is ambivalence itself... that which always affirms or denies in the hypothesis what it denies or affirms in the thesis" (p. 73). This is undecidability.

Penrose's most controversial step is to extend the reality of undecidability to brain–mind via quantum theory. (Edelman considers this to be an avoidance of neuro-physiology itself.) He is very clear that contrary to popular opinion, quantum theory does not simply concern subatomic processes, but the world we inhabit. He says:

> The very existence of solid bodies, the strengths and physical properties of materials, the nature of chemistry, the colours of substances, the phenomena of freezing and boiling... these, and many other familiar properties, require the quantum theory for their explanations. Perhaps, also, the phenomenon of consciousness is something that cannot be understood in entirely classical terms. Perhaps our minds are qualities rooted in some strange and wonderful feature of those physical laws which *actually* govern the world we inhabit, rather than being just features of some algorithm acted out by the so-called "objects" of a *classical* physical structure. Perhaps, in some sense, this is "why" we, as sentient beings, must live in a quantum world, rather than an entirely classical one.
>
> *(1989, p. 226)*

This would mean that Heisenberg's uncertainty, which introduces an impossibility into deterministic measurements, and Bohr's complementarity, which introduces a transitional relation between apparent opposites, describe the reality of brain–mind. This reality can be *seen* in the way Gödel and Penrose call "Platonic."

There is a wonderful contradiction here. Penrose accurately links quantum phenomena to the actual world. As he writes about the most familiar example of complementarity:

> How is it that light can consist of particles and of field oscillations at the same time? These two conceptions seem irrevocably opposed... the dichotomy between particles and field that had been a feature of classical theory is *not* respected by Nature... Somehow Nature contrives to build a consistent world in which *particles and field-oscillations are the same thing*! Or, rather, her world consists of some more subtle ingredient, the words "particle" and "wave" conveying but partially appropriate pictures.
>
> *(1989, pp. 230–231)*

This is why Bohr and Heisenberg considered themselves positivists. They were describing the real world. But their positivism is just as strange as Gödel's Platonism. What is a positivism of uncertainty and complementarity? Of the reality of intermediacy?

There are many other examples of intermediacy in quantum theory. Subatomic processes are not completely probabilistic. For instance, on the subatomic level, as Max Born put it, the motion of particles follows probability laws, but the probability itself propagates according to the law of causality (Pais, 1986, p. 258). This is akin to Penrose's statement that nature comprises something between particles and wave, and so inevitably something between chance and causality. Born took an image from Einstein to describe the relation between a (continuous) wave field and (discontinuous) light quanta. The way in which the wave field *determines the probability* of a light quantum makes it virtual, spectral, what Einstein called a "ghost field" (*Gespenstfeld*) (Pais, 1986, p. 259). Dirac, describing processes of photon—light particle—scattering, found simultaneous absorption and emission of energy, which appears to violate the principle of conservation of energy. However, there is no actual violation because the principle does not apply. The principle does not apply "because of the transient existence of the intermediate state... whence its alternative name: virtual state" (Pais, 1986, p. 338). Pauli had to describe certain anomalies in emission from the atomic core by postulating "a peculiar not classically describable two-valuedness [*Zweideutigkeit*, literally double meaning] of the quantum theoretical properties of the valency electron" (Pais, 1986, p. 272).

The point, then, is not whether Edelman is right that Penrose is wrong to apply mathematical undecidability and physical uncertainty/complementarity to understand the brain/mind relation. Rather, it is that wherever one is describing the reality of auto-hetero-affective processes in which there is both determinism and chance, one can only use the language of hyper-reflexive, ambivalent thought. "Incompossible" and necessary double values (e.g., active–passive, chance–determinism, unique–iterable), oscillation, virtuality, spectrality are aspects of nature as process, including brain/mind and "the" unconscious. Plotnitsky puts it this way:

> The undecidability of mathematical logic [Gödel] does not lead strictly to complementarity as uncertainty does in quantum mechanics; but it does suggest, metaphorically, the possibility—and perhaps the necessity—of a kind of undecidable complementarity. The latter may be found in Derrida,

> where it indicates a relation to, and dependence—theoretical, metaphorical, and historical—on both models, that of Gödelian logic and that of quantum mechanics.
>
> *(1993, p. 71)*

Where Plotnitsky says "metaphorically," I am saying "inevitably," although he does allude to a possible "necessity."

Derrida mentions Gödelian undecidability in his text on Mallarmé, which he says is also a reading of Freud's *Das Unheimliche* (1981b). The uncanny itself is conceptually hyper-reflexive (doubling and dividing of the self), and Derrida reads Mallarmé in terms of what Merleau-Ponty has called "ambivalent thought" and "poetic productivity." What Derrida does not mention, however, is the way in which Gödel elaborated the proof of undecidability. He invented a numbering system in which statements make statements about themselves, i.e., a "hyper-reflexive" text. Goldstein provides a clear description:

> The syntactic features of formal systems—which were meant to obviate intuitions, those breeders of paradox—can't capture all the truths about the system, including the truth of its own consistency... One of the strangest things of all about [Gödel's] proof is that it co-opts the very structure of self-referential paradoxes, those abominations to reason, and reshapes that structure to its own end... All other formulations of his proof—for example... by Alan Turing... —have incorporated features of paradoxes... into their own versions of the proof. These paradoxes, though different from one another, are all of the self-referential variety. The affinity between the incompleteness result and self-referential paradox is therefore very deep, since every proof of incompleteness has some version of self-referential paradoxicality lurking around in the background... Gödel found an ingenious way to make arithmetical language speak of its own formalism. The upshot of the technique is that G [a sentence in the numbering system]—is simultaneously making two different statements.
>
> *(2005, pp. 164–167,* passim*)*

Penrose, like Edelman, understands the brain as non-algorithmic, auto-affective process. But he takes the further step of integrating Gödelian undecidability, derived from self-referential paradox, with uncertainty/complementarity, in order to rethink time and space: "it is hard to see how one could begin to develop a quantum–theoretical description of brain action when one might well have to regard the brain as 'observing itself' all the time... when that theory arrives, [it] will be even further from having a conventional space-time description" (1989, p. 446).

Merleau-Ponty had said that the "intertwining (*entrelacs*)" of space and time are responsible for the fact that my body, "visible and tangible like a thing," "acquires a view upon itself: the objective body and the phenomenal body encroach upon one another" (1968, p. 117). This is the "dehiscence," which opens my body to itself and opens us to the being, the thing (ibid.). This raises the question of telepathy. Merleau-Ponty writes: "Telepathy—Being for the other—Corporeity... The visibility of my body (for me—but also *universal* and eminently for the other) is what is responsible for what is called telepathy. For a minute indication of the other's behavior suffices to activate this danger of visibility... to feel one's body is also to feel its aspect for the other" (pp. 244–245).

That feeling one's body is to feel its aspect for the other is the way in which auto-affection is the opening to the thing. "To touch=to touch oneself, i.e. things are the prolongation of my body and my body is prolongation of world: hence the ontological signification of the body which is also the invisible of vision, the ucs. of cs., the central blind spot" (p. 255). Telepathy, then, is a function of everything Merleau-Ponty has called the "invisible," itself the ontologically transformed unconscious, making the consciously "visible" the "central blind spot." The invisible is the flesh of time as dehiscence, opening, differentiation; the surface unconscious perceives it pre-reflectively. This is perception as "teleperception" (1968, p. 258).

Merleau-Ponty does not allude to Freud on telepathy, as Derrida does. At the end of the last chapter (and in *Interpretation and Difference*, 2006, pp. 114–119), we saw Derrida read Freud on telepathy and allude to *Kant and the Problem of Metaphysics*. I have also emphasized the importance of Freud's explanation of projection and telepathy as "switching," the basic phenomenon of communication from unconscious to unconscious without passing through consciousness. For Freud, this is the process built into analytic therapy, which I have been attempting to rethink as the auto-hetero-affective relation between analyst and patient. This is why I propose to think of "switching" as chiasmatic in Merleau-Ponty's sense: the body–mind flesh of time that explains the possibilities of unconscious perception, akin to the transcendental intuitions of the transcendental imagination. Merleau-Ponty's invisible, phantomatic "flesh of time," then, would be akin to Heidegger's *thing of time*, the auto-affective, self-mirroring *ekstatikon,* the *ens imaginarium*.

To recapitulate: the self-referentiality and double meaning of the fetish necessarily open onto all the ways in which the relation of mind and thing, including the relation of mind and brain, open onto the kind of "hyper-reflective," or self-reflexive, "ambivalent" thinking many disciplines have come upon (physics, mathematics, neuro-physiology, psychoanalysis—and the deconstruction of metaphysics). It is not a question of direct imposition of one discipline upon another, but rather one of rigorously explaining and employing their possible overlapping to develop a new, more encompassing theory of mind, matter, and reality.

Notes

1 I do not know if Hans Loewald read the late Heidegger or the late Merleau-Ponty, but he uses the same language to make the same points in his last paper, "Psychoanalysis in Search of Nature": the unconscious itself is the opening of *naturans* before we are *naturata* (1988).

2 For more on Bohr, see the series of endnotes in the next chapter.

3 Again, Loewald, who says that in the organization of primary narcissism, "memory, as registration or recording [i.e., differentiation], and perception are identical" (1980, p. 155). "Perception," here would have to be taken in relation to the intuition of the non-sensuous sensuous.

6

ORDINARY IRIDESCENCE

In 1991, I published "Fetishism, Reality, and 'The Snow Man.'" I did not know then that this was the beginning of a long-term project. I found in Stevens' "The Snow Man," a poetic expression of what I had started to realize about fetishism, that its oscillating structure between *opposites* was also a disavowal of (sexual) difference, which oscillates within itself. (Or, as Merleau-Ponty says, sexual difference is complementary.) Stevens' canonic poem is a single sentence in which each phrase turns on itself, oscillates. And it is a meditation on whether something such as the Romantic pathetic fallacy is justified or not, i.e., whether man can or should see himself in nature. The poem's famous last line says that the snow man, who is nothing himself, cannot see anything that is not there, but can still see the nothing that is (Stevens, 1982, p. 10). This is a paradoxical, double statement. A snow man, an artifact that will melt into nothing, sees (how can a snow man see?). It sees nothing that is not there, that is, everything; and simultaneously it sees nothing, the nothing that *is*. I read the nothing, which as being itself, which, like time, is nothing objectifiably present. The oscillating structure of each phrase in the poem, then, expresses the reality of the relation between the nothing which is not there, and the nothing which is. This is what Heidegger calls the ontological difference.

Merleau-Ponty, echoing Heidegger, had spoken of "investment of the openness to Being in an Entity—which, henceforth, takes place *through this Entity*... in virtue of the ontological difference" (1968, p. 270). This is to be thought in "the words most charged with philosophy [which] are not necessarily those that contain what they say, but rather those that most energetically open upon Being, because they more closely convey the life of the whole and make our habitual evidences vibrate until they disjoin" (p. 102). The description of the "snow man," an "Entity," opens onto being "in virtue of the ontological difference" through the oscillating, disjoining structure of the poem itself. A snow man, potentially a fetish in the traditional sense that it might embody the projections of the pathetic fallacy, is a thing that *sees* the ontological difference, nothing that is not there and the nothing that is. The words and syntax of the poem itself, an artifact created by the poet, like a snow man, then become this *thing*. Both the poem and the snow man have what Merleau-Ponty called the chiasmatic relation between man and worked over matter that makes every historical object a fetish. This is a *mise en abîme* effect that, as Derrida had said via Ponge, is potentially a "scientific reading of the fetish effect" (1984, p. 107).

"The Snow Man" appeared in Stevens' first collection, *Harmonium*. It does seem to announce a theme to be rehearsed throughout Stevens' career: that poetry itself can give access to what the last line of the last poem in his *Collected Poems* calls "a new knowledge of reality" (1982, p. 534).

Comte's neo-fetishism integrates poetry, philosophy, and mathematics, to produce a positivist "subjective synthesis" expressed in a self-reflexive text. Merleau-Ponty said that the "interminable psychoanalysis of objective knowledge" "does not suppress the past or phantasms but transforms them from powers of death into poetic productivity" (1968, p. 116), and does so through "hyper-reflective," "ambivalent" thinking. Merleau-Ponty had also spoken about feeling oneself looked at by things, such that looking is both active and passive (p. 139), resonating with Freud's primary scopophilia, and Heidegger's general look. The snow man, a thing, *sees.* It sees everything, including man, but sees everything as the nothing that is. It sees what Merleau-Ponty calls the invisible, a seeing that can only occur as an intuition of the non-sensuous sensuous, via something like Heidegger's rethinking of the transcendental imagination.

To link Merleau-Ponty's active and passive seeing to Freud's primary scopophilia and to Heidegger's transcendental imagination is also to follow another theme of Stevens'. Throughout, he explored how poetry itself can produce a "new knowledge of reality" through *imagination*. In his recent biography of Stevens, Paul Mariani sees this theme already in the early work: "Real poetry, Stevens was coming to see, was... something that revealed the imagination in command of some deeper reality" (2016, p. 15). Mariani cites from a late letter of Stevens, in which he explains that poetry "had to nourish itself on reality because that was its only source. The imagination, after all, did not create reality ex nihilo. Rather, it transformed the real that is found all around one. Ultimately reality was coequal with the imagination, and by extension... reality, the imagination, and pure poetry were ultimately one" (p. 279).

Poetry comes from reality, and continually has to replenish itself from reality. If poetry is a product of imagination, one must be clear that poetry replenishes itself from a reality that imagination does not create out of nothing. Rather—and this is the difficult part—imagination *is* reality. If so, then "pure poetry," poetry itself as a product of what one might call "pure imagination," is itself reality, or more emphatically, the saying of reality that produces a "new knowledge of reality." This is the reality intuited by Heidegger's reconfiguration of the transcendental imagination, the reality of "pre-reflective experience" expressed in "hyper-reflective" poetic productivity (Merleau-Ponty, 1968).

In Number 27 of *An Ordinary Evening in New Haven*, Stevens writes:

> If it should be true that reality exists
> In the mind...
> ... it follows that
> Real and unreal are two in one...
> This endlessly elaborating poem
> Displays the theory of poetry,
> As the life of poetry. A more severe,
> More harassing master would extemporize
> Subtler, more urgent proof that the theory
> Of poetry is the theory of life,
> As it is, in the intricate evasions of as,
> In things seen and unseen, created from nothingness.
>
> *(1982, pp. 485–486)*[1]

If reality exists in the mind, real and unreal are two in one. At first reading, this might simply mean that the reality in the mind is an internal, subjective representation of an external objectivity. But an endlessly elaborating poem, i.e., "pure" poetry, the "meta-poem," the poem as reflection on poetry itself, is also the theory of poetry. This theory says something about the real and unreal as one, because it is not an abstraction in the usual sense; it is the "life" of poetry, its wellspring. Further, if one were to submit to the more rigorous, severe, subtler thinking of a difficult, harassing master, one would see the "urgent proof" that the theory of poetry as the life of poetry is also the theory of life "as it is."

But the proof that the theory of poetry is the theory of life is contained in the "intricate evasions" of "as." If the "as"[2] is both life itself and evasion, is it a disavowal of sorts, an evasion "in *things* seen and unseen"? Is an unseen thing simply a not there thing, or is it a *thing* rigorously not seeable, the invisible, the nothing that is? Stevens does write that these intricately evaded seen and unseen things are "created from nothingness." If this cannot be creation *ex nihilo*, then, again, "nothingness," is being itself. The theory of poetry as the theory of life in the intricate evasions of *things* seen and unseen, makes the "oneness" of the real and the unreal, of imagination and reality, the oneness of *things* seen and unseen. How can one not think back to the Heraclitean *Hen*, the one in difference with itself? To the being of beings? Perhaps, then, Merleau-Ponty is a Stevensian "harassing master," because his "poetic productivity" is "free... of all the terms philosophy uses to distinguish me absolutely from things" (Merleau-Ponty, 1968, p. 51).

Number 2 of *An Ordinary Evening in New Haven* seems to me to be an exemplary meditation on all of this. The poem culminates with a statement that addresses the entire question of fetishism.

> Suppose these houses are composed of ourselves,
> So that they become an impalpable town, full of

Impalpable bells, transparencies of sound,
Sounding in transparent dwellings of the self,
Impalpable habitations that seem to move
In the movement of the colors of the mind,
The far-fire flowing and the dim-coned bells
Coming together in a sense in which we are poised,
Without regard to time or where we are,
In the perpetual reference, object
Of the perpetual meditation, point
Of the enduring, visionary love,
Obscure, in colors whether of the sun
Or mind, uncertain in the clearest bells,
The spirit's speeches, the indefinite,
Confused illuminations and sonorities,
So much ourselves, we cannot tell apart
The idea and the bearer-being of the idea.

(1982, p. 466)

"Suppose these houses are composed of ourselves." As the poet walks in New Haven looking at ordinary things, he invites one to a thought experiment. "Suppose…" The opening of "The Snow Man" also considered a kind of thought experiment: "One must have a mind of winter not to see" (1982, p. 9). That is, what would mind be if it was not to see itself in nature, indulge in the pathetic fallacy? Here, the experiment seems to be the opposite: what happens if we do think of houses consubstantial with ourselves? Of the houses as us, not in the sense that we have built them, but that they are actually made up, composed, of whatever we are?

"So that they become an impalpable town." If the houses are composed of ourselves they undergo a kind of derealization. They are impalpable, they cannot be touched, they are not spatial in the usual sense. One might read this as the projection of our minds into things, such that they seem to acquire a "spirit," as in animism. However, these are not the terms of the thought experiment. We are asked to think of the houses actually "composed of ourselves," so that their impalpability is real. We are being asked to see this real impalpability, to see the houses as the reality of the untouchable minds in which we live, the "oneness" of the "real and the unreal."

In Chapter 4, we examined Derrida on Freud's ultimate remark about the spatiality of the psyche. Our usual view of space as extension is what makes it touchable, which, for Kant, becomes the pure intuition of externality. Derrida had said that if Freud is asking us to imagine a spatiality of the mind, he is asking us to imagine a spatiality that cannot be touched—impalpable. Which is why Derrida had said that Freud's remark about the psyche's extension implies that "a psychoanalytic transcendental aesthetic would account for spatiality on the basis of a psychic apparatus which indeed would have to be extended in order to carry within it, of the two pure forms of sensory intuition, an *a priori* form of the external sense" (2000, p. 58).

Hence, Freud implicitly envisages "a kind of pure sensibility, the non-sensuous sensuous" (p. 59), which, for Heidegger, becomes the transcendental imagination, always in relation to the *ens imaginarium*. Would we have to think of Stevens' imagination, the consubstantiality of poetry and reality in a similar way, if we suppose that "these houses are composed of ourselves"?

> So that they become an impalpable town, full of
> Impalpable bells, transparencies of sound...

As one walks in New Haven, one sees houses and hears bells. Bells inevitably recall churches. (The Puritan settlers of New Haven had established it as a theocracy.) As the *visible* houses that make up the town become untouchable, so too do its *audible* (church) bells.[3] They ring transparently. One can see through them. But they do ring. Are they then one with the transparent air through which invisible sound waves ordinarily move? Non-sensuous sensuous sound? And if these are church bells, has religion, the religion of the town, itself become something more or less than theology?

Religion is always a question of mind, of belief. Is this why the impalpable bells are "Sounding in transparent dwellings of the self"? Because the houses, the dwellings, are where we live, our selves, our minds? If we hear the (church) bells non-empirically, then religion too becomes something more than an empirical question of belief. Derrida, analyzing Marx on fetishism, had said that religion is not "just one ideological phenomenon or phantomatic production among others" (1994, p. 165), because religion itself is always "spectral" in the strong sense of the irreducibly virtual, like mind itself. Discourse on fetishism began as a theological question about mind and thing, i.e., as a question about the virtual. Whether he knew it or not, de Brosses' theory of universal fetishism makes both the virtual and the concrete universal characteristics of the mind which always produces beliefs:

> transparent dwellings of the self,
> Impalpable habitations that seem to move
> In the movement of the colors of the mind

Mind: the transparent, impalpable place we inhabit *moves*. Of course, it cannot move in the usual sense of displacing itself spatially. Rather, its motion is the motion of colors of the mind. Two things are stated: the mind has colors, these colors move. According to the logic of the poem these cannot be visible colors, but rather the variations in hue, the invisible vibrating light waves, that are color itself. And light waves, of course, are the possibility of seeing. Stevens is saying that the way we "see," think, imagine, in all the ways they are linked to light, also makes them "colored," in the sense of vibrating light waves themselves. Colors that move of themselves are iridescent. Heidegger called the imagination of Kant's *Anthropology* "iridescent" in its simultaneous receptivity and spontaneity, the qualities he found lodged in the transcendental imagination. "Lightening" itself, is, for Heidegger, the opening that permits what one might call ontological seeing: the "light" required for "vision" of what is never objectively seen. This is the possibility of reception of the "non-sensuous sensuous," a kind of "experience free" intuition. Like the transcendental imagination in relation to time, this lightening is auto-affective: mirroring. But a mirroring of what is always simultaneously itself and other. Hence, it *binds* each to the other in such a way that each remains itself, in its particularity, *as* the relation to the other. Particularity *as* relation: complementarity.

Penrose, as we saw in the last chapter, also said that the complementarity of quantum mechanics is part of our everyday world, responsible for such things as color. This is also why he said that the complementarity of light itself (wave, particle) shows that "somehow Nature contrives to build a consistent world in which *particles and field-oscillations are the same thing*! Or, rather, her world consists of some more subtle ingredient, the words 'particle' and 'wave' conveying but partially appropriate pictures" (pp. 230–231). Further, the "very existence of... the colours of substances... and many other familiar properties require the quantum theory for their explanations. Perhaps, also, the phenomenon of consciousness is something that cannot be understood in entirely classical terms... Perhaps, in some sense, this is 'why' we, as sentient beings, must live in a quantum world, rather than an entirely classical one" (p. 226). Penrose is saying that our very existence as beings who both think and feel (sentient) is a form of complementarity, inevitably opening the question of brain and mind. Merleau-Ponty called for an "ontological psychoanalysis" able to think mind in complementary ways, a psychoanalysis free of the ways philosophy separates ourselves from things. Body–mind.[4]

> The far-fire flowing and the dim-coned bells
> Coming together...

The far fire is the distant sun, the source of the light that *flows* toward us. One does not usually think of light as flowing, like water. (Why this alliterative expression of being "bathed" in light, the light that "washes" over everything? It does emphasize the sound of language.) Dim coned bells: bells whose conic shape is hard to make out, the bells producing impalpable, unhearable sound. Light and sound are vibrations in the air, received by eyes and ears as qualitative sensations—Kant's "intensive magnitude" that Heidegger emphasized in *What is a Thing?* Sensation itself, Heidegger had said, "occupies a peculiar intermediate position between things and human beings, between object and subject" (1967, p. 208), and "reflects the *uncertainty* of the relation between man and thing" (1967, p. 211, my emphasis). For Kant, intensive magnitude, unlike extensive magnitude (the measurable uniformity of space), is the "quantity of quality": how bright, dim, loud, soft is sensation (seeing, hearing)? For Heidegger, this means that all sensory perception contains an "anticipation," a "reaching out" that makes it possible for sensation to be a relation, a "receivable, encountering this and that" (1967, p. 220)—i.e., a *particular, qualitative* encounter. Kant's discovery of anticipation in perception, Heidegger said, is "astonishing" in light of the role of mathematical physics in the *a priori* synthesis, because it puts the particular and the qualitative into sensory reception *a priori*. This would be an *a priori* of the non-measurable particular, the non-conceptual singularity of *this thing*, another aspect of what Derrida had called the signature effect as the "scientific reading" of the "fetish effect."

> Coming together in a sense in which we are poised,
> Without regard to time or where we are

The light and sound of "impalpable sensation" come together "in a sense." This is a sense in which we are "poised," balanced. We are balanced in the coming together of impalpable sight and sound. This balance has no concern for time or space. So we are on the cusp of time and space, Kant's transcendental intuitions that are the *a priori* conditions of empirical sensation, for example, seeing, hearing. Coming together is synthetic. The synthesis of empirical sensation takes place on the synthetic cusp of transcendental intuition. For Stevens, the balancing synthesis of impalpable sensation, the non-sensuous sensuous, as for Heidegger, occurs in a time and space that disregards time and space, i.e., empirical, measurable time and space. For seeing and hearing to be able to come together, as Heidegger would say, they must have a common root, what he called a "seam" that accounts for their union and separation. This seam *is* the cusp of time and space. This is the pivoting point of *différance*, "time becoming space, and space becoming time," *pace* Derrida.

> In the perpetual reference…

To refer to something is to "point" to it. I am referring to… Bibliographically, a reference is a source. On an application, a reference is someone who recommends one. In *Being and Time*, Heidegger spoke about the existential structure of useful things as referential. Things are used in order to do something, always implying reference of something to something, even in an apparently useless broken tool. Reference itself points to usefulness in general, giving it the "sign structure." Signs themselves are "useful things with manifold references" (1996, p. 73). For Heidegger, the fetish as the self-referential conflation of indication and indicated (as for de Brosses and Hegel), was excluded from the sign structure. Stevens, here, does seem to envisage an ontological structure of reference. Non-empirical sensation is synthesized in non-empirical time and space as perpetual reference, i.e., as always pointing to… Derrida, in his essay on Mallarmé, which he said was a rereading of Freud's "The Uncanny" in relation to Gödelian undecidability, found a structure of permanent "allusion" (1981b, p. 219). But Gödelian undecidability itself is demonstrable only in self-referential statements. Could Stevens' "perpetual reference" have a relation to permanent allusion and to self-referential conflation of indication and indicated?

> In the perpetual reference, object
> Of the perpetual meditation, point
> Of the enduring, visionary love

The perpetual pointing to… of the coming together of impalpable sensation in non-empirical time and space is the object of perpetual meditation. The perpetuity of reference is the perpetuity of this contemplation. It is the point that perpetual, enduring, visionary love always converges upon. What is visionary love? Visionary implies imagination, what we envision mentally. We can only envision impalpable sensation, but this does not make it imaginary in the sense of something we make up. Rather, the inevitable visionary meditation of inevitable reference is the condition of mind as the condition of reality. It is imagination as love. And because Stevens' imagination is the reality of the non-sensuous sensuous, intuited by the transcendental imagination, we can ask about the transcendental imagination and love.

For Freud, love as Eros is simultaneously self-preservative and libidinal. As such, it is unifying, synthetic, and "introduces fresh vital differences" into the "organism" (1920, p. 54). Before he had conceptualized Eros, Freud had postulated an unconscious origin of *thought*, as the non-verbal "impress," the trace, of the relation to an object. This is a differentiating synthesis, but one that occurs in the organization of primary narcissism, in which there is no subject–object, passive–active, structure. Merleau-Ponty had envisioned a "science of the body" that is a psychoanalysis of nature, as "flesh," "mother" (p. 267), the opening of pre-reflective experience in which "the seer and the visible reciprocate one another" (p. 139). For Winnicott, in this relation to the mother there are two babies, one feeding from itself and the other from an "other than me" source. Which is why this double, divided self-preservative love is implicitly uncanny, as Freud had hinted at in his derivation of uncanniness from primary narcissism. This love is inscribed in the unconscious origin of thought. Is it, then, the object of perpetual meditation? And "visionary" in an almost mystical[5] sense, the imagining of an ideal which is nevertheless real? Is this Stevens' life itself, the life that is a theory of poetry, of the consubstantiality of reality and imagination?

> Obscure, in colors whether of the sun
> Or mind, uncertain in the clearest bells,

But the visionary is not clear. It is obscure, hard to make out. But still colored, although one does not know "whether" these are the colors of the sun, the source of vibrating light, or the colors of the mind. The colors of the mind in which the impalpable habitations seemed to move. Even the ringing of the clearest bells is "uncertain." That is, even the clear sound of the palpable bells comports an uncertainty. Heidegger on Kant's intensive magnitude: sensation "reflects the *uncertainty* of the relation between man and thing" (1967, p. 211). To describe his finding that the position and momentum of an electron cannot be measured simultaneously Heisenberg used the same word: uncertainty. It is important to note again that both Heisenberg and Bohr considered themselves positivists. (Comte already saw his neo-fetishistic subjective synthesis as positivism.) Uncertainty and complementarity are real, but provide "new knowledge of reality." The point then, as in

Merleau-Ponty's call for an ontological psychoanalysis that takes complementarity into account, is not to impose one discipline upon another, but to see where disciplines converge in their necessary encounters with uncertainty, complementarity, or, from mathematics, undecidability.[6]

> Obscure, in colors whether of the sun
> Or mind, uncertain in the clearest bells,
> The spirit's speeches, the indefinite,
> Confused illuminations and sonorities
> So much ourselves

The obscure colors of the mind and the uncertainty of the clearest bells are the "spirit's speeches." They are what mind says. They are confused light and sound. This is both the obscurity of what mind sees and hears, and the indefiniteness of sensation itself: the color and sound whose vibrations are the conditions of what mind can say, because they are "so much ourselves." So much: emphasis and irreducibility. These confused illuminations and sonorities *are* us in the most emphatic way.

> So much ourselves, we cannot tell apart
> The idea and the bearer-being of the idea.

What mind says, the spirit's speeches, the confusion of light and sound that is mind, produces another confusion, another indistinguishability, something else we cannot tell apart. Mind produces ideas. But ideas are expressed in the sensory material of the language we see and hear. This sensory material carries, bears, the idea. Because the confusion of light and sound *is* mind, spirit, we can have ideas. But ideas, then, cannot simply be abstractions. Their "bearers" are their being.

Previously, we asked whether the idea of perpetual reference could have a relation to the conflation of indication and indicated. Stevens says that we cannot tell apart the idea and the bearer of the idea, because the bearer is the being of the idea. The preceding lines have prepared this statement. What is the poem saying about the conflation of indication and indicated, the question that pre-occupies the history of fetishism? (De Brosses: Egyptian worshipers of different animals could not live peacefully with each other, because divinity resided in their respective animals, "like different words of several languages when they signify the same thing.") The thought experiment of supposing that the ordinary houses of New Haven are "composed of ourselves," a seeming projection that confuses mind and thing, produces the counter-intuitive result that the sensory materiality, the thingliness of the idea *is* the idea. As in Derrida's analysis of Marx on fetishism, for the idea to be a thing, and the thing an idea, requires one to think the non-sensuous sensuous. This thinking is necessarily iridescent. Mind reflecting on itself, the "spirit's speeches," says that the confusion of indication and indicated is the inevitable possibility of oscillation between apparently concrete self-reference and "hyper-reflection," the relation to the thing, "free… of all the terms philosophy uses to distinguish me absolutely from things" (Merleau-Ponty, 1968, p. 51).

In Number 12 of *An Ordinary Evening…* Stevens wrote: "The poem is the cry of its occasion/ Part of the res itself and not about it" (1982, p. 473). The poem speaks of itself as a singular event. It is auto-affective. As such, it does not talk about things, but is a thing, this singular thing, part of the *res*. An auto-affective thing. The auto-affective poem–thing is poetry itself, the "endlessly elaborating poem," the theory of poetry—as the theory of life. Which produces a theory of what supposedly cannot be theorized: singularity. The non-conceptual iridescent singularity of the signature and the fetish. When Derrida says that "what is happily and tragically *universal* is *absolute singularity*" (1988, p. 65),[7] he is announcing the universality of fetishism as auto-affective thing: the poem as the cry of its occasion and as part of the *res.* But life *as* it is cannot exclude the "intricate evasions" of as. Life as auto-affective "poetic productivity," an expansion of Comtean neo-fetishism, evades itself and becomes the enclosed self-reference of a subject who projects ("Suppose these houses were composed of ourselves"). This is another reason why fetishism as traditionally conceived is also universal. It is the result of brain–mind,[8] the auto-affective spirit–thing becoming the mind that is not part of the *res.* Which paradoxically makes "mind" the (restricted) fetish of brain–mind.

Stevens' poem does not address this process and its inherent destructiveness. There is no analyzing fetishism without taking destruction into account, as we have seen elliptically throughout. De Brosses spoke of the inevitable "wars" between the worshipers of the cat and the rat, while saying nothing about the violence of the Spanish whose fetish, for the Indians of Cuba, was gold. Kant and Hegel concretely used their understanding of fetishism to endorse their assumptions of the natural inferiority of the Negro and their positions on the slave trade. Fetishism always repeats itself as it operates blindly. De Brosses, Kant, and Hegel do not see the concreteness of their idealization of European whiteness, inevitably justifying the supposed dangerous inferiority of the non-white, who then becomes the object of violent control. Comte, however, saw in fetishistic "fixity" a possible check to the violence of carnivorous human nature, which extended to his opposition to the slave trade. While one can never forget Heidegger's reprehensibility during the Nazi era, his thinking evolved into an account of the destructive violence of technology as the end of metaphysics. In a similar vein, Merleau-Ponty spoke of the "interminable psychoanalysis of objective knowledge" that "does not suppress the past or phantasms but transforms them from powers of death into poetic productivity" (1968, p. 116). I understand him to mean both the general, historical past and the individual past—the crux of psychoanalytic therapy—as powers of death.

I did not mention Derrida in the preceding list, but the question of violence is explicit from his earliest work on. His reading of Freud is based on the ideas that the unconscious is always open "to the effraction of the trace," i.e., the breaking in of difference, and that there is no writing that does not call for protection against itself, precisely because it is inseparable from violence. Auto-hetero-affection is never without destruction. This is another way of thinking about the disavowal of difference. To take one more example from Derrida on Freud (discussed in *Interpretation and Difference*, pp. 161–173), the unconscious as "archive" is inseparable from destruction of the archive. Toward the end of *Archive Fever*, Derrida says, "*L'un se garde de l'autre, pour se faire violence*" (1995, pp. 169–170), a multivalent sentence that can say: one keeps for oneself something of the other; one protects oneself against the other; to do violence to oneself; to make oneself violence.

I would like to extend this thought back to Heidegger on the "transcendental need" of the finite creature for the play-space that is the opening to the thing; and to Winnicott on the anxiety of play on the edge of internal and external, such that "games and their rules" are a source of control. In the inevitable keeping for oneself of the other of the finite creature, in the need for the play-space, in the differential trace of the other, there is also a controlling violence of oneself and the other. In *Difference and Disavowal*, I called this aggression in primary narcissism, in which destruction of the other equals destruction of oneself. Stevens' visionary love meets Freud's death drive.

I am also alleging that what I have called the process of brain–mind becoming an independent mind, mind as the fetish of brain, entails a similar violence. Why? Brain–mind is capable of memory, the open, differentiable unconscious. Edelman understands memory as a stochastic, auto-affective process with a generator of diversity, but also saw the inevitability of defense, for him, repression. Defense, then, is an attack of brain–mind on itself, the auto-immune response. Once Freud models all defenses on fetishism as the formation of substitutes for an intolerable reality, the general structure of disavowal of difference is also the disavowal of complementarity in a large sense—for Freud, the primary intermediacy of drives, and for Heidegger, the primary intermediate of the transcendental imagination (from which Kant recoiled). The primary intermediate drives are what account for the possibility of active and passive versions of the drive substituting for each other, and for the historicity, the temporalization of sexuality.[9] To return to another passage I have so often cited, in *Analysis Terminable and Interminable*, Freud uses the intermediacy of universal bisexuality as an illustration that Eros itself often leads to conflict due to what he calls an "element of free aggressiveness," the death drive (*neikos*) as the antagonist of love (*philia*). To all of which must be added Freud's idea that Eros, like originally unconscious thought, raises tension levels, binds, and differentiates, and that the death drive lowers tension levels, unbinds, and dedifferentiates. Eros is akin to complementarity in that both presume maintenance of tension, the tension of the differentiating trace and the tension of sustaining a view of physical reality in terms of the co-existence of mutually exclusive properties. Intermediacy as the opening to temporalized, complementary (sexual) differences (see Merleau-Ponty previously) is conceivable as the general fetishism of brain–mind as an oscillating, iridescent, *uncontrollable* process. But brain–mind, the "signature of the transcendental imagination," can attack itself, and become the restricted fetishism, the concreteness, of a tension-lowering, unbinding, dedifferentiating, mind that attempts to control via projection of fantasy. This is fantasy as exemplified by the conscious, tension-reducing hallucinatory dream experience, which is the "birth" of the subject opposed to the object. This is the subject violently intolerant of its fundamental need for, and structuring by, its uncontrollable opening to the other. As in Freud's *philia* and *neikos*, there is the complementarity of, on the one hand, the visionary love of the brain–mind, and, on the other, the self and other directed violence of concreteness in the service of tension reduction.

Stevens does not know that the indistinguishability of the idea and the bearer-being of the idea contains this essential paradox. But it is always there in the ordinary day of the psychoanalyst, because analysis is always concerned with the modification of defenses. Loewald understood the tension lowering effect of all defenses as a function of the death drive, and of a regression of the organization of psyche and reality in the direction of a closed system.[10] When Merleau-Ponty speaks of the past and phantasms as powers of death, I read him to be saying something like this. The difficulties in life that every patient brings to analysis are grounded in the blind, self-destructive ways that he or she uses defense to maintain an illusory sense of control. And when Merleau-Ponty speaks of the transformation of the past and phantasms into poetic productivity, I further read him to imply that within the power of death there is embedded life as the "flesh of time," the complementarity of *philia* and *neikos*.

This is also why his call for an "ontological psychoanalysis" is essential. This can never mean dismissal of everything in psychoanalysis that is psychological, i.e., the infinitely complex content derived from each patient's actual history, emotional life, fantasies, anxieties, and defenses. But the analyst also needs to remember that this content derives from those aspects of the unconscious mind that Freud called deterministic, the aspects that determine the self-destructive forms of fetishistic control intrinsic to each patient's problems. But this defensively fetishistic control is itself an evasion, a disavowal of the ontological processes of brain–mind, body–mind. These processes are ontological because they concern the non-present aspects of difference: time, space, oscillation, repetition, substitutability, complementarity, and undecidability. These processes are the intuition, the pre-reflexive tracing of the non-sensuous sensuous, the primary intermediate, which is never without a tension that is both affective and cognitive. The result is that there is in everyone what we called in Chapter 4, an idiom, a signature, unique and iterable (complementary)—tragically always subject to destruction. Again Derrida: "what is happily and tragically *universal* is *absolute singularity.*"

These ontological processes are the unreal reality, the life, on which analysis, like poetry for Stevens, nourishes itself. Absent an understanding of such processes, analysis risks becoming an exercise in closed self-referentiality on the part of both patient and analyst. Throughout *Difference and Disavowal*, I tried to show that this is precisely what happens in the endless, stalemated analyses of conspicuously concrete patients. But this has to be understood as an example of the risk built into analysis. This is the risk that the analyst will not understand that ontological processes are the essence of analysis, which makes the analyst, as Freud says, the "guardian of a process." The analyst functions as such a guardian by maintaining the analytic frame—the space, the time, the repetition, the neutrality of the analyst's difference, which are the analytic environment. These are what make possible what Loewald so importantly called "internalization of a process," rather than "identification with an object" (1980, pp. 83–84). This process *is* auto-hetero-affection: the patient's modification of his/her own mind through the otherness of the analytic frame.

The transformation of the past and fantasy from powers of death into "poetic productivity" is also a way of conceptualizing the traditional psychoanalytic view that effective treatment increases the capacity for self-reflection. Self-reflection is an openness that closed self-reference intricately evades. In simple terms, self-reflection is the capacity simultaneously to say, "I am, and I am not, that." Yes, that history, those emotions, those fantasies, anxieties, defenses, are me, my psychology; but I can accept them without having them determine me, I can live in the difference from myself that is my idiom, my signature, that is and is not my psychology. History is time, and time itself is both permanence (I am always my past) and change (I am other than my past). Time itself, then, is complementary—the ontological principle built into the unconscious as historical. When the analyst encounters the defensive use of one side of this complementarity against the other, i.e., a deterministic past against opening to change, the analyst must maintain the tension of not interpreting in a deterministic, causal way, precisely because such interpretations do not address the defense against opening to the non-deterministic process.

> Number 18 of *An Ordinary Evening...*
>
> It is the window that makes it difficult
> To say good-by to the past and to live and to be
> In the present state of things as, say, to paint
> In the present state of painting and not the state
> Of thirty years ago. It is looking out
> Of the window and walking in the street and seeing,
> As if the eyes were the present or part of it...
> The life and death of this carpenter depend
> On a fuchsia in a can—and iridescences
> Of petals that will never be realized,
> Things not yet true which he perceives through truth,
> Or thinks he does, as he perceives the present,
> Or thinks he does, a carpenter's iridescences,
> Wooden, the model for astral apprentices,
> A city slapped up like a chest of tools,
> The eccentric exterior of which the clocks talk.
>
> *(1982, p. 478)*

One looks out of a window from inside a house. This is perhaps the house *not* composed of ourselves, i.e., the house as object external to a subject. This kind of looking is not the auto-affective looking and being looked at by things. (Not the seeing of the snow man.) This looking in the usual sense makes it difficult to say good-by to the past, and *to live*. To live in the present state of *things*, taking "things" here to mean more than what they conventionally mean when one says, "the present state of things." Thinking again of the singularity of the thing, I also think of what Derrida says in *Specters of Marx* about the absolute difference, the singularity of the "here and now" (1994, p. 31). Stevens compares this living in the present state of things to painting in a way not tied to the past. Painting is the form of "poetic productivity" directly related to color. This way of painting is both looking out of the window and walking in the street, inside and outside the house, the poet looking at houses on an ordinary evening. This simultaneous seeing from inside and outside makes the eyes the present—"or part of it." In other words, a seeing that is part of the *res*, the self-reflective seeing of the idea as the bearer-being of the idea. Then the painter is a carpenter, one who makes objects out of wood. In other words, the painter produces a painting, just as a carpenter might produce a table. The life and death of this carpenter, i.e., whether he will say good-by to the past and live, or whether he will not and die (*philia* and *neikos*, opening and closure), depend upon a "fuchsia in a can."

A fuchsia is the flower that has given its name to a purple-red color, because it is composed of both purple and red elements (sepals and petals). This flower is not in a vase, but in a can, displayed in an ordinary object now emptied of its usual contents, the way painters will often put paint or turpentine in a can. A kind of carpenter's still life—a flower in a can on a table.

How do the life and death of the carpenter–painter depend upon the fuchsia in a can? By virtue of color ("the colors of the mind"). As multi-colored, the flower, and the color fuchsia, are iridescent. The life and death of the carpenter–painter depend upon the iridescence of petals that will never be realized, i.e., upon unreal petals, petals of the imagination. But the real and the unreal themselves are two in one, the iridescence of imagination and reality. (Non-sensuous sensuous iridescence.) These petals, as unrealizable except in the reality of imagination, are *things* "not yet true." They are virtual things, perceived "through truth," i.e., intuited through truth as what is conventionally real.

But perhaps the carpenter–painter only thinks, in the usual sense, that he perceives these virtual, iridescent petals. Perhaps he only thinks the here and now not determined by the past. Perhaps these iridescences are wooden, fixed. I think that Stevens is saying that just as there is a movement of the colors of the mind, an iridescence of (brain–) mind, there is also a fixity of mind, the looking out of the window tied to the past. A carpenter can make a wooden model for his apprentices to follow. What, though, are "astral apprentices," apprentices of the stars? Are they apprentices of light, of color itself? Or are they worshipers of idealized, external objects, what was called "Sabism" in the eighteenth century? Is this the model of a city (New Haven) hastily assembled like a carpenter's chest of tools? Tools as useful things, as in *Being and Time*? The tools that themselves always point to reference itself (the "perpetual reference object/Of the perpetual meditation")? In *Being and Time*, the analysis of tools that exemplifies relatedness to things (and excludes fetishism), is part of the careful preparation for making the structure of care, being in the world, the structure of time itself, time as *ekstasis.* Stevens' wooden iridescences, as the model of a city slapped up for the astral apprentices like a chest of tools, is the "eccentric exterior of which the clocks talk." Time as the odd, or more precisely decentering exterior, the outsidedness that clocks speak of. For Kant, time is the pure *internal* sense, but for Heidegger, time as *ek-stasis opens* the subject to the world. Kant compared time with the monogram of the transcendental imagination, and Derrida said that when the *mise en abîme* succeeds it is the *other*, the *other* thing, the "ec-centric exterior," that signs. Clocks speak of all of this. If clocks could talk, they would say that time is both fixed, permanent, "wooden," and change "iridescent." The fetish as concrete and oscillating. It all depends upon the iridescence of a fuchsia in a can.

I am reading the fuchsia in the can in relation to the ordinary analytic setting. The fuchsia as an analogon to the iridescence of the transcendental imagination, in its relation to singularity and "the eccentric exterior of which clocks talk." The ordinary as a can analytic setting, the analyst's "tools" *and* the clock that times the session, holds the opening of the auto-hetero-affective transcendental imagination—a question of life or death.

Notes

1 "An Ordinary Evening in New Haven" from *The Collected Poems of Wallace Stevens* by Wallace Stevens, © 1954 by Wallace Stevens and copyright renewed 1982 by Holly Stevens. Used by permission of Alfred A. Knopf, an imprint of the Knopf Doubleday Publishing Group, a division of Penguin Random House LLC. All rights reserved. Also reprinted by kind permission of Faber & Faber, Ltd.

2 Here, one would have to refer to Heidegger on the "as structure" of interpretation as developed in *Being and Time*. For Heidegger, phenomenological interpretation describes beings *as they are*, the preparation for his analysis of truth as disclosure. See *Interpretation and Difference,* pp. 46–50. To this, one would have to add Derrida's contention that there is no "as such" of *différance* itself.

3 Here I begin a series of notes on Nils Bohr, the "inventor" of complementarity. *Atomic Theory and the Description of Nature* is a series of essays on the implications of the quantum theory, implications Merleau-Ponty envisaged, beginning with the question of the effect of measurement on subatomic particles. Bohr begins with this question too, seeing it not only as a physical one, but as a psychological one as well. He says that the investigation of acoustical and optical phenomena, i.e., the physics of hearing and seeing, has been crucial to the development of "psychological analysis," by which I assume he means experimental psychology. But because in psychology "it is our own mental activity which is the object under investigation," even the "'objectivity' of physical observations becomes particularly suited to emphasize the subjective character of all experience" (1968, p. 1). By which, as Merleau-Ponty made clear, Bohr does not mean subjective in the sense that everything is created by our minds. Rather, the "impossibility of distinguishing in our customary way between physical phenomena and their observation places us… in a position quite similar to that which is so familiar in psychology, where we are continually reminded of the difficulty of distinguishing between subject and object" (p. 15).

4 Bohr: "the nature of our consciousness brings about a complementary relationship, in all domains of knowledge, between the analysis of a concept and its immediate application" (p. 20). There is an "analogy between fundamental features of the quantum theory and the laws of psychology" (ibid.). "Behind these analogies" there may be not only epistemological "kinship," but also "a more profound relationship… behind the fundamental

biological problems which are directly connected to both sides" (ibid.). More on psychology and biology in the following footnotes.

5 Bohr: both Einstein's relativity, which depends upon the state of motion of the observer, and quantum mechanics "are concerned with the recognition of physical laws which lie outside the domain of our ordinary experience and which present difficulties to our accustomed forms of perception" (1987, p. 5). Quantum phenomena are "fundamentally unvisualizable" (p. 12). As the uncertainty principle prohibits "a sharp distinction" between "a phenomenon and the agency by which it is observed," stationary states in the atom "may indeed be said to possess... just as much, or if one prefers, just as little 'reality' as the elementary particles themselves" (pp. 11–12; Stevens: the real and the unreal are two in one). The linkage of atomic phenomena and their observation, then, "compels us to caution in the use of means of expression. The intent is not to introduce a mysticism which is incompatible with the spirit of natural science" (p. 116). In other words, something like the vocabulary of mysticism seems inevitable here. Bohr uses his own example: "we can scarcely avoid speaking of a choice between various possibilities on the part of the atom" (p. 13). But to use an expression like "free choice on the part of nature" "implies an external chooser, the existence of which is denied by the use of the word 'nature'" (pp. 19–20). Bohr knows that this sounds like animism, or what is usually called mysticism or magic. But the discoveries of uncertainty, complementarity, and the interactions of matter with matter, as in the effect of the means of observation on the particle observed, and later the famous two-slit experiment, demand these kinds of "ambiguous," paradoxical expressions. The word "complementarity" itself reminds us that "all our ordinary verbal expressions bear the stamp of our customary forms of perception, from the point of view of which the existence of the quantum of action is an irrationality. Indeed, in consequence of this state of affairs, even words like 'to be' and 'to know' lose their unambiguous meaning" (p. 19).

6 This was Plotnitsky's point, cited previously (Chapter 6, p. 141), about an "undecidable complementarity" of complementarity and uncertainty from physics and undecidability from mathematics, which he finds in Derrida. Plotnitsky is quite aware that this kind of thinking requires a "self-referential transformational economy" (1993, p. 84), a "reconsideration of the functioning and limits of reflexivity" (p. 288).

7 I found this quote in Fred Moten's *In the Break: The Aesthetics of the Black Radical Tradition*. Moten refers to Stevens in his chapter on Amiri Baraka: "the poem—which is to say the music... the interanimation of poem and music... 'refreshes life' so that this phenomenon (something akin to but more than what Wallace Stevens calls 'the first idea') is given us" (2003, pp. 95–96). "[A]n object whose objectivity *is* in that it transforms... what Stevens would call... in a phrase more precise than the one ('the first idea') I echo above, 'a supreme fiction': abstract, pleasure-giving, changing, yet material" (p. 101). A shout out to CRB, who alerted me to Moten's work. More on the tragic aspect below.

8 Bohr: the quantum theory uses complementarity—again the necessity of mutually exclusive properties—to account for "the characteristic stability of the properties of atoms" (1987, p. 23). In other words, one must take into account both uncertainty, the "free choice" of particles, and identifiable stability: hydrogen is hydrogen, oxygen is oxygen. Bohr extends this proposition to the relation between the physical and the psychical, brain and mind: "the *peculiarity of the phenomena of life,* and in particular the self-stabilizing power of organisms, [might] be inseparably connected with the fundamental impossibility of a detailed analysis of the physical conditions under which life takes place" (ibid.). This holds for the "psychical aspects of life... the unavoidable influencing by introspection of all psychical experience that is characterized by the feeling of volition, shows a striking similarity to the conditions responsible for the failure of causality in the analysis of atomic phenomena... [there would be] an unpredictable modification of psychical experience produced by any attempt at an objective tracing of the accompanying physical processes in the central nervous system... In associating the psychical and physical aspects of existence, we are concerned with a special relationship of complementarity

which it is not possible thoroughly to understand by one-sided application either of physical or of psychological laws" (pp. 23–24). Further on, Bohr emphasizes that there is no complete causal chain from brain processes to emotional, mental experience (p. 100).

9 Bohr, on the "historicity" of the atom, sounding like Heidegger and Loewald (see *Difference and Disavowal*, 2000, pp. 91ff.): Bohr is addressing "the singular position of time in problems concerned with stationary states, the observation of which, by means of collision or radiation reactions" permits a distinction between different stationary states, and allows us to disregard the previous history of the atom. But the "fact that the symbolical quantum theory methods ascribe a particular phase to each stationary state the value of which depends upon the previous history of the atom, would for the first moment seem to contradict the very idea of stationary states. *As soon as we are really concerned with a time problem, however, the consideration of a strictly closed system is excluded*" (p. 82, my emphasis).

10 See *Difference and Disavowal*, 2000, pp. 91ff.

References

Assoun, P.-L. (1994). *Qu'est-ce que le fétichisme?* Paris: Presses Universitaires de France.

Bass, A. (1991). Fetishism, reality, and 'The Snow Man.' *American Imago*, 48: 295–328.

Bass, A. (1992). The philosophy of electrical science. In *Logomachia: The Conflict of the Faculties*. R. Rand, Ed. Lincoln, NE: Univeristy of Nebraska Press.

Bass, A. (2000). *Difference and Disavowal: The Trauma of Eros*. Stanford, CA: Stanford University Press.

Bass, A. (2006). *Interpretation and Difference: The Trauma of Eros*. Stanford, CA: Stanford University Press.

Bohr, N. (1987). *Atomic Theory and the Description of Nature*. Woodbridge, CT: Ox Bow Press.

Comte, A. (1852). *Catéchisme positiviste*. Paris: Carilian-Goeury.

Comte, A. (1853). *Système de politique positive*. Paris: Dalmont.

Damasio, A. (1994). *Descartes' Error*. New York: Penguin.

David, M. (1966). Lettres inédites de Diderot et de Hume écrites de 1755 a 1763 au président de Brosses. In *Revue philosophique*, No. 2.

De Brosses, Charles. (1988). *Du culte des dieux fétiches*. Paris: Fayard.

Derrida, J. (1974). *Of Grammatology*. G. Spivak, Trans. Baltimore, MD: Johns Hopkins University Press.

Derrida, J. (1978). Freud and the scene of writing. In *Writing and Difference*. A. Bass, Trans. Chicago, IL: University of Chicago Press.

Derrida, J. (1981a). Plato's pharmacy. In *Dissemination*. B. Johnson, Trans. Chicago, IL: University of Chicago Press.

Derrida, J. (1981b). The double session. In *Dissemination*. B. Johnson, Trans. Chicago, IL: University of Chicago Press.

Derrida, J. (1982a). Différance. In *Margins—Of Philosophy*. A. Bass, Trans. Chicago, IL: University of Chicago Press.

Derrida, J. (1982b). Ousia and gramme: Note on a note in *Being and Time*. In *Margins—Of Philosophy*. A. Bass, Trans. Chicago, IL: University of Chicago Press.

Derrida, J. (1982c). The pit and the pyramid: Introduction to Hegel's semiology. In *Margins—Of Philosophy*. A. Bass, Trans. Chicago, IL: University of Chicago Press.

Derrida, J. (1984). *Signéponge/Signsponge*. R. Rand, Trans. New York: Columbia University Press.
Derrida, J. (1986). *Glas*. J. Leavey and R. Rand, Trans. Lincoln, NE: University of Nebraska Press.
Derrida, J. (1987). To speculate—On "Freud." In *The Post Card*. A. Bass, Trans. Chicago, IL: University of Chicago Press.
Derrida, J. (1988). "This strange institution called literature": An interview with Jacques Derrida. D. Allison, Trans. In *Derrida and Différance*. D. Wood and R. Bernasconi, Eds. Evanston, IL: Northwestern University Press.
Derrida, J. (1992). *Given Time*. P. Kamuf, Trans. New York: Routledge.
Derrida, J. (1994). *Specters of Marx*. P. Kamuf, Trans. New York: Routledge.
Derrida, J. (1995). *Archive Fever*. E. Prenowitz, Trans. Chicago, IL: University of Chicago Press.
Derrida, J. (2000). *Le toucher—Jean-Luc Nancy*. Paris: Galilée.
Derrida, J. (2007a). My chances/*Mes chances*. In *Psyche—Inventions of the Other*. P. Kamuf and E. Rottenberg, Trans. Stanford, CA: Stanford University Press.
Derrida, J. (2007b). Telepathy. In *Psyche—Inventions of the Other*. P. Kamuf and E. Rottenberg, Trans. Stanford, CA: Stanford University Press.
Dulaure, J.-A. (1825). *Histoire abrégée de différens cultes. Tome premier*. Paris: Guillaume.
Edelman, G. (1992). *Bright Air, Brilliant Fire*. New York: Basic Books.
Fedi, L. (2002). *Fétichisme, philosophie, littérature*. Paris: L'Harmattan.
Freud, S. (1895). Project for a scientific psychology. In *The Standard Edition of the Complete Psychological Works of Sigmund Freud* (henceforth S.E. followed by a volume number). Vol. 1. London: Hogarth Press.
Freud, S. (1900). The interpretation of dreams. S.E. 4–5.
Freud, S. (1905). Three essays on the theory of sexuality. S.E. 7.
Freud, S. (1911). Formulations on the two principles of mental functioning. S.E. 12.
Freud, S. (1913). Totem and taboo. S.E. 13.
Freud, S. (1915). Instincts and their vicissitudes. S.E. 14.
Freud, S. (1919). The Uncanny. S.E. 17
Freud, S. (1920). Beyond the pleasure principle. S.E. 18.
Freud, S. (1921a). Group psychology and the analysis of the ego. S.E. 18.
Freud, S. (1921b). Psychoanalysis and telepathy. S. E. 18.
Freud, S. (1922a). Some neurotic mechanisms in homosexuality, jealousy, and paranoia. S.E. 18.
Freud, S. (1922b). Dreams and telepathy. S. E. 18.
Freud, S. (1923). The infantile genital organization. S.E. 19.
Freud, S. (1924a). Neurosis and psychosis. S.E. 19.
Freud, S. (1924b). The loss of reality in neurosis and psychosis. S.E. 19.
Freud, S. (1925). A note on the "Mystic Writing Pad." S.E. 19.
Freud, S. (1926). Inhibition, symptom, and anxiety. S.E. 20.
Freud, S. (1927). Fetishism. S.E. 21.
Freud, S. (1930). Civilization and its discontents. S.E. 21.
Freud, S. (1937). Analysis terminable and interminable. S.E. 23.
Freud, S. (1940a). An outline of psychoanalysis. S.E. 23.
Freud, S. (1940b). The splitting of the ego in the process of defense. S.E. 23.
Freud, S. (1941). Findings, ideas, problems. S.E. 23.
Goldstein, R. (2005) *Incompleteness: The Proof and Paradox of Kurt Gödel*. New York: W.W. Norton.
Hegel, G.W.F. (1956). *The Philosophy of History*. J. Sibree, Trans. New York: Dover.
Heidegger, M. (1953). *Kant und das Problem der Metaphysik*. Frankfurt: Vittorio Klosterman.

Heidegger, M. (1962). *Being and Time*. J. Macquarrie and E. Robinson, Trans. New York: Harper and Row.

Heidegger, M. (1967). *What Is a Thing?* W. Barton and V. Deutsch, Trans. Chicago, IL: Henry Regnery.

Heidegger, M. (1969). *Identity and Difference*. J. Stambaugh, Trans. New York: Harper and Row.

Heidegger, M. (1971a). The origin of the work of art. In *Poetry, Language, Thought*. A. Hofstadter, Trans. New York: Harper and Row.

Heidegger, M. (1971b). The thing. In *Poetry, Language, Thought*. A. Hofstadter, Trans. New York: Harper and Row.

Heidegger, M. (1972). The end of philosophy and the task of thinking. In *On Time and Being*. J. Stambaugh, Trans. New York: Harper and Row.

Heidegger, M. (1987). *Nietzsche: Vol. 4*. D. Krell, Ed. New York: Harper and Row.

Heidegger, M. (1990). *Kant and the Problem of Metaphysics*. R. Taft, Trans. Bloomington, IN: Indiana University Press.

Heidegger, M. (1996). *Being and Time*. J. Stambaugh, Trans. Albany, NY: State University of New York Press.

Heidegger, M. (2001). *Zollikon Seminars*. M. Boss, Ed. Evanston, IL: Northwestern University Press.

Hume, D. (2007). *A Dissertation on the Passions: The Natural History of Religion*. T. Beauchamp, Ed. Oxford: Clarendon Press.

Iacono, A. (1992). *Le fétichisme: histoire d'un concept*. Paris: Presses Universitaires de France.

Kant, I. (1960a). *Observations on the Feeling of the Beautiful and the Sublime*. J. Goldthwait, Trans. Berkeley, CA: University of California Press.

Kant, I. (1960b). *Religion within the Limits of Reason Alone*. T. Greene and H. Hudson, Trans. NY: Harper.

Kant, I. (1998). *Critique of Pure Reason*. P. Guyer and A. Wood, Trans. Cambridge: Cambridge University Press.

Klein, M. (1932). Early stages of the Oedipus complex. In *The Psychoanalysis of Children*. New York: Delta, 1975.

Kofman, S. (1978). *Abérrations: Le devenir femme d'Auguste Comte*. Paris: Aubier Flammarion.

Kurke, L. (1966). *Coins, Bodies, Games, and Gold: The Politics of Meaning in Archaic Greece*. Princeton, NJ: Princeton University Press.

Loewald, H. (1980). *Papers on Psychoanalysis*. New Haven, CT: Yale University Press.

Loewald, H. (1988). Psychoanalysis in search of nature: Thoughts on metapsychology, "metaphysics," projection. In *The Annual of Psychoanalysis*. Vol. 16. Madison, CT: International Universities Press.

Macherey, P. (1989). *Comte, la Philosophie, et les Sciences*. Paris: Presses Universitaires de France.

Mariani, P. (2016). *The Whole Harmonium: The Life of Wallace Stevens*. New York: Simon and Schuster.

Marx, K. (1977). *Capital*. B. Fowkes, Trans. New York: Vintage.

Mauss, M. (1974). *Oeuvres*. Tome 2. Paris: Editions de Minuit.

Merleau-Ponty, M. (1968). *The Visible and the Invisible*. A. Lingis, Trans. Evanston, IL: Northwestern University Press.

Moten, F. (2003). *In the Break: The Aesthetics of the Black Radical Tradition*. Minneapolis, MN: University of Minnesota Press.

Nietzsche, F. (1968). *The Will to Power*. W. Kaufmann, Ed. New York: Vintage.

Nietzsche, F. (1995). *Human, All Too Human*. I. Handwerk, Trans. Stanford, CA: Stanford University Press.

Pais, A. (1986). *Inward Bound*. Oxford: Oxford University Press.

Penrose, R. (1989). *The Emperor's New Mind*. Oxford: Oxford University Press.
Pietz, W. (1985). The problem of the fetish, 1. In *Res*, 9 (1985): 5–17.
Pietz, W. (1987). The problem of the fetish, 2. In *Res*, 13 (1987): 23–45.
Plotnitsky, A. (1993). *In the Shadow of Hegel: Complementarity, History and the Unconscious*. Gainesville, FL: University of Florida Press.
Schmidt-Hellerau, C. (2001). *Life Drive and Death Drive: Libido and Lethe*. New York: Other Press.
Schurmann, R. (1990). *Heidegger On Being and Acting: From Principles to Anarchy*. Bloomington, IN: Indiana University Press.
Stevens, W. (1982). *The Collected Poems*. New York: Vintage Books.
Stiegler, Bernard. (1998). *Technics and Time 1: The Fault of Epimetheus*. R. Beardsworth and G. Collins, Trans. Stanford, CA: Stanford University Press.
Taussig, M. (1993). *Maleficium*: State fetishism. In *Fetishism as Cultural Discourse*. E. Apter and W. Pietz, Eds. Ithaca, NY: Cornell University Press.
Winnicott, D.W. (1971). *Playing and Reality*. New York: Routledge.
Winnicott, D.W. (1975). Transitional objects and transitional phenomena. In *Through Pediatrics to Psychoanalysis*. New York: Basic Books.

INDEX